Minds and Gods

Minds and Gods

The Cognitive Foundations of Religion

TODD TREMLIN

Foreword by E. Thomas Lawson

OXFORD

UNIVERSITY PRESS

OXFORD
UNIVERSITY PRESS

Oxford University Press, Inc., publishes works that further
Oxford University's objective of excellence
in research, scholarship, and education.

Oxford   New York
Auckland   Cape Town   Dar es Salaam   Hong Kong   Karachi
Kuala Lumpur   Madrid   Melbourne   Mexico City   Nairobi
New Delhi   Shanghai   Taipei   Toronto

With offices in
Argentina   Austria   Brazil   Chile   Czech Republic   France   Greece
Guatemala   Hungary   Italy   Japan   Poland   Portugal   Singapore
South Korea   Switzerland   Thailand   Turkey   Ukraine   Vietnam

First published by Oxford University Press, Inc.
198 Madison Avenue, New York, New York 10016

www.oup.com

First issued as an Oxford University Press paperback, 2010

Oxford is a registered trademark of Oxford University Press

Library of Congress Cataloging-in-Publication Data
Tremlin, Todd.
  Minds and gods : the cognitive foundations of religion / Todd
Tremlin; foreword by E. Thomas Lawson.
      p. cm.
   Includes bibliographical references and index.
   ISBN-13 978-0-19-973901-1
   1. Psychology, Religious. 2. Thought and thinking—Religious
aspects. 3. Faith. I. Title.
   BL53.T68 2006
   200'.1'9—dc22   2005023088

Printed in the United States of America
on acid-free paper

For Dicksie, who waited patiently—and believes.

Preface

Thankfully there is no need to use this preface—as is so often the case—as an apology for yet another book on a given topic. The field today being called the "cognitive science of religion" is indeed yielding a number of scholarly monographs and collections, but the field is too young and too expansive to have yet been adequately represented or summarized. If anything, there is an under abundance of available reports for people wishing to become familiar with this fruitful new approach to human religiosity. Furthermore, the best and most revealing work currently informing the field is found in the form of experiment summaries, conference papers, and journal articles—a rich yet disparate body of material seldom seen by any but the most committed professionals.

These first words, then, invite students and scientifically literate readers to encounter the cognitive science of religion at a level that is, hopefully, both clear and engaging. This book is meant as an introduction to some of the field's major themes, theories, and thinkers as well as fresh analyses suggested by ongoing research. No doubt those already well versed in the cognitive science of religion or its many tributaries will find much here to criticize (coverage that is too brief, analogies that are too rough, generalizations that are too broad), but the discussion purposely aims at outline and implication rather than erudition and novelty. The story told here is about everyone, so it ought to be easily followed by anyone. Likewise, it ought to provoke not only interest but also introspection. Toward that end, the style of presentation is deliberate: the cognitive perspective on religion is best communicated through instances of common human behavior rather than through complicated theory and jargon.

Take as an example one impetus for this book: Dick Miller, my father-in-law, is remarkable in a number of ways, but one frequently noted by acquaintances is how, in his mid-seventies, he continues to operate a one-man tree-trimming service. While Dick's work and mine are worlds apart, it is obvious (I've had occasion to assist him on several jobs, carrying equipment and chipping brush) that tree trimming—and, more to the point, Dick himself—presents a perfect example of the type of mental abilities featured on the following pages. In the course of cutting branches or falling trees, Dick has to calculate such difficult vectors as the fall line of the trunk: the direction based on cut angle and structural balance, the distance based on height. Getting these measurements right is rather crucial when nearby homes and property are at risk. Dick manages this consequential task with nothing more than vision and intuitive judgment; no elaborate instruments, no trigonometry carefully worked out on paper.

Yet trigonometry certainly is being done, and with great speed and accuracy (Dick has had no more than a couple near misses in over thirty years of falling trees). Just how such mental work is so efficiently—and so *naturally*—carried off is precisely the type of question those of us studying the mind find worth asking. Experience alone is clearly not the answer. In Dick's business there is no allowance for trial and error. Moreover, no two jobs are the same; a new set of variables must be weighed each time. So the answer must be related to the operation of the brain itself. Dick's skill illuminates one of many innate processes of human cognition, in this case an arithmetic (based on spatial relationships) as effective as the explicit procedural formulas learned in school. Similar illustrations will color this book's discussion of "minds."

As to the talk of "gods," Dick serves as an exemplar as well. For just as Dick looks upward and calculates the dimensions of a tree, so too he looks upward and concludes that there is a divine being that cares about life on earth, knows what we humans think, and makes specific demands on our behavior. For Dick, the existence and characteristics of a supernatural being (in his case, a supernatural being expressed in Christian terms) come as naturally to mind as does the trajectory of the limb he is about to cut. Dick's basic understanding of god is as automatic, as intuitive, and, it turns out, as innate as the mental math that supports his livelihood. The point of this book is that knowledge of tree trimming and knowledge of gods are not unrelated; both have natural cognitive foundations. Unearthing these foundations is our project.

Concentrated focus on the processes and products of human thought, an enterprise today engaging the efforts of a broad group of researchers, is a noteworthy academic development. The recognition that the brain lies at the center of the human world—as organizer and interpreter of incoming information, as constructor and communicator of outgoing ideas—is revolutionizing the humanities and social sciences. In fundamentally restructuring traditional understandings of human thought and behavior, cognitive science is bringing provocative new insights and methods to traditional areas of specialization, including anthropology, archaeology, linguistics, philosophy, psychology, sociology, and others. It also offers a powerful theoretical framework for compiling a truly interdisciplinary knowledge.

The scholarly inquiry into religion is no exception. Cognitive science has begun to impact this field of study with equal force—and just in time. Old and largely unsatisfying approaches to the uniquely human phenomenon of religion are being replaced by testable explanatory techniques adopted from the natural sciences. As a result, we now have powerful new answers to longstanding questions about the origin and persistence of religious thought, the processes governing the acquisition and transmission of religious ideas, and the relationship between religion's ubiquitous features and its cultural variations.

I am deeply indebted to those who introduced me to the cognitive science of religion, as well as to those who have since become my colleagues in the field. First among the former is Tom Lawson, who not only ushered me into the world of the mind and its implications for religious studies but also many others working in the field. That a cognitive science of religion now exists is due in no small part to Dr. Lawson's profound scholarly vision. The foreword he has graciously contributed to this book commends itself, and I am honored by its presence. Individuals who fall into the latter category include Justin Barrett, Pascal Boyer, Brian Malley, Luther Martin, Bob McCauley, Illka Pyysiäinen, Jason Slone, and Harvey Whitehouse.

I also thank those individuals who read and commented on early versions of this book, in particular Tom Lawson, Tim Light, Luther Martin, Jason Slone, and Brian Wilson. Special appreciation is extended to Staci Doty, who worked tirelessly on the manuscript and provided invaluable assistance with formatting and other irksome tasks. Finally, I thank Cynthia Read, executive editor at Oxford University Press for her many kindnesses, Julia TerMaat, and all of the folks at OUP for their diligent work on my behalf.

Note: Portions of the discussion laid out in chapter 6 (including the tables found therein) were first presented in a short essay titled "Divergent Religion: A Dual-Process Model of Religious Thought, Behavior, and Morphology" in *Mind and Religion: Psychological and Cognitive Foundations of Religion*, edited by Harvey Whitehouse and Robert N. McCauley (AltaMira Press, 2005).

Foreword

The cognitive science of religion is no longer a gleam in the eye of its earlier visionaries. It is now established as an increasingly substantial program of scientific inquiry rigorously pursued by cognitive scientists in both Europe and North America. As with any successful scientific program, it not only involves individuals pursuing specific theoretical and experimental work, but it also means finding support in new institutional forms. The most significant of these are academic programs such as the Institute of Cognition and Culture at Queen's University in Belfast and a similar program at Aarhus University in Denmark, as well as a group of scholars associated with the Institute for Advanced Studies in Helsinki. There are also a number of scholars in the United States who have played a major role in the development of this discipline. In addition, the *Journal of Cognition and Culture* (now in its sixth year of publication) has proved to be a major venue for the publication of theoretical and experimental studies in the cognitive science of religion. Furthermore, a number of conferences focusing on the many issues and problems involved in connecting cognitive and cultural forms in both the United States and various European countries have already been held, bringing together the ever increasing number of cognitive scientists now working in this field of inquiry. More such events are in the planning stages. The number of publications, both books and journal articles, is accelerating and is beginning to make an impact in associated fields such as cognitive, developmental, and evolutionary psychology. It is, therefore, with a great deal of pleasure that I welcome *Minds and Gods* by Todd Tremlin as a fine addition to the literature of the cognitive science of religion.

Tremlin calls our attention to an interesting fact: Religious ideas and the practices associated with them are ubiquitous. Scratch beneath the surface of any society and you will find religious ideas and practices in spades. The long view back and the wide view sideways highlights the presence and persistence of religion. This fact is, no doubt, irritating to those intellectuals who have always treated religion with suspicion, if not outright hostility, and hoped for its immediate or eventual demise. But as an ancient Greek philosopher has said: The world is full of gods. What *Minds and Gods* proceeds to show is why this is the case. Telling the story right takes knowledge, focus, imagination, cleverness, and hard work. These qualities can be found in abundance in this book.

The cognitive science of religion has been a long time coming. Many obstacles to a deep scientific understanding of religious behavior have slowed the growth of our knowledge about religious ideas and the practices they inform. This is not because scholars have had little interest in religion. The history of western thought shows that from its earliest days philosophers have wrestled with the problem of making sense of the reference of religious ideas, their truth-likeness, their origins, and their causes. Religious practices, too, have been embraced and decried. Since the Enlightenment, the status of religious belief has come under severe scrutiny. Religious belief has also found its apologists who were willing to pull out every logical trick in the book to preserve its intellectual status. What was missing from this long intellectual encounter with religion was a serious, dare I say objective, analysis and explanation of the origin, structure, and causes of religious ideas and the way that such structures inform religious practices. To understand the significance of Tremlin's contribution to the resolution of these difficulties we need a clearer picture of the obstacles.

The first of these is the overemphasis on the *interpretation* of religious ideas and practices and the paucity of work developing an *explanatory understanding* of why religious ideas arise in the first place and why such ideas and the practices that attend them persist no matter what the social and cultural conditions are. Given the Enlightenment project and its assumptions about human rationality, one would have expected religion to disappear from the human scene or at least be hidden in little isolated villages of irrationality in the backwaters of the earth. As we well know, that did not happen. While the attendance at religious observances might have diminished in some religions, the fact of the matter is that religious ideas and practices are not only alive and well but also increasing across the globe. This successful persistence of religion needs to be explained.

This need for explanation, however, points to the second obstacle to a more penetrating understanding of religion. Resistance to developing an explanatory understanding of religion by both the humanities and the social sciences is endemic to both of these noble enterprises but for different reasons. In the case of the humanities, the focus has never been on identifying the causal factors that precipitate religious ideas. Rather, it has involved either a positive or negative evaluation of these ideas, according to some assumed norm and according to some cultural context or other. Certainly many of these interpretations of religious ideas and practices heighten our sensitivities to the intricacies of religious belief. They do not, for all of that, explain why the ideas are there in the first place. Novelists have been particularly adept at pointing to the cultural role that religious ideas play in the human story. But even powerful imaginative stories are not enough in the quest for knowledge of the intricacies of human behavior.

While I do not wish to call into question the scientific aims of social scientists, nor, for that matter, their methods, I do think that some of the underlying methodological decisions that mark the history of these sciences has unnecessarily cut them off from the genuine contributions that the natural sciences, particularly biology and psychology, can make to their putative explanations. Ever since Durkheim, insistence on the methodological autonomy of the social sciences has retarded the power of social scientific explanations because this has forced social scientists to look only to socio-cultural variables for explanations of the phenomena in question. Surface correlations between social and cultural forms, while interesting, are not enough to assuage the scientific drive for ever deeper causal explanations and the search for the specific mechanisms involved. However, sufficient critique of the standard social science model has been presented not to cover this territory again. I would point out, however, that some social scientists have themselves rebelled against the strictures imposed by the standard model and have begun to seriously explore the interface between the natural and the social sciences to the benefit of both areas of scientific inquiry. The discipline of evolutionary psychology has been particularly importance in building bridges between, for example, anthropological and psychological inquiry.

Evolutionary psychology has taken a hard look at the surface variability of cultural forms and begun to identify significant regularities that underwrite such variability. This discipline has aided and abetted the work of cognitive scientists who have focused upon the problem of how the mind works, what the processes are in such working, and what products these processes construct. Evolutionary explanations of why the mind is able to engage in such construction are particularly relevant to our understanding of how and why the cognitive and the cultural are connected. Obviously, humans differ from each other in significant ways. However, despite their significance, the importance of such differences is not sufficient to exclude the search for regularities across human minds. One way of getting a grasp of these regularities is by paying attention to the constraints that both limit and enable human minds to produce the kinds of concepts that they typically do. And there is no better way of focusing upon the constraints that play a role in the production of such concepts than starting with the cognitive development of infants. Here developmental psychology has done yeoman work in transforming our knowledge of "the scientist in the crib." The literature on the subject is already vast and compelling.

Crucial to cognitive development is the very early recognition of agents and agency as well as the recognition of the difference between agents and everything else in the world. From an evolutionary standpoint, such knowledge has significant adaptive value. The forces of natural selection are unkind and the ability to distinguish between rocks, trees, and animals was important in ancestral environments and remains so today. Cognitive scientists have developed both interesting theories and designed clever experiments in order to uncover the various forms of intuitive knowledge that come very quickly in the development of the human mind as it strives to figure out and understand its environment. One way of describing these forms of knowledge is via the notions of folk physics, folk biology, and folk psychology. These forms of knowledge appear to be "domain specific" and independent of each other in both structure and development. That means that they are sensitive to particular environmental cues specific to the form of knowledge being acquired. They have been called "modes of construal." I will leave it to the reader to search the literature for references to folk physics (what are the material properties of things in the world made and how do they typically interact with each other) and folk biology (what are the properties of animate things and how do they reproduce, grow, and die). Folk psychology, however, requires our attention.

Folk psychology is a theory about how human beings and other animals represent their cohorts and cousins in their environment in terms of desires, beliefs, intentions, expectations, intuitions, and so on. Scientific psychology takes these features of commonsense knowledge and theorizes about their relationship to brain states, their role in cognitive development, their biological origins through the processes of natural selection, and their function in human reasoning. Of particular interest to cognitive scientists is the deep-seated nature of folk psychology in our commonsense knowledge and its resistance to more abstract concepts underlying human behavior. This resistance has been the bane of philosophers who would like human beings to grasp the significance of scientific theorizing for providing better understandings of human behavior than those delivered by common sense. What these philosophers sometimes forget is how useful such common sense knowledge is in our commerce with the world in which we live and especially with the people and other animals that populate that world. For example, attributing desire to a leopard on the ancestral plains of Africa is a very useful notion to possess if you spot that animal looking at you from some distance away. Who can deny the importance of such an attribution to the carnivore in question?

It is, however, in the social situations that humans typically find themselves from the day of their birth that the commonsense knowledge delivered by folk psychology becomes particularly important. And here the notion of agency plays a crucial role. What distinguishes agents from everything else is their intentionality. Intentionality is the notion that human minds have representational states. To have a representational state is to possess the means for conceiving of something in a specific way. For example, when I have a concept about something is the referent of our notion about something actual, possible, or impossible? To be an agent means that the concept under consideration is something that is capable of knowing something about something, intending to do something about something, and can evaluate, upon the basis of the evidence provided in the immediate context, whether that agent in fact did know and do something as conjectured. Of course, these processes can end up being wrong. I could misinterpret the glance, the movement, the sigh, the turning of the face. But I could also be right and being right makes a difference in my relationship to that other. Sometimes my very life might depend upon my being right, whereas if I am wrong there is no great loss. As the saying goes: It's better to be safe than sorry.

Tremlin has seized upon this recognition of the importance of the attribution of agency to others in *Minds and Gods* and runs with it in intriguing new ways. In order for human beings to develop god concepts, we need first to understand how agent concepts emerge from our mental basements. The easy way out would have been to start with a notion of the mind as a blank slate and simply argue that such concepts are nothing but the consequence of the process of socialization. Ultimately, of course, socialization does not really explain very much because it ignores the problem of what capacities a person needs to possess in order to be the subject of socialization. In other words, it simply postpones the explanation. Tremlin has taken the harder route, first, by paying very close attention to the evolutionary story that has produced such significant knowledge about why we have the bodies and minds that we do and why we perceive and conceive of the world in the way that we do. He has also focused on the work already accomplished in the cognitive science of religion and provides an excellent introduction to that literature. In addition, he shows not only that religion is about gods, but also that god concepts are fascinating by-products of mental processes that, in turn, can be accounted for by the processes of natural selection. Most importantly, however, he has persuasively shown that because the concepts of agents with some counterintuitive properties so easily take hold in human minds and, in fact, play a central role in religious systems, they should be understood as providing an impetus for the development of religious systems. As if this were not itself significant enough a contribution to the cognitive science of religion, Tremlin has also introduced the notion of what is known in cognitive science as dual processing. Dual processing involves two different cognitive processes that operate at different levels of mental representation. The first of these is a rapid, inference-rich mode of processing that points to the fact that our minds are quick responders to environmental stimuli. The rapidity with which we make judgments on the basis of fleeting cues from the surround is astounding. This mode of reasoning is inferentially rich. It does not take much for a young child to infer further relevant properties of an object when presented with either the representation of that object or the object itself. Knowing that something is an agent rather than a rock permits the child (and, therefore adults as well) to make all kinds of additional judgments about the agent.

There is also a slower reflective process where we can think about our rapid judgments. This is a meta-level of reasoning. When I think about what I just did, did I do the right thing in this instance? Why do I hesitate when I should not? What is the nature of thought? Why is there religion anyway? Did the universe have a beginning? Unlike the inferences I make when I know that I am perceiving an artificial object, for instance that clocks don't breath but they are reasonably good indicators of the time of day, higher order reasoning provides no quick and dirty inferences for answering such questions. Some higher order forms of reasoning take years of training before we are provisionally satisfied with the conclusion we reach. Some even require the language of mathematics in order to provide solutions. And some forms of reasoning end up with nonsense.

What can we learn from this idea about the levels of thought? For one thing, the more abstract the notion the more difficult it is to deal with. In religious contexts this means that appeals to the quick and dirty notions that so easily populate our minds tend to be more successful in contributing to the persistence of particular religious systems than those theological systems that require sustained abstract reflection. This attitude has proved to be the bane of theologians who are always ready to argue for the elimination of "superstitions" and the curtailment of ritualized behavior. This does not mean that such models of abstraction will die out. Theology has a long and sometimes distinguished intellectual history. But the institutionalized forms that provide the playground for the manipulation and development of such abstractions never succeed in playing the decisive role that the theologians constantly hope for as they dream of bettering the thoughts of typical religious participants. It is sometimes all too obvious that the religious system works quite well without depending to any significant degree upon such theological notions. Sometimes theology seems to do little more than provide soothing background noise. Even if this is an unnecessarily harsh characterization of theology's place in religious systems, at least it must be said that such notions are not the motor that drives religious ideas and the practices these ideas inform, nor does it play any significant role in the growth and decline of religious traditions. In fact, the picture that is emerging in the cognitive science of religion is that there is not one motor, even when we focus on the quick and dirty processes, but that there are *many* motors. It all depends on the level of analysis involved. What Tremlin has accomplished lies in his identifying the role that god concepts play as part of the complex causal story that is now being told in the cognitive science of religion. That is a considerable achievement.

E. Thomas Lawson
Institute of Cognition and Culture
Queen's University of Belfast
Northern Ireland

Contents

Minds and Gods

Introduction

In the sprawling shrine complex of Kataragama on the island nation of Sri Lanka, men and women from different religions come together each year to fulfill vows to this ancient Hindu god by offering him baskets of fruit, rolling on hot sand, walking over burning coals, piercing their bodies with metal lances, even hanging themselves from hooks impaled in their backs. Unlike some other gods in the Hindu tradition, Kataragama identifies with common people and has the power to answer worldly petitions, from cures for illness to help in passing government exams. He does not expect sacrifice in advance, but once a favor is granted, he demands his due.

Throughout the Gulf region of the Arabian Peninsula, Muslim men and women not only have faith in Allah but also believe in beings named jinn, malevolent spirits, and demon possession. In order to safeguard their families from such beings and the misfortune or illness they bring, Bedouins and townspeople alike have long employed a rich tradition of charms, decoys, and disguises. One of the most common methods of deflecting malevolent forces is the use of amulets, small containers or pieces of jewelry stuffed with passages from the Qur'an believed to shield the owner from harm. Many spirits, while dangerous, can also be fooled. A traditional method of protecting infants, for example, is to purposely speak ill of them, or even give them disparaging names, in order to trick evil beings into thinking them unworthy victims.

In the Pomio Kivung, a popular cargo-cult movement among the Baining peoples of East New Britain Island, Papua New Guinea, many hours are spent each day preparing elaborate meals to feed the spirits of ancestors who come to feast in special thatch-roof temples. The most important of these ancestors is a heavenly assembly of spirits known as the "Village Government." While the ancestral spirits of deceased kin are also given food offerings, cultivating relations with the Village Government is especially important because it is this divine assembly that, after judging the Baining peoples worthy, will one day return to earth in the bodies of white people, bringing with them the technological knowledge and material resources to turn the Baining's land into a utopia of Western-style industry and wealth.

At the baptism of a teenage girl in a Pentecostal church in Los Angeles, the pastor invokes the triune nature of god—"Father," "Son," and "Holy Spirit"—as he immerses the young lady in a pool of water. Unlike many other deities around the world, this being is to be worshiped and prayed to, but no sacrifices are required. In this case, god is said to have offered *himself* for sacrifice, and lifelong devotion to this being is the salvific exercise of his followers. Across the street, members of a Roman Catholic church worship the same god, yet they also spend a great deal of time offering prayers to a woman named Mary, *theotokos*, "Mother of God," as well as to a wide range of saints possessing special powers of their own.

Across the Japanese landscape, simple wooden arches called torii mark sacred sites—groves of trees, rocks, waterfalls, and mountains—where nature deities, or kami, reside. Kami are the energies that animate nature. They created the world; they embody the sun, moon, wind, sea, and fire; they gave birth to Japan's first human emperor; they prompt rice to grow in fields and lava to flow from volcanoes. In order to honor or engage the power of kami, these beings are treated as persons and given names. In large public shrines and at small altars in private homes, the kami are regularly revered with offerings and plied with prayers for personal health, success at work and school, and other worldly affairs.

Around the world and throughout history, in cultures as diverse as Mesopotamia and Mesoamerica, among people as different as the Yamana of Tierra del Fuego and present-day New Yorkers, religion shares at least one feature in common—belief in gods. These beings come in many forms. They may be the absolute, all-powerful deities of monotheistic religions like Judaism, Christianity, and Islam, or beings with very human behavior, such as certain gods in Roman and Hindu religion. They may play important roles in maintaining human or cosmic harmony, like the Wakan Tanka of the Lakota Sioux in America and the Orisa of the Yoruba in Africa, or they may be dangerous or foreboding forces to be avoided or placated, like the Pört hozjin, a Scandinavian spirit that lives under fireplaces and floors. Thus the term "god" can be misleading, as it is usually understood, at least in the West, to designate some eternal, supreme deity rather than the ghosts, ghouls, spirits, minor gods, or any of the seemingly endless possibilities found in cultures, communities, and cults across the globe. The term "supernatural being" might be better, for it speaks to the full range of unusual agents that populate the systems of belief and practice that we call religion.

Are there exceptions to this rule? No. While a handful of religions have been characterized as nontheistic or fundamentally unconcerned with the existence of gods—Theravada Buddhism, for example—even a cursory examination of such traditions reveals that supernatural beings are neither excluded from the overall structure of these religious worlds nor wholly incidental to their outworking. Theravada Buddhists interact with a complex cosmology filled with supernatural beings, and they openly treat the Buddha with the same reverence garnered by any god, despite a "formal" belief that the historical Buddha is now dead and inaccessible to petition. As we shall see, this discrepancy between formal beliefs and "folk" ideas is a compelling feature of religion. When a tradition's official teachings point its members away from gods deemed unorthodox or else forbid particular behaviors thought to be unfaithful, people often do them anyway. Even very real, very human people—like Siddhartha Gautama, Confucius, the Virgin Mary, and honored kin—are deified to varying degrees and added to the pantheon of religion.

What makes supernatural beings "supernatural" varies widely as well. Some gods are at once omniscient, omnipotent, and omnipresent, while others have limits on their access to knowledge, are powerful just in particular ways, or can only be in one place at one time. Some gods are superlative and live for ever; others die or can lose their station. Some supernatural beings have a definite, material shape yet can move freely through walls, fly, influence other objects, or read minds. Some supernatural beings are highly emotional; some care little for life on earth; some need to eat despite being incorporeal.

Conversely, it is extremely difficult to think about or picture a given god without invoking some resemblance to human beings. Hindu gods look and act like humans, from Shiva represented as the Lord of Dance to Krishna's flirtatious exploits with milkmaids. Bodhisattvas live in heavenly paradises with plenty of room for those who call on them. Ghosts, spirits, and ancestors once *were* human. Even when religious discussions turn to a transcendent deity like the Christian god, this being too is described with human metaphors, thought about and interacted with as a personal being, and is believed to have literally taken human form in the *person* of Jesus Christ. In short, gods are a special category of agents that in some ways resemble or are at least spoken about as having human-like qualities yet also possess powers, capacities, and faculties that exceed or break the basic rules of mundane human existence.

In whatever ways they are envisioned, gods are central to the study of religion. This connection is not always acknowledged. Some see religion in purely social terms, and turn gods into symbols for other ideas or else simply consider them irrelevant. That supernatural beings matter, however, is demonstrated by their universality across religions, by their centrality within religions, and by their psychological relevance to religious persons. As Illka Pyysi-äinen points out, "when people no longer can believe in the real existence of counterintuitive beings [his preferred term for 'gods'], religion loses its power" (2001b: 70). What distinguishes religion from a neighborhood Elks lodge, a college fraternity, a political party, or other kinds of social organizations centers precisely on belief in gods. This is a distinction of consequence. The collective systems of thought and action that we call religion often include vast institutions, gather in huge numbers of people, and inculcate lifelong ideas and behaviors. These religious systems, in turn, have and continue to play a significant role in the warp and woof of society at large.

While belief in supernatural beings is so common that it seems trivial, this same triviality obscures some compelling questions. Why *do* people believe in supernatural beings? And why, specifically, do they believe in *these kinds* of supernatural beings? This book is concerned with answering these questions. What is different about the answers offered here is that gods are described not primarily as theological concepts or as social or cultural constructs but as the products of human cognition. Explaining why people believe in gods requires first explaining the way people think. Describing the variety and nature of god concepts and their place in religious systems requires first describing the structure and functions of the brain. Understanding the origin and persistence of supernatural beings requires first understanding the evolved human mind.

Why is the subject of the human brain foundational to the discussion of gods and religion? A more complete, detailed explanation of the relation of heavenly gods and earthly minds is the reason for this book. By way of introduction, however, two very general responses provide the proper starting point.

First, our mind is, quite literally, the center of our universe. Every sensation that comes to us from the world "out there" is received, organized, and given meaning by the tissues of the brain. Fingers, eyes, ears, and the body's other sense organs are crucial to this process of reception, but in fact they are merely gateways and conduits for the brain. It is within the brain that all our perceptions of the external world are gathered, connected with other stored information, and interpreted—from basic stimuli like heat, taste, and light to complex symbols like mathematical theorems and spoken words. Working with such inputs, our brains literally generate what we assume the external world to be. As E. O. Wilson recognizes in his own attempt to ground knowledge: "The mind is supremely important. . . . Everything that we know and can ever know about existence is created there" (1998: 105).

This is only half of what the brain does, for it also—and more fundamentally—lies at the center of our inner world. At the physical level, the roughly one hundred billion neurons that comprise the human brain control the biological processes of the body, from managing the movement of limbs to initiating the onset of puberty to orchestrating tonal match when singing a song. At the conceptual level, the brain turns basic sensory input into meaningful information, maintains an extensive field of memory, creates a unified sense of "self," produces complex thoughts and novel ideas, and communicates with the outside world, principally through language. In short, the brain is central to what comes into the body and what goes out; it interprets and interacts with the external world, and it governs the physical systems and mental conceptions of our internal world.

The second reason for connecting gods and minds is that supernatural beings, as well as the religious systems of which they are a part, are among the plethora of mental conceptions acquired, represented, and transmitted by the human brain. Therefore, if the arising and nature of god concepts are to be understood, it is necessary to explore what goes into the acquisition, representation, and transmission of concepts generally. At the level of human cognition, ideas about gods and religion are not "special" kinds of thoughts; they are produced by the same brain structures and functions that produce all other kinds of thoughts. As Tom Lawson notes, "whatever it takes to explain how minds work generally will be sufficient to explain how religious minds work" (2000: 79). Of course, god concepts are different in content from other kinds of ideas—and examining what makes them distinctive and therefore universally successful is a major goal of this book—but the immediate point is that understanding any type of mental representation, including ideas like "god," must begin with the architecture and operation of normal brains.

While inquiry into the nature of the mind has a long history, it is only within the last several decades—a period of time often referred to as the "cognitive revolution"—that a comprehensive picture of human cognition has begun to emerge. Study of human cognition was initiated by, and continues to benefit from, dilemmas and discoveries in seemingly unrelated fields. For example, ongoing research into artificial intelligence has profound parallels with the investigation of biological thought. The study of the cognitive abilities of other animals, most notably the primates, begs comparison with our own species. Observation of childhood development seeks to articulate the debated relationship between innate endowment and learning. Medical scrutiny of patients with damaged brains and persons born with mental impairments prompts inquiries into the workings of "healthy" thought. These and other areas of study raise compelling questions about human intelligence and provide creative methods for finding equally compelling answers. Indeed, it is the interdisciplinary character of what may be broadly called "cognitive science"—now gathering in neurology, psychology, biology, archaeology, paleontology, anthropology, linguistics, philosophy, and other fields—that has allowed such rapid growth in our knowledge of the brain.

Of this expanding knowledge about human cognition, three insights are of crucial importance to the discussion to follow. First, we now recognize that though the brain literally looks to be, and is experienced by each of us to operate as, a single, seamless organ, it is in fact an astoundingly complex machine comprised of numerous specialized parts, or "modules." These modules are dedicated to specific tasks that, for the most part, are executed unconsciously. Again, this applies both to tasks related to receiving and interpreting information from the outside world and to those responsible for maintaining internal life and thought. No one is aware, for example, of the computational processes that add color to the objects we see, or of the mental signals that guide the release of hormones, or of the various component parts that go into the formation of a single idea like "friend." Understanding the modular architecture of the brain and what such a structure means for conceptualization is essential for explaining the ideas we produce, including gods.

Second, the specific modules and functions of the brain that we see today are the result of millions of years of natural selection. The modern mind has been shaped by evolutionary responses to the many environmental pressures faced by our early ancestors. How we presently think is a direct result of adaptive solutions to past problems. In this sense, characterizing the brain as "modern" is, structurally speaking, a bit of a misnomer. When taking into account our ancestral history of roughly 6 million years, we have not been "modern" for very long. The critical period in the development of the modern mind took place from about 1.8 million to 11,000 years ago. Thus at the most basic level of cognition, our modern brains still function much like the brains of the Pleistocene hunter-gatherers. This turns out to be one of the keys to understanding the nature and persistence of religious thought.

An evolutionary approach to the brain leads to a third significant insight about human cognition. Because the modern brain, with its many specialized devices and corresponding processes of thought, is characteristic of humans *as a species*, the way people think and the ideas they produce are largely the same for everyone everywhere. As Leda Cosmides and John Tooby point out, "the representations produced by these universal mechanisms [of the human brain] constitute the foundation of our shared reality and our ability to communicate" (Baron-Cohen 1995: xii). It is because all humans possess the same cognitive hardware that we can speak to each other—an activity that really amounts to the transfer of mentally constructed ideas. This means that concepts are tractable not only between people who are related or who live in the same country but also between cultures. Ideas as basic as a greeting or as complex as an ethical norm pass readily from mind to mind, regardless of one's gender, ethnicity, or society. Readers around the world, for example, can easily grasp the ideas found in this book, if presented in their own language—a universal cognitive ability that is itself based on a set of evolved mental skills.

What this means is that culture is not the barrier to the study of people and their systems of thought and practice that it has long been made out to be. In fact, "culture" is not a thing in itself at all but is, as Dan Sperber puts it, "the precipitate of cognition and communication" (1996: 97); that is, the products of mental activity that are shared by other like-minded people. To

speak of culture is really to speak of ideas—and the behaviors they engender—
that have been embraced, institutionalized, and perpetuated by a community.
With this *truly* revolutionary insight has come the revisioning of a host of
academic disciplines. Recognizing that the evolved human mind stands at the
nexus of basic biology and complex culture has finally bridged the gulf separating the natural sciences from the humanities and the social sciences. Whatever the subject at hand—art, politics, family relationships, war, and so on—
it maintains an intimate and immediate footing in the adapted information-
processing mechanisms of the modern brain.

In all of this, the study of religion also finds its place, for religion too is a
symbolic-cultural system produced by minds. "Gods" are ideas—and particularly successful ones at that. But fully grasping this fact, and then applying it
as an *explanation* for religion, is an activity only recently begun. Among the
roadblocks to a scientific study of religion is the long-standing view that religious thought is somehow unlike other kinds of thought, and that it therefore
cannot be explained in the same way that ordinary ideas can be. At the heart
of this perspective is the belief that a "scientific" explanation of religious
thought reduces away whatever it is that makes it "special." Another traditional
misconception of religious studies is that the tremendous diversity within religion found round the world makes it impossible either to generalize about
human religiosity or to construct a single explanatory theory.

Obviously, even the few insights of cognitive research outlined above call
into question such perspectives on religion as well as past approaches to its
study. As is true of any class of ideas, "gods" are the natural products of evolved
human psychology, and they are therefore open to a cognitive explanation. And,
since the modern mind is fundamentally the same everywhere, religious ideas
turn out to be neither as diverse nor as culturally relative as previously supposed. The cognitive approach reveals that the types of ideas that lie at the core
of religious systems are limited, necessarily constrained and shaped by the
specialized kinds of minds we all possess. As Pascal Boyer's work demonstrates, the supernatural concepts on which all religions are based comprise a
surprisingly short "catalogue of supernatural templates"—there are only so
many ways to build a god (2001: 78).

Findings like this one illustrate the promise that the "cognitive science of
religion" holds for our understanding of human religiosity. The appearance of
a major theoretical approach is a rare event in any field—and rarer still in the
field of religious studies. Yet over the course of only a couple decades and still
with a small number of people working in the field, the cognitive science of
religion is already proving itself to be the most significant and fruitful approach
to the subject ever undertaken. By probing the connection between the processes and products of the adapted human brain, cognitive research is laying
the foundation for a science of religion capable of supplying a meaningful,
testable description of one of the most fascinating aspects of human behavior.

Minds and Gods: The Cognitive Foundations of Religion seeks to contribute to this new science of religion by exploring the features of human cognition that lead, naturally, to thinking about, believing in, and constructing religions around gods. The central claim of this book is that understanding the origin, composition, and persistence of religion and the supernatural beings it features requires an understanding of the evolved human mind. This argument unfolds in two parts. The first four chapters explore the cognitive foundations of god concepts, discussing in both evolutionary and developmental terms the suite of mental structures and functions involved in the acquisition, representation, and use of these religious ideas. Due to a long history of adaptations designed for interaction with the world "out there"—in particularly with *others* "out there"—humans today possess a powerful set of cognitive endowments that make their minds particularly good at producing and transmitting god concepts—and, as a consequence, religion itself. The final chapters look at the cognitive foundations of religion. By connecting individual cognition with human culture, they show how the ideas that we have of gods in our minds relate to and shape the public religious systems that coalesce around them.

Chapter 1, "The Prehistoric Roots of the Modern Mind," pursues the question of what the past has to do with the present. Tracing the course of evolutionary history that led to the rise of *Homo sapiens* uncovers some of the selective pressures and adaptive strategies that gave shape to the brains we all use today. Chapter 2, "The Architecture of the Modern Mind," shifts the perspective back to the present by asking what our long developmental history has to do with the nature of human cognition. Given our ancestral world, what kinds of mental structures and functions should we expect to find in the brain, and what do we find? Just as important, what roles do such structures and functions, formed as they were in the crucible of Pleistocene life, continue to play in the construction of even our most complex and "modern" forms of thought?

Chapter 3, "Minds, Other Minds, and the Minds of Gods," begins to discuss directly what evolutionary adaptation and individual brain development have to do with religious thought. Isolating the innate predispositions and intuitive processes of cognition aids in explaining the composition of ideas about supernatural beings, shows what it is about god concepts that makes them a natural part of our cognitive repertoire, and clarifies the computational constraints placed on religious thought. Chapter 4, "Gods and Why They Matter," introduces readers to a peculiar yet revealing feature of religious thought—the differences between god concepts as portrayed in official theological systems and the way that god concepts are represented and processed by the human mind. It also looks more closely at the properties of god concepts that make them seem both plausible and relevant to life, especially their crucial links with human social psychology, and that lead many people to accept that supernatural agents are real.

Chapter 5, "Gods and Religious Systems," shifts the focus from how individual minds handle god concepts to the pivotal role such concepts play in religion. This discussion begins with another argument for the centrality of gods in the cultural systems we label "religion"—their ubiquity in conceptual and ritual schemes—and goes on to show that gods are necessary for fostering the commitment, motivation, and transmission potential such systems require. Chapter 6, "Cognition and Religious Systems" uses dual-processing models of thought drawn from social psychology and neuroscience to clarify, in detail, the often incongruent relationship between cognition and culture in the domain of religion. This work, in turn, grounds a new understanding of the selective forces at work on the shape and stability of religious systems and offers a new perspective on common but poorly explained episodes of change in religious systems, including personal conversions, doctrinal and ritual innovations, revival movements, syncretism, and the formation of new religions.

As noted in the preface, *Minds and Gods* is primarily intended to serve as an introduction to the cognitive science of religion. The original contribution of this book lies in expanding the present boundaries of the discussion. First, the book pays closer attention to human evolutionary history. This is certainly nothing new to the field, but it does make explicit what has largely remained implicit in other works. For example, in their analysis of Pascal Boyer's *Naturalness of Religious Ideas* (1994), Bernard Spilka and his colleagues write: "This is a cognitive theory of religion premised upon 'universal cognitive processes.' Natural selection is mentioned, but somehow the biological basis of these notions is never developed" (Spilka et al. 2003: 60). The exact evolutionary forces and stages that gave rise to these universal cognitive processes may be conflicted, but a general outline of them is essential to the cognitive explanation for religious thought and behavior. Second, greater attention is paid here to religious systems in addition to the religiosity of individuals. A subtle argument running throughout the book, and finally focused on in chapter 6, suggests that the natural constraints and dispositions of human cognition shape the content, development, and durability of actual religions.

On the whole, however, this entire volume owes its existence to previous and ongoing research by many talented people exploring human cognition and its connection to cultural artifacts. It therefore stands as a summary of some of the more important theories, clever experiments, and conclusions currently shaping our understanding of how religion works.

I

The Prehistoric Roots of the Modern Mind

What Does the Past Have to Do with the Present?

When Charles Darwin wrote his monumental work *On the Origin of Species* in 1859, he chose to say next to nothing about the implications of his theory of evolution for our own species—*Homo sapiens*. Yet few of his contemporaries failed to read between the lines. If correct, the mechanisms of natural selection had to apply to *all* life on earth. Darwin's reticence proved well founded, for his revolutionary idea, even without reference to human beings, set off a maelstrom of public debate and criticism.

Despite the outcry, Darwin carefully worked out the final phase of his argument, *The Descent of Man*, which appeared in 1871. The keenness of Darwin's scientific insight is illustrated not only by his knowledge that evolutionary theory would rewrite "natural history," but also that its effects should be detectable at biological depths below mere physical appearance. While admitting that serious research into the subject was still many years away, Darwin saw that the forces driving biological adaptation should reach even to the most sacred aspect of humanity—the mind itself:

> In the distant future I see open fields for far more important researches. Psychology will be based on a new foundation, that of the necessary acquirement of each mental power and capacity by gradation. Light will be thrown on the origin of man and his history. (1859: 488)

Today, evolutionary psychologists and related specialists are indeed demonstrating the formative role played by natural selection in shaping the structures and functions of the human brain. The assumption behind such research, of course, is clear: We can understand the mind of the present only by first recognizing that it is the product of selective pressures in the past. As Steven Mithen notes, investigation into the nature of the modern mind must begin with our *prehistory*, "for it was during that time that the distinguishing features of the human mind arose" (1996: 7).

That such a claim should come from an archaeologist is both obvious and fascinating. It is obvious because prehistory is Mithen's business; it is fascinating because archaeology is now deeply interested in human cognition. This is an illustration of the interdisciplinary power of the emerging field of cognitive science, which, just a decade and a half ago, Merlin Donald lamented was still based mainly on the study of literate, postindustrial minds and the capabilities of computers (1991: 5). Many traditional sciences are reorienting themselves toward cognitive concerns, thereby making substantial contributions to the multidimensional story of human thought.

Any meaningful model of the modern brain's structures and functions must be based directly on the possibilities and constraints of evolutionary theory. From the perspective of evolutionary psychology, current mechanisms of the brain are biological adaptations that have accumulated over the long course of our species' developmental history. Aligning the present characteristics of the mind with past selective pressures is not to ascribe predetermined goals to evolutionary forces; it is simply to recognize, and attempt to reconstruct, the process of cause and effect that produced the contemporary mind. Meeting this challenge requires both a panoramic view of human evolution and an extrapolation of the kinds of selective pressures that, progressively, resulted in the adapted brains we all use today. Once the proper connection is made between our biological past and present, it leads on to the further connection between our biology and culture.

It is normal to begin the story of human history at a point some 6 million years ago, when humans and modern apes shared a common ancestor. But this vast temporal distance means that there is little hard evidence of our first relative. Fortunately, the period of evolutionary history that is central to the emergence of the modern mind—a period of time spanning roughly 2 million years ago to the present—is both less distant and more accessible. Fossil remains and prehistoric artifacts that date to this period provide clues to the behavior, and therefore the cognitive capacities, of the hominids that comprise our ancestral train.

This period of prehistory is so important because it features the specific environmental conditions and selective pressures that shaped the modern mind. Throughout this expanse of time our ancestors lived as hunter-gatherers, directly competing for food with other animals while trying to avoid becoming food themselves. Under such conditions, pressure to develop physical and mental advantages was intense. The fossil record shows that certain hominids answered with crucial adaptations on both fronts. We are now able to isolate a number of adaptations that represent key turning points in the development of our species.

In outlining the cognitive evolution of modern humans, this chapter will clearly be focused at the level of brute existence, for it is precisely the reward of life or death—the successful continuance of a species or its extinction—that is the endgame of natural selection. Winning this game in our hunter-gatherer past required powerful new mental capacities that, after becoming permanent fixtures within our ancestral lineage, still continue to inform our thinking today.

Describing these cognitive adaptations calls for examining the nature of prehistoric life on the ground—a life, as Tennyson's description goes, "red in tooth and claw." It calls for finding the obstacles to daily existence that only one hominid species managed to overcome, and for exploring the mental abilities that enabled it to do so. This is not to say that the kinds of mental mechanisms that would eventually lead to higher, modern modes of thought, such as art and philosophy, were not yet being set in place—they where. However, the primary concern of survival in a decidedly hostile environment called for more immediate, more pragmatic developments. As Jerry Fodor nicely puts it, "it is, no doubt, important to attend to the eternally beautiful and true. But it is more important not to be eaten" (1985: 4).

Milestones in Human Evolutionary History

Approximately 5 million years ago, in an East African landscape very different from today, there lived a small primate with a profound future. While this outwardly unremarkable animal and all of its kin would soon die out, its momentary success as a forager gave rise to two closely related yet divergent families of descendants—modern apes, which include chimpanzees and gorillas, and humans. We have no direct record of this common ancestor. It is precisely the lack of fossil evidence that has dubbed the creature the "missing link." That this common ancestor existed, though, is demonstrable at the genetic level. By comparing the genetic makeup of modern apes and humans— chimpanzees and humans, for example, share ninety-eight percent of their genetic material—and measuring the rates of DNA mutation, molecular biologists have reliably honed in on both the time of biological convergence 5 million years ago and the existence of this common ancestral ape, which could in no way imagine its grandiose legacy.

The choice of Africa as the seat of human evolution is clear. This vast continent, which comprises about one third of the habitable landmass of the entire planet, contains nearly every type of natural environment known and, consequently, more kinds of animals are found here than anywhere else in the world. The most obvious argument for Africa, however, is the physical evidence itself. Of the rich store of hominid fossils discovered so far, those that are the oldest and represent the greatest variety of species all come from eastern and southern Africa. In East Africa, the majority of fossil specimens come from sites in Hadar and Middle Awash in Ethiopia, Koobi Fora and Omo in Kenya, and Olduvai Gorge in Tanzania. In South Africa, important finds come from places like Makapansgat, Sterkfontein, Taung, and Swartkrans. Genetic research also suggests Africa as the Eden of human origins. Contemporary studies of mitochondrial DNA reveal that the gene pool shared by Africans today is more diverse, and therefore older, than that of people from other parts of the world. This finding supports the theory that anatomically modern humans originated in Africa around 100,000 years ago—the descendents of a statistical genetic progenitor known as "mitochondrial Eve"—and later migrated to other lands.

Aside from the genetic evidence for a common ancestor of apes and humans, we know nothing about the first million years of hominid evolution. Barring hard evidence, there is no way to project a reliable picture of life at the time. But the fossil record begins to unfold in earnest at a point 4.4 million years ago. It is generally agreed that the trajectory of hominid evolution following the split from the common ancestor resulted in four categories of hominid: the genus *Ardipithecus*, dating to 4.4 million years ago; the gracile and the robust australopithecines, ranging from 4 to 1 million years ago; and the genus *Homo*—our own genus—which emerged around 2 million years ago. A fifth genus of hominid, *Kenyanthropus*, was added to this list in 2001, following the discovery of a new, distinctly unique skull on the western shore of Lake Turkana in northern Kenya. The diversity of known hominids expands still further at the basic biological unit of species. All told, about eighteen species of hominids have been identified, although several of these classifications continue to be contested, as well as the theories regarding their descent relationships. The most recent addition to our ancestral tree, *Homo floresiensis*, was unearthed in 2003 in a cave called Liang Bua on the Indonesian island of Flores. This spectacular archaeological find has yielded several specimens of a dwarf-size hominid species that existed in remote isolation alongside modern humans as recently as 13,000 years ago.

The fossil record begins with *Ardipithecus ramidus*, the oldest known hominid. The first fossils of *A. ramidus*, which date to about 4.4 million years ago, were discovered in the Middle Awash region of Ethiopia in 1994. Subsequent fieldwork has yielded teeth, cranial, and skeletal fragments from some fifty individuals. Investigation of this fossil evidence reveals a creature more apelike than any other hominid, including important skeletal similarities and dentition typical of leaf eaters. At the same time, the hominid characteristics of *A. ramidus* are also evident. Estimated to stand about 40 inches tall and weigh about 65 pounds, A. ramidus held its head upright, had smaller canine teeth, and was at least capable of walking on two legs. Also important to the description of A. ramidus is the environment in which it lived. Analysis of the accompanying sediment shows fossilized wood, seeds, and monkeys—evidence that A. ramidus lived in forests. This finding places A. ramidus in a different ecological niche than that of later hominid species.

The next oldest set of fossils belongs to Australopithecus anamensis, a new genus of hominid that emerged between 4.2 and 3.9 million years ago. First discovered at Kanapoi, Kenya, in 1965, more than twenty new fossil specimens were found in the region in the mid-1990s. Likely a contemporary of A. ramidus, this hominid is larger and heavier—perhaps twice as large. While the exact nature of A. ramidus's locomotion is not clear, leg bones of A. anamensis show that it almost certainly walked on two legs. It likely shared A. ramidus's diet of fruit, leaves, and seeds, yet A. anamensis's habitat was riverine woodland as opposed to forest.

Starting at about 3.9 million years ago, the trail of hominid evolution is both enriched and complicated by the appearance of two related yet regionally diverse species known as the gracile australopithecines. In East Africa lived Australopithecus afarensis, one of the best-known early hominids. While current fossil specimens represent some 120 individuals, the most famous find is "Lucy," a 3.2 million-year-old skeleton uncovered in Hadar, Ethiopia, in 1974. Nearly half complete, Lucy's remains reveal a hominid more human-like than either A. ramidus or A. anamenis. Lightly built, with long arms relative to the legs, A. afarensis stood between 3 and 5 feet tall and weighed an average of 110 pounds. Facial features include a low, flat forehead, projecting face, and prominent brow ridges. The design of Lucy's pelvis and leg bones shows that A. afarensis was clearly bipedal, a fact further attested to by a trail of 3.6 million-year-old footprints preserved in volcanic ash in Laetoli, Tanzania. Yet A. afarensis also had curved fingers and toes, suggesting that it still spent time in trees. While current interpretations differ, A. afarensis is commonly held to be the pivotal ancestor along the evolutionary line toward human.

Another contender for this distinction, however, is a newly-announced hominid, Kenyanthropus platyops. Represented by a mostly complete cranium and dental fragments discovered at Lomekwi in Kenya in 1999, K. platyops dates to between 3.5 and 3.2 million years ago, making it a contemporary of Lucy. While no skeletal remains exist that might tell more about the body structure of K. platyops, the skull displays an unusual combination of characteristics that have prompted researchers to designate the specimen as a new genus. While K. platyops shares many traits in common with A. afarensis, including brain size, its well-preserved facial features are distinctly different— and closer to human. Rather than the ape-like projecting face of the australopithecines, K. platyops has a broad, flat face with small teeth. The striking contrasts between these two contemporaries illustrate the process known as adaptive radiation, in which members of an evolving group contending with different environments or ways of life quickly diversify.

Another contemporary of *A. afarensis* is *Australopithecus africanus*, which emerged in South Africa at about the same time that Lucy was living in East Africa. Fossil specimens of some 130 individuals have been found in places like Gladysvale, Makapansgat, and Sterkfontein, most dating to between 3 and 2.4 million years ago. The most famous representative of this species is the "Taung Child," which raised the ire of the scientific community when it was unveiled in 1925. In stature, *A. africanus* was slightly smaller than *A. afarensis* and shows an average weight of about 100 pounds. The skull of *A. africanus*, however, features more human-like characteristics, such as a higher forehead, shorter face, and less prominent brow ridges. Like its East African relative, *A. africanus* combined both bipedal and arboreal locomotion and pursued a similar vegetarian diet.

Other recent discoveries have resulted in the naming of two new though contested australopithecine species. A fossilized mandible and teeth dating to between 3.3 and 3 million years ago was found in 1995 in Chad—the most western location of australopithecine remains found in Africa. While this specimen shares anatomical features in common with *A. afarensis*, the number of differences, taken together with its geographical distance, has been used to justify the species designation *Australopithecus bahrelghazeli*. Two years later, near the village of Bouri in the Afar region of Kenya, skull and jaw fragments were unearthed that date to between 2.5 and 2.3 million years ago. Named *Australopithecus garhi*, this specimen exhibits features of both the gracile and robust hominids and therefore could represent an important transitional species.

While the relationships between these early hominids remain unresolved, it is clear that following the gracile australopithecines the hominid line split in two: one branch leading to a set of more robustly built australopithecine species before eventually coming to an end; the other branch continuing toward modern humans. The known robust hominids, sometimes classified under the genus *Paranthropus*, include two East African species, *Australopithecus aethiopicus*, whose fossils date to 2.5 million years ago, and *Australopithecus boisei*, dating to 2.3 million years ago, and one South African variety, *Australopithecus robustus*, which emerged around 2 million years ago. The bodies of the robust australopithecines where more heavily built than those of the graciles but remained of similar size and weight. The structure of their skulls, however, is distinctive. All three robust species have broad, flattened faces, big, thickly enameled teeth, massive lower jaws, and a sagittal crest of bone on the cranium that anchored large muscles used for chewing. These physical features suggest that the robust australopithecines had adapted to harder, low-quality foods found in savanna—a markedly different environment from the ones occupied by earlier hominids—and perhaps, at least in the case of *A. robustus*, a diet that included meat.

The robust australopithecines became extinct around 1 million years ago, their end attributed to overspecialization and climate change. Along the second trajectory of hominid evolution, however, a new genus emerged, one capable of adjusting to shifting environmental conditions. This was the genus *Homo*, and its first representatives appeared in eastern Africa a little more than 2 million years ago. The classification and descent relationships of the habilines are still much debated, but two species commonly thought to be direct human ancestors are *Homo habilis*, first found in Olduvai Gorge, Tanzania, in 1960, and *Homo rudolfensis*, unearthed at Koobi Fora, Kenya, in 1972. The crucial anatomical features distinguishing the habilines from the australopithecines include bigger bodies, smaller teeth, larger brains, and more dexterous hands.

Larger brains and improved dexterity were obviously crucial both to the habilines' present competitive success and future cognitive development, but one characteristically "human" result of these physical changes was the design and use of tools. While the australopithecines may also have utilized wood and stone—perhaps as hammers and digging tools—stone tools of regular design appeared just over 2 million years ago and are commonly attributed to *H. habilis*, or "handy man." Among this collection of tools are sharp stone flakes and the stone nodules used to make them. These tools were utilized both directly—the stone flakes, for example, used to cut plants and butcher meat—and to shape other tools out of wood. This early tool technology is known as the "Oldowan" industry after Olduvai Gorge in Tanzania, the site where it was first discovered.

A third early *Homo* to emerge in East Africa, and which appears to be an important transitional species, is *Homo ergaster*, dating to 1.8 million years ago. In contrast to both *H. habilis* and *H. rudolfensis*, this species features a larger, thinner cranium and increased brain size. *H. ergaster* was also tall and lean, its body proportions essentially the same as modern humans. The best-known example of *H. ergaster* is the "Turkana Boy," found on the banks of Lake Turkana in 1984. This specimen—the most complete early hominid yet found—is of a male between 10 and 12 years of age. Already more than five feet tall at the time of death, this juvenile would likely have grown to over six feet in adulthood.

The fossil record of the early *Homo* species ends at about 1.6 million years ago, when they are displaced by a prolific new species, *Homo erectus*. The widespread presence of *H. erectus* is attested to by a particularly rich body of fossil evidence dating from 1.5 million to 300,000 years ago. The earliest examples of *H. erectus* come from sites in northern Kenya. These bones reveal a large, robustly built creature with an external projecting nose, strong jaws, and a flat, thick skull with a large brow ridge and a brain capacity considerably larger than that of the habilines.

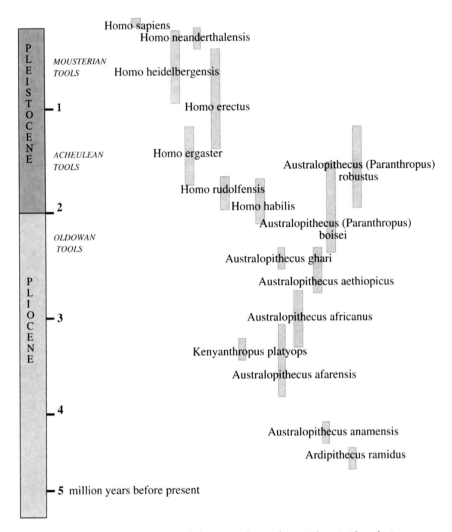

FIGURE I.I. Ancestors, dates, and descent relationships in hominid evolution.

In addition to important biological changes, *H. erectus* represents a milestone in human evolution in several other respects. First, *H. erectus* developed a superior tool technology, known as the "Acheulean" industry. In comparison to crude Oldowan artifacts, the stone tools of *H. erectus* were more complex in design and took greater skill to make. The key innovation of the Acheulean technique is the shaping of an entire stone to a specific tool form and then systematically chipping the stone from both sides to produce a bifacial cutting edge. Examples of new Acheulean tools include bifacial handaxes, picks, and cleavers. These tool kits, prevalent throughout the world, attest to a mastery of hunting skills. There is also evidence, such as charred animals bones and the remains of hearths, that *H. erectus* was the first hominid to control fire. Co-ordinated mass hunting and learned tool design signal the presence of a complex social ordering of everyday life.

Second, the rise of *H. erectus* marks the beginning of migrations of early humans out of Africa. This geographic dispersion is confirmed by extensive fossil evidence of *H. erectus* living not only in Africa but also throughout Europe and Asia. Remains of *H. erectus* have been discovered in places as diverse as Dmanisi in the republic of Georgia, in China, and throughout the Indonesian islands. Indeed, with the exception of modern humans, *H. erectus* was the most wide-ranging hominid to have lived.

The widespread movement and material culture of *H. erectus* demonstrate that at this point in evolutionary history, hominids reached a momentous new stage. In the first place, they had clearly become adaptable to new and changing environments. The differences between the climates and ecosystems of Africa and those occurring throughout Asia would have been significant, yet *H. erectus* appears to have thrived. Likewise, their success also suggests that hominids were now the dominant species wherever they lived. While no doubt still vulnerable to other large predators, it is safe to claim that their newfound skills in toolcraft and social cooperation changed their environmental status from hunted to hunter. This consequential new position likely extended to encounters with each other, or at least between differing hominid species. Fossil remains found in Gran Dolina, Spain, dating to 780,000 years ago and currently attributed to the species *Homo antecessor*, show numerous cut marks at muscle connections. This finding is considered by some to be the earliest documented case of cannibalism.

Starting at about 500,000 years ago, the fossil record shows the emergence of new populations of early humans living in Africa and Europe that appear, both anatomically and behaviorally, still closer to modern people. In Africa, specimens of archaic *Homo sapiens* have been found in Kenya, Zambia, and elsewhere. From sites in England, France, Germany, and Spain comes evidence of *Homo heidelbergensis*, the Western descendant of *H. erectus* or one of the African hominids. Both of these species had robust, muscular bodies, but it is their crania that are most striking. The braincases of these species are taller and rounded—much like the skulls of modern humans—and show another increase in brain size.

Archaic *Homo sapiens* lived until 100,000 years ago. However, at a point some 150,000 years ago, a new—and arguably the most famous—human relative rose to prominence, *Homo neanderthalensis*. Named for cranial and skeletal remains discovered in 1856 in Germany's Neander Valley, Neanderthal is now represented by hundreds of specimens that reveal common character traits, but also a confusion of morphological relationships. Indeed, just as the original arguments over the validity of Neanderthal was responsible for initiating the science of paleoanthropology, so questions about the species' fate and contribution to human phylogeny are subjects of intense debate today. Some researchers see Neanderthals as simply geographic variants of *Homo sapiens*; others believe they are a separate species that evolved from an earlier archaic form but, failing to compete with rival *H. sapiens*, finally went extinct around 30,000 years ago, having made little impact on the contemporary human genome.

Though a highly variable species, the preserved anatomy of Neanderthals reveals a strong, stocky being struggling to eke out a living during the harsh period of ice ages. Male Neanderthals were 5.5 feet tall on average and weighed 150 pounds. The facial features of Neanderthal include a low, slopping forehead, large nose, pronounced jaws, and double-arched brow ridges. Though the skull itself is less round than that of anatomically modern humans, the size of the brain is actually slightly larger, likely due to Neanderthal's greater muscle mass. Also noteworthy are reconstructions of the vocal tract, which demonstrate Neanderthal's capacity for vocalization and speech, though this was probably already present in other species.

Found throughout Europe and parts of Asia, the remains and artifacts of Neanderthals also witness to significant cultural advances. Though capable hunters, the Neanderthal's skills were further tested by the severe cold and limited resources of the European ice age. The use of fire was crucial to survival in glacial conditions, as were items like clothing, bedding, and forms of shelter. While the stone tools of Neanderthals remained simplistic, they are closely associated with the "Mousterian" industry of tool making, a further improvement on the Acheulean technique. The main innovation of Mousterian toolcraft involved first preparing the stone cores in a way that standardized flakes and blades could be systematically struck off and then retouched. This process not only introduced stages into the creation of stone tools but also led to the refinement of old designs and the creation of new ones. A variety of points used in spears appear as well as implements like sidescrappers for dressing animal hides. The development of complex tools such as spears, in which two or more parts are combined, foreshadowed the rapidly improving tool-making cultures to come.

Accompanying advancements in Neanderthal material culture is striking evidence that Neanderthal cognition had opened new conceptual spaces as well. There is evidence that Neanderthals looked after those who were injured or infirm, implying deeply rooted social bonds, and there are numerous and widespread examples of intentional burial of the dead, sometimes with the inclusion of objects like personal decorations or flowers. Such activity suggests self-conscious awareness, the development of social rituals, and a growing symbolic understanding of the world.

Neanderthals survived in Europe until 30,000 years ago. Their disappearance is commonly ascribed to their failure to compete with anatomically modern humans, who, according to fossil remains found at sites in Africa and Israel, were already present by 100,000 years ago. The first modern humans are physically distinguishable from Neanderthals: their bodies are taller, more lightly built, and adapted for a warm climate; their faces feature a shorter nose, smaller teeth, minimal brow ridging, and a prominent chin; their skulls are higher and globe-shaped, with the front of the braincase set directly above the face. In addition to large brains, early humans also possessed the anatomical apparatus necessary for complex speech patterns, such as the modern supra-laryngeal vocal tract.

For a long period of time these first modern humans shared the world with archaic *Homo* species and Neanderthal and show few cultural advances or behavioral changes. Then, beginning about 60,000 years ago, modern humans moved in rapid succession through a series of Upper Paleolithic tool industries—including the Aurignacian, Gravettian, Solutrean, and Magdalenian periods—bringing to bear significant design innovations and using the full range of natural materials, including bone, horn, and ivory. They also began to operate within a vastly expanded conceptual world. Starting at about 40,000 years ago personal decoration like jewelry is joined by abstract and representational art in the form of sculpture, engravings, and cave paintings, the most famous of which are found in Lascaux, France. Burials are more elaborate and ritualized, including the use of red ochre and grave goods. Additionally, the first modern humans migrated with great proliferation, extending their range out of Africa to the Middle East, Europe, and Asia, finally building boats for the crossing to Australia around 50,000 years ago. At about 35,000 years ago the Beringia land bridge allowed them access to the Americas.

Homo sapiens's superior intelligence and ability to exploit the natural environment is clear; by 30,000 years ago they are the only representatives of their genus left on earth. And yet they have barely begun to exercise their dominance and newfound creativity. Over the final thousands of years of human history—a tiny percentage of the 5 million years just covered—the pace of cultural innovation accelerates. Modern humans learn to manipulate the world and express themselves in profound ways, from reflective activities like philosophy to major social and technological enterprises that include empire building and experimental science. Along the way modern humans shift from the lifestyle of hunter-gatherers to a sedentary existence based on agriculture and the domestication of animals. They trade in their Stone Age tools for metal implements, develop complex sociopolitical relationships, codify oral communication as written words, and, in the absolute last moment of time, display an intellectual brilliance capable of producing computers, spaceships, and nuclear power.

The course of evolutionary history highlights two features of modern humans. On the one hand, *H. sapiens* are clearly different from their predecessors. As the cultural explosion of the last 50,000 years demonstrates, modern humans are capable of achievements far beyond those of the Neanderthals, who, for some 70,000 years, were contemporaries. From a purely anatomical perspective, such abilities aren't obvious. Modern humans are principally distinguished from earlier hominids by skeletons perfected for bipedal locomotion, by distinct skull, dental, and facial morphology, and by larger brains, yet there is little reason to think these physical differences of great consequence. Indeed, in many ways the modern human physique is far more vulnerable to the natural world than that of earlier hominids, and it should not be forgotten that several of these species thrived for roughly a million years in environmental conditions significantly more hostile than today's Holocene world. But the physical differences of modern humans are accompanied by substantial behavioral changes that herald their success. As interesting as the characters in the story of human evolutionary history look from the outside, it is what was taking place inside their heads that proved paramount.

On the other hand, a focus on superior mental abilities cannot loose sight of the fact that the modern mind is the result of evolutionary development. This is no less true of its spectacular cultural products. As Daniel Dennett points out, "all the achievements of human culture—language, art, religion, ethics, science itself—are themselves artifacts (of artifacts of artifacts . . .) of the same fundamental process that developed the bacteria, the mammals, and *Homo sapiens*" (1995: 144). Evolution is slow and constructive: random advantageous differences within species become permanent adaptations that eventuate into new forms. Thus all of the hominids discussed above, from the australopithecines to *H. sapiens*, stand in relation to each other—some as direct precursors, others quite distant. Because physical morphology and mental abilities are tractable across time, it is impossible to understand the present anatomy and psychology of modern humans without reference to our evolutionary past.

These two features of modern humans—novel ability and biological inheritance—open two trajectories of research. The first explores what it is that makes contemporary minds so different from ancient ones. This is a difficult task. The natural answer revolves around assumptions about brain size. Yet as noted above (and to be discussed further in the next section), Neanderthals had a brain as large, if not actually larger, than *H. sapiens*. Nevertheless, archaeological evidence shows Neanderthals to be incapable of matching the cultural innovations of their competitors or of summoning the imagination to do so. So brain size, while important, is not the whole answer. The intellectual Rubicon seems, rather, to be related to matters of cognitive structure and processing. Cognitive archaeologist Steven Mithen, for example, locates the profundity of modern humans not in brain size per se, but in a fundamental reorganization of mental processing that took place around 60,000 years ago (1996). This idea, and various other proposals regarding the architecture of modern minds, will be discussed further on.

The other trajectory of research—and the one central to this book—explores the mental inheritance links between the past and the present. *Homo sapiens* may be smart, but their current mental abilities rest on biological foundations developed and passed along by their ancestors. This claim calls for caution. We are not simply, as Scott Atran provocatively frames the question, "stone age minds" in a "space age world" (2002), but neither are we wholly disconnected from prehistoric life. The argument throughout this book tracks the investigations of evolutionary psychology, insisting on crucial similarities between prehistoric and modern thought despite the obvious differences, and claiming that many forms of thought, including religious thought, owe a great deal to the mind's prehistoric roots. A reversal of Atran's conceit is therefore called for: We are "space age minds" from a "stone age world."

Elucidating the mental links between the past and the present involves returning again to the long story of human evolution. This time the purpose is not simply to identify our ancestral heritage but to uncover the specific environments and selective pressures that gave rise to the adapted human brain.

Selective Pressures and Adapting Brains

Today people in developed nations awake in comfortable beds inside sturdy, well-heated houses. They don prefabricated clothing chosen for the weather that they purchased from a store, along with many other essential products. They eat balanced meals kept fresh by refrigeration which are quickly and efficiently cooked. They go about their day in relative peace, without fear of being attacked by others or needing to look out for hidden dangers. They navigate the social world with great freedom of expression, picking friends and mates according to personal taste. If this picture of modern life were typical of human history as a whole, there would be little reason to consider links between the ancient world and the mind. But life today is obviously not what life was like even a few centuries ago, let alone during the vast expanse of evolutionary history. The environments and selective pressures that made humans human had nothing in common with contemporary cities, nor even with the agricultural lifestyle often marked as the start of human civilization some 10,000 years ago. Understanding the present design of the mind requires reaching much farther into the past, to places comprised of jungles and savannas rather than parks and concrete—places far less safe and predictable, times far less secure and fruitful—where interaction with the world, both the natural and the social, was quite literally a matter of life and death.

What hasn't changed from prehistoric to modern times is the game of life itself. As Tim Friend has colorfully noted, there are some 10 million species on this planet, and for the most part all are concerned with the same four things: Sex, Real Estate, Who's boss? and What's for dinner? (2004). While there is a wide range of theories regarding the driving forces of human evolution and the ways in which its various stages unfolded over time, these four elements of daily existence, together with the vicissitudes of life in a hostile, ever-changing ecology, comprise a short list of the kinds of powerful selective pressures at work on our early ancestors.

Limning the contours of this process is obviously difficult. The timescales involved are immense, and it is all too easy to conflate them in the search for "defining human traits." Bipedalism, for example, evolved over 4 million years ago, but the creatures that first exploited it could hardly be called human. Other human characteristics, such as tool use, the capacity for language, the conquest of fire, even large brains, arose progressively over millions of years, but again in hominids not yet human. Truly human traits—that is, traits displayed by the truly human—emerged only 100,000 years ago, what amounts to the smallest moment in the course of life's development on earth. Yet it is precisely across these evolutionary stepping-stones that we must follow after our ancestors, and the messy, muddy ground around these footholds is equally important to an understanding of what we have become. Evolution is interactive; it takes place at the interstices between an organism and its environment. Its method is natural selection, the only process capable of producing complex design, and its means is adaptation through genetic mutation, changes in form or function that better solve survival problems. None of this need involve oversight or foresight. William Paley might be quite right about watches, but eyeballs and other biological systems—which are far more complex than watches—can indeed have natural makers. For every successful mutation there are many more that prove flawed and fail to propagate. But this is the basic blueprint for constructing a modern human, and it points up the need to clarify the changing environmental conditions and challenges of life that drove adaptation in the direction it went rather than another.

From an ecological perspective, the human ancestral line passed through dramatically shifting landscapes, climate changes, and biozones, all of which played a significant role in molding the modern body and mind alike. During the last 5 million years the earth's landmasses continued to drift and collide, forming mountain ranges, creating new passages, and rerouting watercourses. In this same period radical oscillations in climate, including numerous glacial and interglacial phases, reset regional temperatures, affected rainfall patterns, and raised and lowered sea levels. Such global reshuffling had a profound effect on the world's flora and fauna, defining the variety of plant life that anchored the food chain and driving the diversity of animals feeding within it. The composition of local habitats and the level of diversity they breed relate to the speed and nature of adaptation, as competition and encounters with others rapidly selects beneficial mutations. This history of geological upheaval and climatic swings is as complex as it is consequential; fortunately, we can limit the dimensions of this changing world to humankind's place of origin. "We are what we are today," writes Lee Berger, "because we've been shaped by our environment—and it was the African environment that hosted almost every major evolutionary change we've experienced on our journey toward being human" (2000: 8).

One of the most dramatic set changes on Africa's ecological stage took place at the end of Miocene epoch approximately 6 million years ago. For millions of years Africa had been blanketed in lush tropical forests, offering easy travel, safe shelter, and abundant water and foodstuffs to the arboreal primates that flourished there. Then a new ice age, which had begun in the middle Miocene, drastically altered the African environment. Though the ice itself never reached Africa, falling global temperatures cooled the continent significantly. As more and more water became locked up in ice, sea levels plunged—the Mediterranean shrank to an inland sea—and Africa experienced an extensive period of acidification. The net effect of this climatic change was the devastation of Africa's rich Miocene forests. With the start of the Pliocene epoch 5.2 million years ago, Africa featured a very different landscape with a new set of selective pressures for the creatures struggling to survive in it.

While Africa's equatorial rainforests remained, savanna and riverine woodlands now dominated much of the continent, a rather traumatic shift in scenery for primates equipped for life in trees. Vast tracts of grassland made movement between wooded areas both difficult and dangerous, yet also necessary in the face of severely curtailed resources. These grasslands welcomed the arrival of grazing animals, but also of predators whose lives were made easier by the open country. In the face of shifting ecosystems, Africa's primate population was forced to adjust their lifestyles or perish along with many other species that could not.

Environmental changes precipitate physical changes. Given Africa's revised terrain, it makes sense that one of the first crucial anatomical adaptations promoting success in this new world was reliance on the hind legs. Why we became bipeds is widely debated, but its import is not. The shift to bipedalism was likely *the* adaptation responsible for the irreversible divergence of ape and hominid. What makes the earliest hominid finds significant—what marks them as hominid in the first place—is the evidence they show of physical capacities for bipedal locomotion, demonstrated most dramatically by the vertical entry of the spinal cord into the base of the skull. Yet it is still a chimpanzee-size skull we see. So this anatomical juxtaposition provides an important object lesson in evolutionary speculation; namely, we must avoid teleological readings of physical change. As Craig Stanford points out, "the earliest humans were more or less upright apes" (2001: 3). The transition to bipedal walking was not achieved so that tools could be designed and wielded (these were still 2 million years away) nor to spur explosive brain growth (almost 4 million years away) but simply because upright locomotion provided selective advantages over quadrupedal posture.

The ability to stand and move upright would certainly have enabled the first hominids to peer over tall savanna grasses as they moved cautiously between forested areas, yet primatologists like Stanford are skeptical of the "savanna scenario" as the sole stimulus behind bipedalism. Other direct benefits of upright posture include a more energy-efficient means of locomotion, reduced body heat, appearing larger to predators and group mates, improved food-gathering techniques, and the ability to exploit woodlands and grasslands simultaneously. This last ramification of bipedal, hands-free living, was crucial to early humans' continuing success; becoming ecological generalists would have provided much-needed flexibility for coping with Africa's altering habitats. It is widely suspected that the demise of hominid species such as the robust australopithecines was, as for other kinds of animals, the result of over-specialization.

Hands-free living, while providing many immediate practical advantages, also opened up a new space of developmental possibilities for the first hominids. Standing on two legs allowed for novel forms of interaction with the three-dimensional world, a world for which primates already possessed a well-developed, color-sensitive visual system. Two free hands can not only gather food more efficiently, for example, but also carry it from place to place. Free hands also enable their owners to manipulate objects in the environment, such as rocks and sticks. Ever-increasing dependency on the hands in conjunction with increasing mental acuity would have fine-tuned dexterity to the point of, while not anticipating tool construction, allowing for it. Even without taking complex tool use into consideration, the advantages and creative potential of free, grasping hands are aptly illustrated by the way modern chimps regularly use rocks to crack open nuts, denude stems to fish termites from their mounds, and mash leaves into sponges for sopping up drinking water.

Powerful adaptations like bipedalism should not be overwrought, however. It is all too easy to equate upright posture with more impressive capacities. The earliest hominids represent just the first fork down a long evolutionary road, and they were certainly not the dominant animals in their environment. Indeed, for a substantial extent of evolutionary history, hominids were the hunted rather than the hunters. Graphic evidence comes from cave sites in South Africa containing hominid bones, mainly australopithecine. Contrary to the Hollywood canard of protohumans as hunting "cavemen," these well-gnawed skeletal remains were apparently dragged to their final resting places by the leopards, hyena, and other predators that hunted *them* (Brain 1983). Africa's retreating forests and roving carnivores only accentuated the danger of predation. As intermediate members of the food chain, the early hominids felt intense pressure to detect and escape from predators, a pressure that would have remained even after they too developed the ability and desire to hunt.

One of the reasons that hunting is seen as important to hominid development, though, is that meat, the yield of hunting, feeds brains as well as bodies. Large brains are clearly advantageous, but they are also expensive to power. While accounting for only two percent of the body's total weight, brain tissue consumes twenty percent of its energy. Pound for pound, the brain burns up ten times as much energy as the rest of the body. Meat, as a dense parcel of fats and proteins, provides a concentration of nutrients available nowhere else. Developing a diet with substantial amounts of meat would have been essential to support the expansion of brains that tripled in size over the course of 5 million years. Just such a shift in diet is demonstrated, interestingly, not only by the size and structure of the modern brain but also by the size and structure of the modern gut. Expansion of the brain requires a commensurate reduction of growth in other organs, usually the digestive system. This is precisely what has taken place in humans, "virtually a gram for gram trade-off between the expansion of the human brain and the reduction in the weight of our digestion organs" (Allman 1999: 169). This trade-off works, however, because carnivores do not require complex digestive systems. Meat, unlike plant matter and other less digestible foods, contains nutrients that are easy to break down.

Nevertheless, it is unlikely that meat consumption directly kick-started brain growth. Meat eating would not have been innovative at the time. Chimps and several other primates also eat meat, and they will devour it when the opportunity arises. Chimps are even known to spontaneously organize hunting parties that target colobus monkeys, brush pigs, and other mammals. Furthermore, the fossil record shows that early hominids were largely foragers, subsisting on fruits, nuts, roots, and vegetation. The skulls and jaws of the robusts, for example, were unequivocal grinding machines, ideally designed for processing tough, low-quality vegetable matter, another testimony to Africa's ancient habitat. No doubt the early hominids, like chimps, took small rodents, baby animals, and other sources of meat when fortune offered—and much has been made about the "scavenging" lifestyle of hominids to offset the image of "Man the Hunter"—but hunting as a serious enterprise was likely a later development in hominid history, best equated with *H. erectus*, though perhaps with *H. habilis* too.

In any case, hunting illustrates another facet of the relationship between the environment and behavior. Though chimps love meat, they actually hunt only rarely and opportunistically. Meat is delicious and provides valuable energy, but hunting for it expends a great deal of energy, too. Despite being rich storehouses of fruits and leaves, forests are relatively scarce in meat. The payoff for a time-consuming, frenetic, even dangerous hunt is usually not worth the size of the kill, especially if it has to be shared. When early hominids finally did turn to hunting as a mainstay, they would have looked to Africa's savanna, with its teeming herds of protein, where creatures refitted for terrestrial life could test their prowess.

These two central goals of daily life, finding food while avoiding *becoming* food, can both be advanced through a single strategy displayed by most primates—group living. As a survival strategy, the benefits of group living are obvious, such as effective protection against predation. The more individuals that make up a group, the more eyes, ears, and noses there are to detect the approach of predators. The scattering of large groups also confuses predators, which usually hunt by honing in on single individuals. While flight is the usual reaction to warning calls in the wild, animals that stand together in groups can often, if pressed, turn away a would-be attacker. If all else fails, being a member of a group reduces the chances that any one individual will fall victim to predation, adding a subtle twist to the adage that there is safety in numbers. Group living is particularly relevant to the African landscape, past and present. Savanna favors the group more than the loner, the opposite of the forest. This dynamic has shaped the lifestyles of Africa's herding animals, as well as the carnivores that stalk them. A gregarious lifestyle has more positive rewards as well. Foraging efficiency goes up within consortiums of feeders, which can collectively cover more ground, keep better track of seasonal bounties, and benefit from sharing. Living in groups also makes it easier to defend food resources or territory from others. In addition, in many primate species the group as a whole plays significant roles in the development of offspring, including protection and instruction.

While group living by itself may not be a sufficient cause for higher intelligence, there is plenty of evidence linking social organization and brain size. The mammal species that possess the greatest brain-size-to-body-size ratios are generally those that live in complex social arrangements, such as porpoises, dolphins, whales, elephants, and wolves. This relationship is especially true, as one would expect, for the primates, which have larger brains for their body weight (about 2.3 times larger) than most other mammals. Humans have the largest brains relative to body size of any species. Our brains, in fact, are nine times larger than would be expected for a mammal of our body size, and still six times larger than for a primate of our size. Most interesting of all is the discovery of what *part* of the brain has expanded in relation to social organization. Though researchers expected to find a correlation between brain size and group size, what they actually found was a significant relationship between group size and the size of the neocortex relative to the rest of the brain (Sawaguchi and Kudo 1990; Dunbar 1992). The suite of mental skills most closely associated with higher cognition is connected with the neocortex, and in humans this structure accounts for approximately eighty-five percent of the brain's weight.

Findings like these suggest that group living not only served as an effective adaptation of continuing value to our hominid ancestors but also that it provided the context for new evolutionary developments, particularly cognitive ones. Group living itself imposes powerful selective pressures. While groups accrue a wide range of benefits for their members, they also present a number of serious challenges. Steven Pinker wonderfully portrays some of the exigencies of social life:

> There are disadvantages to the madding crowd. Neighbors compete over food, water, mates, and nest sites. And there is the risk of exploitation. Hell is other people, said Jean-Paul Sartre, and if baboons were philosophers no doubt they would say that hell is other baboons. Social animals risk theft, cannibalism, cuckoldry, infanticide, extortion, and other treachery. (1994: 193)

Every social animal walks a fine line between reaping the advantages of group living and minimizing the disadvantages. Walking this line often requires brains rather than brawn. It is easy to recognize the rough edges of group life in impressive battles for male dominance, feeding order, sexuality, and other familiar animal behaviors, but beneath such visible displays there exists an unseen, highly intricate matrix of social relationships that touches every aspect of daily life. Successfully negotiating this matrix called for increasing competence in the domain of social intelligence.

The requisites for human-like social intelligence are several, but two in particular illustrate how living in tightly knit social groups continued to shape the hominid mind: "cognitive capacity" and "strategic thinking." Each of these terms encompasses a broad range of mental skills that have served as the basis for extensive comparative studies in primate intelligence (for example, Whiten and Byrne 1997; Tomasello and Call 1997; Parker and McKinney 1999). Cognitive capacity here refers generally to the mental hardware that is necessary for acquiring various levels of social cognition. Strategic thinking is used to describe the often cunning ways that individuals employ information within their social context.

At the functional level, interaction between individuals that goes beyond mere responses to behavioral cues requires some basic cognitive capacities. First, individuals must have the mental ability to keep track of others in their group: who they are, what they are like, what their relationship is to you. This is why group size is so closely tied to brain size: there is a limit to the number of individuals that one can personally keep track of in a constantly changing social world, and that limit relates to computing power. According to Robin Dunbar, chimpanzees can coexist in communities averaging about fifty-five members while group sizes of about 150 individuals would be predicted for primates with brains the size of modern humans (2000). Those who see the growth of hominid neocortex through time to have been driven by the need to increase group size point to such pressures as entry into more risky habitats, the need to defend ecological resources, and protection against rival hominid groups. Dunbar himself favors the notion that "the need to evolve alliances to provide access to limited ecological resources (almost certainly permanent water) was most likely to have been the key pressure selecting for increased brain size," particularly at the time ancestral hominids adopted a more nomadic or migratory lifestyle (2000: 249).

A second basic feature of cognition underpinning advanced social intelligence is awareness that other individuals think, that they possess beliefs and desires, and that their beliefs and desires can intersect with one's own. Such implicit knowledge is part and parcel of what is today called a "theory of mind," which in simplest terms means the ability to put oneself in the mind of another. In interacting with others we automatically presuppose that they have mental states, and the way we interpret those mental states is crucial to the process of social interaction. Put another way, we are all "mind readers," constantly monitoring what we believe others know, think, and feel—particularly as each of these things relate to ourselves.

Theory of mind has practical application, of course, because much of daily life entails personal inferences about the minds of those with whom we come into contact. When we meet up with friends or lovers we assume these are folks who like and love us as well. Confronting those we dislike usually brings corresponding assumptions about their own states of mind. Theory of mind is also at play when we seek to deceive, outwit, or anticipate a rival. Lies work (or at least we hope they do) because we make assumptions about the knowledge another mind holds or has access to. Conversely, theory of mind makes possible cooperation: we agree with like-minded people. We also regularly use theory of mind to place ourselves within the social order. We read minds as we converse, factoring in facial clues and body language. We guess at the impressions we make on strangers, wonder at our current standing with the boss, and estimate the feelings of those to whom we are attracted. As Matt Ridley affirms, "one of the things that marks humanity out from other species, and accounts for our ecological success, is our collection of hyper-social instincts" (1996: 6). Psychologists confirm what is a correspondingly "hyper" theory of mind: each of us is guided most fundamentally not by what other people think of us but by what *we think they think* of us.

Such evaluative thinking displays an extremely important feature of theory of mind; namely, that it can be extended to increasing depths referred to as "orders of intentionality." Self-awareness, recognizing that I have a mental state (I believe x to be true) equates to first-order intentionality. Obviously, this ability sets us apart from machines and other objects lacking self-awareness. Ascribing mental states to others (I believe that you believe x to be true) is a form of second-order intentionality. This is the common level of analysis noted above; when we wonder on the fly what others might be thinking. Yet intentionality can continue to still deeper levels, as in third-order intentionality (I believe that you believe that I believe x to be true) and fourth-order intentionality (I believe that you believe that I believe that you believe x to be true). In theory this regress is infinite, but studies suggest that humans are capable of handling—though with difficulty—up to six orders of intentionality.

Theory of mind is a critical component of human thought, and it develops very quickly in all normal persons. As we'll see later on, the ability to postulate and ponder the inner workings of minds other than your own plays a central role not only in social cognition but also in such human endeavors as fiction and imaginative thought, including religious thought. There is wide debate, however, about whether other primates possess theory of mind. Extensive experimental work has probed this question (Premack and Woodruff 1978; Povinelli and Nelson 1990; Call and Tomasello 1999) and the consensus appears to be that while monkeys are incapable of second-order intentionality, it certainly shapes ape society. Chimpanzees, for example, recognize the difference between knowledge and ignorance in other individuals and can distinguish between intentional activities and accidents. Second-order intentionality is also clearly seen in the episodes of tactical deception that color ape life. Chimps regularly deceive their groupmates to obtain food and sex and to circumnavigate the political order. Such deception requires thought about the beliefs of others so that one can then influence those beliefs by altering information. This activity is akin to lying, which even human children cannot do until their own theories of mind mature. Thus while it is not possible to credit chimps with higher orders of intentionality, they do demonstrate a cognitive capacity that evolution continued to sharpen along the hominid lineage. Dunbar concludes that while chimps "only just aspire" to second-order intentionality, hominids pressed to deeper and deeper levels of mind reading because larger brains "allowed them to set aside more computing power for these purposes" (2000: 245).

While apes may not be the profound philosophers of mind that people are, they nevertheless use their limited attribution of mind to striking effect as they circulate among their peers—and in this respect they are most illuminating models for the development of social cognition and behavior in humans. As the passage by Pinker cited previously alludes, the social world is every bit as challenging as the physical one. Group living might bring forms of altruism, but then again it might not. Friends may abound, but enemies are nearby, too. In daily life one can expect encounters with cheaters and freeloaders, backstabbers and two-timers, in addition to the need to keep abreast of group politics, sexual mores, and social etiquette. For those who live in complex social arrangements, learning to network can be as important as finding adequate food and safe shelter is for solitary animals.

This is what "strategic thinking," the second facet of social intelligence, is all about. Carving out a successful life requires not just knowing that those around you have goals and intentions of their own, but also putting that knowledge to use for your own beneficial ends. However negative it may sound, one must be socially clever because social creatures exploit one another. Richard Byrne and Andrew Whiten coined the provocative term "Machiavellian intelligence" to capture this reality of group living, arguing that primate intelligence arose as an adaptation for social manipulation (1988). Living with conspecifics who are after the same things as you are results in mental parlay rife with deceit, favors, bribery, nepotism, cheating, retribution, friendships, alliances, coalitions, and power plays worthy of the famous Italian Renaissance prince.

In such a competitive environment, the value of increasing intelligence multiplies. The basic need to keep track of others includes more than memorizing faces and kinship. To succeed among peers, individuals must become adept at pairing such implicit knowledge with explicit information. Knowing what others are like, what their beliefs and desires are, and how you might play into them requires the ability to properly read signs, signals, and minds. Thus group living turns largely on the acquisition of reliable information—information that must be continuously filtered, checked, revised—and once such information is acquired, applying it in advantageous ways. It is the behavioral application of information-rich social intelligence that bears witness to strategic thinking.

Information takes many forms, of course. There is information about the world at large that is essential to the entire group, such as the location of ripe fruit or imminent danger. Vervet monkeys on guard duty sound a warning when predators are spotted, using different vocalizations to communicate what to watch out for: a loud barking call for leopards, a short cough for eagles, and a chattering sound for snakes. There is information about individuals that is vital for group stability and peace: which male gorilla holds supremacy at the moment and who supports him, which females are receptive to mating. There is information crucial to interpersonal relations. Chimps maintain a running tally of favors and grudges held toward other groupmates, organizing daily commerce on elaborate systems of quid pro quo. Information, then, is not only necessary to the day-to-day functioning of social life but can also be viewed as a commodity. One might decide to keep information to oneself, share it with select individuals, or disseminate it to the whole group, depending on specific needs and goals. In friendship, sex, and politics, strategic use of information is an invaluable skill. This is true whether we're speaking of apes, hominids, or humans, of the Pliocene, Pleistocene, or the present.

Despite the difficult demands of group living, it should not be forgotten that cohabitation evolved for positive reasons. New adaptations arise only if their benefits outweigh their costs. Intra-group pressures are a side effect of living with others, which itself proved more advantageous than living alone. What is more, group living is responsible for the development of the very attitudes and behaviors that are sometimes said to confound evolutionary origins. Words like "virtue," "trust," and "morality" have a transcendent ring to them, but they fit perfectly well into a natural world where cooperation benefits everyone (Axelrod 1984; Cosmides and Tooby 1992; Ridley 1996). The most successful animals are those possessing cooperative instincts and social bonds. Common behaviors like long-term parenting, benevolence, generosity, even sacrifice do not render self-interest and mutual aid incompatible; rather, they highlight the subtle forms of reciprocity that are a hallmark of life on earth. As Robert Wright affirms, "altruism, compassion, empathy, love, conscience, and the sense of justice—all of these things, the things that hold society together, the things that allow our species to think so highly of itself, can now confidently be said to have a firm genetic basis" (1994: 12). But of course, genetics doesn't determine *behavior*; it remains the decision of each individual whether they will turn genetic traits into character traits.

It is highly likely that the challenges and opportunities associated with group living were responsible for pushing hominid cognition along the developmental trajectory that culminated in the modern human mind. This development was fueled by many evolutionary feedback loops, only a few of which are mentioned above. In the face of sweeping environmental change, protohumans responded with alternative lifestyles and anatomical alterations. Success in these new ways of life depended in part on increasing group size, the better to meet internal needs and confront external threats. Increasing group size drove the growth of larger brains and honed social intelligence. Large, well-organized social groups produced greater quantities of high-quality foods like meat, which in turn helped feed this brain growth. Much has also been made of meat as one of the first forms of currency, a coveted resource that could be traded, just as it is in contemporary primate societies, for social gain. Skilled hands played their role in the process, too, allowing for the production of tools and escalating efficiency at hunting and gathering. In short, the solutions to problems faced in our ancestral past served as the building blocks for our present.

Missing from this picture, however, is the evolutionary development most often held up as the quintessential attribute of humanity—language. Though students of animal behavior, particularly primatologists, would argue vehemently over what constitutes language, it is clear that human vocalization entails much more than simple communication, a skill that most living things are capable of. Human speech reflects the unique adaptations of minds that make possible a symbolic structuring of the world, the sharing of which has profound consequences for practical living. It is the use of language that has resulted in the unique complexity of human social behavior and organization—from the intricacies of marriage and family life to the formation of governments and nations—as well as the discovery and furtherance of knowledge that has made *H. sapiens* the dominant species on earth.

The evolution of language is a controverted subject sometimes mired in debates over linguistic definitions and concepts. Here primatologists help to clarify the origins of language by reminding us of what language really is: "*Language is a social behavior*. It evolved in a context in which getting points across had some survival and reproductive value" (Stanford 2001: 152). Vocal communication is an adaptation to group living, and as such is another variable in the positive feedback loop resulting in modern human intelligence. It should be noted, for example, that part of the increase in brain size displayed by the genus *Homo* is due to the enlargement of the several brain structures that are dedicated to the perception and production of speech.

For Dunbar, the evolution of language is immediately linked to the two primary demands of group living: maintaining social bonds and staying informed about others (1997). Among primates, group cohesion and social relationships are sustained through grooming. Some species can spend as much as twenty percent of their day grooming one another, though individuals focus most of their attention on relatives and close friends. Social interaction of this sort is impossible in large groups, where direct personal contact would simply be too time consuming. With increases in hominid group size, a more efficient method of social bonding was required. Language filled this need. With respect to efficiency, conversation is superior to grooming in at least two ways. First, while grooming is an intensive, single-minded task, conversation can easily take place in combination with other activities. Second, while grooming involves only one other individual at a time, speech can be addressed to several individuals simultaneously.

The real revolution of language, however, lies in the way it fulfills two crucial social functions at once. As a bonding mechanism, conversation is more efficient than grooming, but it also allows for an unprecedented exchange of information. Much of the content of speech includes information about the environment important to daily life. Yet the emergence of language in the context of group living also serves as an effective means for gaining information about others. Just as talk can reach more people than hands, talk allows us to learn about people without actually engaging them ourselves. Conversation about third parties greatly expands our base of social knowledge—who's trustworthy, who's a cheat, and so on—and it also conveys a deeper understanding of individuals, since other peoples' experiences of them can be added to our own. Herein lies the source of our fascination with gossip. As Dunbar reports, analyses of everyday human conversation reveal that we spend about two-thirds of our time musing over social relationships (1993, 1997). Our oversize, gregarious brains are matched by a proportionate propensity to talk about others. A contemporary behavior like gossip is one of the most visible bridges between past and present. While it's easy to disparage the tremendous popularity of such cultural events as "reality TV," the success of this seemingly vacuous programming makes perfect sense in light of evolutionary psychology. And we mustn't neglect the other side of the coin here. While large amounts of conversation are devoted to learning about others, we expend quite a bit of effort using it to advertise *ourselves*, since buoying up our own reputations is equally important in the game of society.

The fossil record suggests that language appeared relatively late in human evolution, and is best aligned with the appearance of archaic *H. sapiens*. It was at this time that the predicted correspondence between group size and brain size was reached and, as anatomical studies reveal, the larynx had descended to its current position. A "voice box" set deep in the trachea is necessary for creating the full range of sounds that comprise human speech. Additionally, it is at this point that an asymmetry in the two hemispheres of the brain can be detected; then, as today, the left half of the brain, where language centers are located, is larger than the right. Once established, language continued to mirror new cognitive developments. The information content of language did not remain focused on ecological and social news but became the conveyor of cultural knowledge as well. Just as chimps learn to fish for termites by watching their elders, so hominid hunting techniques, tool craft, and other life skills could be perpetuated through direct instruction. As a system of symbols, language also provided a format for abstract communication ranging from long-term planning and inter-generational education to belief systems and artistic expression. These mental activities appear to differ from our own only by degree; the separation between humans and other species, however, is certainly one of kind. Our ability to think and communicate our thoughts through language allows us to evaluate, transform, store, and pass on information to degrees that no other animals can match.

Into the Cognitive Niche

The story of human evolution has many versions. Most people working in the field agree on the overall narrative, but opinions vary widely on the details. Filling in the scenes of humankind's developmental history, particularly its cognitive history, involves a fair bit of speculation. The relevant expanse of time and limited hard evidence severely curtail the level of certainty one can muster with respect to evolutionary cause and effect. As new discoveries are made—and a consortium of disciplines contributes them regularly—additional chapters are added to the story, while others are fleshed out or even rewritten. It is important to note, though, that regardless of the unfolding of specific events, the story's plot remains unchanged. As a scientific explanation, Darwinian theory has demonstrated a remarkable integrity.

In the attempt to understanding the nature of the modern human mind, three large lessons can be taken from a reading of this story. The first is that who we are today, including how and what we think, is the result of natural selection. Mental capacities, just like physical form, represent adapted solutions to past problems. *Our minds evolved in conjunction with our ancestral ways of life.* The second lesson is that however and whatever the present structures and functions of human minds have come to be, these structures and functions are *species typical.* Unlike many other animal groups, the genus *Homo* is a set of one. While there are differences between common human ethnic divisions—skin color, language, lifestyles, and so on—there is, nonetheless, no consequential biological difference between any people anywhere. So it is not only possible but also proper to speak of the modern mind in the singular. All humans possess the same brain. More important still, all humans use their brains to *think* the same way. They do not necessarily think the same *things*—though, as we'll see, they usually do that, too—but as thinking itself goes, all humans everywhere use the same set of cognitive processes to generate their particular set of thoughts.

The third large lesson of evolutionary history for students of the modern mind involves how best to place humans in nature. All life on earth now exists or survived for its time in the past because it was designed and equipped to exploit a particular environmental niche. Intense competition for limited resources requires species to specialize in ways that enable them to carve out space for themselves in a crowded world. The spectacular diversity of living things today is the result of successfully finding new places to live and reproduce. Hominid evolution was not different in this respect. Faced with changing habitats, cunning competitors, and ruthless predators, early humans also felt tremendous pressure to ecologically relocate or perish. The direction of their development was both novel and effective: they got smarter.

On the surface this strategy seems obvious—at least its advantages seem obvious. But notice, too, that it is a strategy that is extremely rare. Despite all the advantages of intelligence, it is just one option open to natural selection, one, in fact, hardly ever taken and pushed to a high level in only one species. There are two main reasons for the paucity of smart creatures. One is that "smart" is a relative term. If by smart one means the ability to survive—the only meaningful goal of life—then every extant creature must be considered smart. The bottom line of existence is more existence, not writing poetry or building cars. So on this criterion the "smartest" animals would be wriggly things like insects and reptiles, which have lived on through hell and high water, and in many cases largely unchanged, for a vastly longer stretch of Earth's history than any mammal, let alone humans.

With respect to "smart" as we commonly mean it, the obstacle is one of economy. Intelligence is at least structurally related to bigger brains. Intelligence is the product of computing power, and that requires brain space not already devoted to other basic tasks. Here the neocortex, the outer layer of the brain largely unique to mammals, is implicated. But developing a bigger brain requires serious justification. In the constructive work of natural selection, just as in house building, the project will not continue if cost exceeds profit. As we have already seen, brain tissue is an extremely expensive material to produce and maintain. Starting already in the womb, the largest portion of the nutrients available for growth, some seventy percent, is routed to the brain. Newborns, whose brains are still developing at a rapid rate, continue to divert about sixty percent of their body's energy for the purpose. This metabolic greed continues throughout the life span, though in adults the brain's energy consumption finally falls to about twenty percent.

There are many other problems that come with carrying around a big brain. Animals with big brains have to spend more time feeding to get the fuel they need, and the more time spent feeding the greater their exposure to predators. Heightened fuel demands also make one vulnerable to times of famine and draught. Having large heads increases their owners' susceptibility to serious injury, whether during fights or accidental falls. For females, giving birth to large-headed children is a life-threatening proposition, particularly if their pelvis has already been compromised for upright walking. The anatomical limitations imposed by a restricted birth canal means that large-brained animals like humans need to go through an extended period of development outside the womb that includes a phase of utter helplessness and many years of dependency. This, in turn, translates into a small number of offspring for parents, who must devote their time and their resources to child rearing. Finally, lots of computing power does not necessarily equate with speed, which in the wild, on the hoof, is one of nature's best defenses. In situations of life and death, reacting with reflection rather than instinct will often be fatal.

For all of these reasons, animals with big brains are rare in nature, and only in our species have brains ballooned to such proportions. That the route to intelligence was taken at all, however, implies that intelligence can overcome the additional challenges. While large brains require constant feeding, smart creatures find more efficient gathering and hunting techniques and eat better foods. They devise more effective defenses against danger and wiser strategies for preserving territory and kin. They see tools where other animals see only rocks and sticks. High intelligence like our own can go even further, allowing us to enter entirely new habitats, to exploit multiple ecosystems at once, even to reshape the environment to fit our needs. All it takes is the requisite brainpower.

For this reason, students of human evolution like John Tooby and Irven DeVore have aptly identified our place in nature as the "cognitive niche" (1987). Where every other species can boast a particular physical prowess, either subtle or brute, humans bully with their wits. If forced to face any of a great number of animals hand to hand, even the strongest man would not fare well. Let the man bring along a spear, an axe, or even just a sturdy branch he's shaped into a club and the odds get considerably better. But why even take this risk? Why not find ways to avoid dangers altogether, or at least confront them with the help of others, thereby lessening the danger still further? There is a host of new possibilities open to consideration, if only one is clever enough to consider.

The brain, of course, is where considering occurs. That the brain would become the seat of intelligence makes sense given that "considering" amounts to the processing of information and the processing of information is what brains are designed to do. At the most rudimentary level brains process information about the bodies to which they belong, using this information to keep the functions of life running smoothly. Brains also process information received from the outside world and answer this stimuli with an appropriate bodily response. At first blush this may not be extremely impressive, particularly since it applies to worms as well as to whales, yet it should be. Even the simplest brain, like each bit of living flesh, is a marvel of engineering with an astounding evolutionary history. The immediate point, though, is that brains, from the primitive to the complex, are fitted to the same task—gathering and translating information. It is certainly no small thing to make a little, weak, and simple information processor large, powerful, and complex, but it's precisely the place where one would begin. Eschewing redundancy as well as waste, natural selection works with what it has.

It also makes sense that natural selection would move hominids ever further in the direction of improved information processing. Regardless of the species, survival turns on making correct choices with respect to food, safety, and mates, and these choices are substantially aided by more and better information. The type and quality of the information processor that each kind of animal possesses mirror the specific set of problems it has to solve. As we have seen, the selective pressures at work on Plio-Pleistocene primates came not only from the natural environment but also from the social one. Group living contributes a set of problems that require mental solutions. The result was what is frequently referred to as a "cognitive arms race," in which increasing improvements in the acquisition and use of information bestowed advantages. As Tooby and DeVore point out, the products of this cognitive arms race are reflected in the adapted brain. In the cognitive niche, fitness equals intelligence.

Before turning to look at what the *human* brain is like and how it thinks, it is necessary to clarify a crucial anatomical point. Throughout this chapter much has been made about brain size. We humans have the largest brains relative to our bodies of any animal that has ever existed, and it is no coincidence that we are by far the smartest as well. Part of the obsession with brain size is the intuitive logic that bigger is better, and when it comes to functions like processing power and storage this is certainly true. The fossil record also graphically illustrates the centrality of brain size. The first skull fragments to be recovered date to between 3.9 and 3.0 million years ago, and the evidence becomes richer as one travels forward in time. If a flipbook were made using images of each successive fossil find the most striking movement to be seen while flipping through its pages would be the morphing, expanding cranium. From the conical, chimp-size skull of little Lucy to the spacious orb of *H. sapiens*, the heads of hominids have swelled and rounded to accommodate progressively larger brains. Even this anatomical redesign was not sufficient to meet the demand; cortical tissue is a sheet of folds and fissures that allows still more surface area to be packed into a limited space. Endocasts (models of the inside of a skull) tell us the capacity of these ancient skulls and reveal important clues about the structure of the brains they held. The bottom line is that the hominid brain nearly doubled in size every 1.5 million years.

The fossil record tells us something else as well, something a bit more subtle yet of tremendous importance. When it comes to intelligence, a bigger brain is better, but it isn't everything. Note, for example, that the Neanderthals had brains as big as ours and yet the available evidence suggests that they made no significant advancements on the lifestyle of the day. The cultural signs of higher intelligence, such as complex tool design and art, were left by others. What is more, the overall expansion of the hominid brain was not linear. During the course of evolution the brain actually grew and shrank several times, with two major spikes in brain size occurring around 2 million and one-half million years ago. The first event is usually correlated with the appearance of the toolmaker *H. habilis*, but the second event remains unexplained. Finally, what is normally recognized as the "cultural explosion" beginning about 50,000 years ago was indeed the work of *H. sapiens*, but this date falls well after the size of the modern brain had stabilized. Given this pattern of brain expansion and visible behavior, Mithen argues that "there is no simple relationship between brain size, 'intelligence,' and behavior" (1996: 11).

Having a big brain is important, then, but there must be more to it than sheer mass. Talk of a "growing," "expanding" brain conjures up images of a ball of tissue pulsing and heaving into larger and larger forms. The development of the modern human brain, and hence of modern human intelligence, is not the result of repeated mental overhauls. Natural selection does not implement grand sweeping changes, nor is intelligence merely the result of a protohuman brain that was somehow super-sized. The secret to the power of the modern brain is primarily structural in nature, the way it is wired internally, the processes by which it achieves its calculations—in short, the way it thinks. Architecturally speaking, mammalian brains share a common design, and the similarities are even more apparent in primates. It's mainly what goes on *inside* the human brain, the structures and functions of cognition itself, which makes us so different.

2

The Architecture of the Modern Mind

What Does the Present Have to Do with the Past?

Even upon close inspection, the brain is a rather uninspiring sight, a mass of pinkish-gray, jelly-like material whose function is as inscrutable as its wrinkled, bulbous form. And yet this three-pound organ, the composite of approximately one hundred billion nerve cells and supporting tissue, is the seat of all that is human—more, it is the nexus of every human's world. It is the brain that oversees the life of the body, monitoring its well being, regulating its growth and development, coordinating its movements. It is the brain that interprets what exists beyond the body, translating and organizing the various forms of stimuli sent to it via the sense organs into recognizable patterns. It is the brain that creates a sense of individual self, washing experiences and perceptions with colorful emotions, harboring a lifetime of personal memories, decoding and formulating expressive language, and executing an astronomical number of thoughts ranging from the simple to the sublime.

By anyone's lights, the modern human brain is extraordinary; a marvel of organic engineering whose blueprint is only partly understood. Yet all of it, from its peculiar shape to its powerful calculations, is the result of selected adaptations accumulated over the course of hominid history, a testimony to the handiwork of evolutionary processes. This vital connection between present and past cannot be neglected by any study of human thought. In the same way that our now largely hairless skin still responds to cold with goose bumps and our slate of internal organs includes obsolete parts, the contemporary skull carries around an assemblage of neural tissue designed long ago. Nevertheless, this compact mass of tissue represents nature's best effort at intelligence as a tool of survival, and it is impressive indeed.

The previous chapter sketched in some of the details of the formative history of the human mind. This one will provide a similar line drawing of the brain itself: What are its structures and functions? How did these structures and functions come to be? How does cognition work? Most important of all, what does a brain assembled in an ancient world so very different from our own have to do with the way we think today? Answering these kinds of questions requires the aid of the powerful new discipline called evolutionary psychology, a recent synthesis of evolutionary biology and cognitive psychology. The fundamental premise of evolutionary psychology is that the complex design of the modern brain evolved through natural selection. Understanding the processes and products of the mind therefore requires close attention to their evolutionary background. As Robert Wright says, "if the theory of natural selection is correct, then essentially everything about the human mind should be intelligible in these terms" (1994: 28). True to such predictions, the work of evolutionary psychology is yielding striking insights into the architecture of the mind and human behavior alike.

There is a second side to the study of human cognition, however. While we were designed to live in an ancient natural world, we no longer do. It has been tens of thousands of years since humans have subsisted in conditions conducive to evolution. When one learns to tame and manipulate the very environmental and biological forces that drive natural selection, they lose most of their punch. That means that our brains, whatever they are like, are currently being put to use in novel and, importantly, nonadaptive ways. A day in the life of a Pleistocene hunter is a far cry from a day on the stock exchange or an assembly line. Stone Agers probably reflected on the world around them, but it is doubtful that atomic theory helped shape their conclusions.

This situation highlights two significant aspects of human thought that will become clearer as we look more closely at mental products such as religion. The first is that the mind is flexible; though our brains have been genetically predisposed to specific ways of thinking, we are quite capable of plying them to more generic and creative ends. For example, you can co-opt our innate theory of mind to personify and berate your insentient computer—something most of us in fact do when they seem to turn against us. Following on this is the further recognition that a great deal of what we think *is* rooted in mental predispositions. This reality is inherent to the kinds of brains we all have. The human capacity for imagination is immense, but it is also constrained by the functional design of our minds. A host of behaviors and varieties of thought that typify twenty-first century life can be characterized as nonadaptive by-products of cognitive mechanisms originally designed to serve other purposes. What most excites evolutionary psychologists is the discovery of the mind's innate faculties, their adaptive origins, and their contemporary expressions.

Alongside the adaptationist frame of reference contributed by evolutionary biology, the most valuable conceptual tool for understanding the nature of the human mind has been cognitive psychology's analogical comparison of brains with computers. Over the years, many attempts to describe the mind have been colored with technological comparisons, but likening brains to computers is much more than metaphorical language. Brains *are* computers. It makes no difference that computers are conglomerates of plastic, metal, and silicon while brains are wet, organic tissue. Computers, as Alan Turing defined them, are sets of operations for processing information (1950). The physical nature of the machine itself is only tangentially important since many kinds of devices, from an abacus to Turing's own mathematical abstractions, can process information. With respect to "hardware," then, both brains and computers are information processors that accomplish tasks by executing sets of computational operations.

In terms of "software," the analogy between brains and computers is exacting as well. What is essential to a computer is not its materials but what it does, its activities—in short, its programs. The programs of the brain, the computational activities it executes in its work of information processing, are reflected in the mind. Though attention to the brain's overall design and circuitry is certainly important to understanding what human thought is like, it is even more crucial to focus on the bundle of internal programs that comprise the brain's mental software. While perhaps drifting a bit back into metaphor, it is useful to call the brain hardware and the mind its software. A computational theory of mind, however, is by far the most powerful explanatory approach to mentation ever conceived; it is both accurate and amenable to testable hypotheses. It also provides a clean answer to the perennial mind-body problem. From the perspective of cognitive psychology, the mind is the activity of the brain.

This chapter describes some of the features of the modern mind by reporting on the work of evolutionary psychologists and other specialists who are hacking into the programs that comprise the brain's mental software. Though what we know, and what we think we know, about the inner workings of human thought has filled many volumes, the following, more modest survey will concentrate on a handful of cognitive processes that play a direct role in the subject of the rest of this book—the phenomenon of *religious* thought. While it is the brain's software that interests us most, first a brief overview of the hardware itself is in order.

The Development and Structure of the Brain

The story of the human brain does not begin at birth but at conception. The blueprint for each piece of biological hardware is located in a child's genes, a unique arrangement of DNA contributed, half each, by mother and father. Within hours of the union of sperm and egg, the factory that will build the newest human computer has already geared up for production. This single fertilized egg rapidly multiplies into a staggering number and diversity of new cells that will become a person. The construction of the brain and all the rest is guided by a schematic millions of years in the making. There is no room for error. The network of brain cells must be wired just like everyone else's, allowing each of us to perceive the world in the same way, to think in the same terms, to behave in similar ways, and to understand the same symbols and language.

The real work of brain construction starts at about day fourteen, when the sphere of multiplying cells begins to fold in on itself. A section of the outer layer of the embryo migrates inward, resulting in the formation of three cell layers, the mesoderm, endoderm, and ectoderm. It is from the ectoderm that the brain develops. In this earliest stage, the brain consists merely of a thin layer of cells on the surface of the embryo called the neural plate. The neural plate next folds in two, creating the neural groove. This groove then closes completely, forming a hollow structure called the neural tube, which provides the building material for the central nervous system. One end of the neural tube will extend to become the spinal cord. The central portion will provide the brain's ventricular system. The structures of the brain itself will emerge from the opposite end of the neural tube. All this development occurs with breathtaking speed. By the eighth week of growth, each of the major components of an adult human brain is already present in the fetus.

The building block of the brain, as for all organs, is the cell. There are two main types of brain cells: neurons, which analyze and transmit the electrochemical signals that are the basis of mental communication, and glial cells, which provide developmental, structural, and functional support to the neurons. Neurons are elongated cells of varying lengths composed of three structures: a cell body called the soma, a system of branching dendrites attached to the soma, and a nerve fiber extending out of the soma called the axon, which carries the electrical signals between connecting neurons. The axons of most neurons are insulated by a sheath of myelin, a substance made of fat that speeds the conductivity of nerve fibers.

Neurons communicate with each other using impulses that race from the dendrites of one neuron, through its soma, and out its axon to the dendrites of the next neuron. These impulses are propagated electrically within each cell and transmitted chemically between them. In a typical process of intercellular communication, the dendrites of one neuron receive a signal from the axon of another neuron using chemicals known as neurotransmitters. When an electrical signal reaches the tip of an axon, it stimulates small vesicles that contain neurotransmitters. These chemicals are released across the microscopic gap, or synapse, separating each neuron and attach to specialized receptors on the dendrites of the adjacent cell. This stimulus sparks a fresh electrical charge in the receiving cell that travels from the dendrites to the soma where it is analyzed, integrated, and transmitted along the axon again. Neurons are able to produce an electrical impulse using charged ions—positively charged potassium and sodium, and negatively charged chlorine—which, when depolarized, propagate signals along the cell membrane to the end of the axon. When the electrical signal arrives at terminals in the tip of the axon, neurotransmitters are released that convey it onward once more.

The work of the brain requires more than cell-to-cell signal transmission, however. Even the simplest behavior involves the organization of thousands of neurons. Feeling, acting, and thinking are the result of complex neural circuitry in which neurons are grouped together by function into systems controlling discrete sensory, motor, and cognitive tasks. So as one part of the prenatal factory continues to churn out more and more brain cells, another part is intensely focused on getting them arrayed and connected up in the right ways.

This task is achieved through a three-stage process involving cell proliferation, differentiation, and migration. In the first stage, beginning with the closure of the neural tube, brain cells proliferate in huge numbers. So great is the commitment to brain cell production that the brain weight of a newborn is proportionately much larger in relation to body weight than is the brain weight of an adult. Within months, though, more than half of these young cells die off, having exceeded the brain's structural needs. In the second stage, differentiation, newly created cells specialize, joining either the family of neurons or neuroglia. Glial cells are far more numerous than neurons and account for much of the brain's total volume. In the final stage of migration, the neurons travel to their permanent positions within the brain and begin to establish their crucial interconnections with other neurons. The fixing of brain circuitry through migration is a concerted operation involving glial cells as well as neurons. The neuroglia, whose name means "nerve glue," are responsible for both guiding and anchoring the neurons to their assigned locations. Radial glial cells send out long tendrils that construct scaffolding for the neurons to move along. The brain's growth and final form is the result of the thickening and expansion of this tissue formation.

Describing the finished brain's structural components requires zooming out from single cells to a global view of the brain itself. When that is done, one of the reasons for humans' superior intelligence becomes clear. Mental acuity is in part related to brain architecture, even if its exact mechanics are hidden from view. While all central nervous systems have many parts in common, the brains of humans are visibly different from all others.

The mechanical design of the human brain can best be described according to its three anatomical divisions. These include the large, domed-shaped cerebrum, whose matching hemispheres comprise the bulk of the brain; the cerebellum, two small spherical hemispheres hanging below and to the rear of the cerebrum; and the brain stem, a complex of structures attached to the bottom of the brain that gradually tapers off and exits the skull as the spinal cord. The primary functions of these three divisions, taken in reverse order, reveal what is common and what is distinctive about the human brain.

The brain stem is responsible for maintaining basic bodily functions like respiration, heart rate, digestion, and blood pressure. The upper portion of the brain stem, or midbrain, acts as a relay station for neurons transmitting input signals from sense organs to the cerebral cortex and, in turn, outgoing motor reflex commands. In the middle of the brain stem sits a bulging bundle of nerve fibers called the pons. Like the midbrain, the pons functions as a relay station for messages, in this case between the two cerebral hemispheres and between the cerebral cortex and the medulla oblongata. The medulla oblongata, the third and lowest division of the brain stem, routes incoming and outgoing signals between body and brain in such a way that the right half of the brain communicates with the left half of the body and the left half of the brain with the right half of the body. Running vertically through the entire length of the brain stem is a canal called the reticular formation that governs states of alertness and sleep.

The cerebellum looks like a miniature version of the cerebral hemispheres it sits beneath, hence its Latin name. These two laterally positioned lobes, which include several anatomical subdivisions, are located to the rear of the brain stem and connect to its three majors structures. The cerebellum is primarily responsible for maintaining posture, balance, and coordination. Utilizing motor and sensory input from the brain stem, the cerebellum helps to smooth basic movements like walking as well as to fine-tune the muscle control involved in more specialized skills such as writing and athletics.

Positioned above the brain stem and forming the core of the cerebrum are three interconnected sets of brain structures that comprise the limbic system, the basal ganglia, and the diencephalon. The limbic system, often referred to as the "emotional brain," includes the hypothalamus, pituitary gland, amygdala, hippocampus, fornix, mammillary bodies, and other related tissues. Constantly implicated in new and different brain functions, the limbic system contributes significantly to emotion, memory, and motivation. The basal ganglia are collections of nuclei and neural fibers crucial to the function of the motor system. The diencephalon includes two major structures, the thalamus and hypothalamus. Located in the heart of the brain between the two hemispheres, the thalamus acts as the nervous system's central relay station; all sensory input to the brain, with the exception of the sense of smell, passes through the thalamus. The hypothalamus, which sits just beneath the thalamus, is important for both the autonomic nervous system and the endocrine system. The hormones produced by the hypothalamus regulate vital body functions, and the structure also governs basic feelings and drives like hunger, thirst, and sexual desire.

The suite of mental skills most closely associated with human thought— reasoning, language, imagination, personality—originates in the cerebrum, which, true to its name, accounts for approximately eighty-five percent of the brain's weight. The exterior layer of the cerebrum, called the cerebral cortex, is the brain's most familiar feature, with its gray skin of convoluted grooves (sulci) and ridges (gyri). Yet this gyrencephalic landscape is a wonder of biological design, evolution's answer to brain growth that outstripped cranial volume. This extensive system of grooves and ridges, which hides nearly two-thirds of the cortex's actual size, allows about sixteen square feet of cortical surface to be folded up within the skull.

The cerebral cortex is divided into four lobes outlined by prominent sulci and named for their overlying cranial bones: the frontal, parietal, temporal, and occipital lobes. These regional divisions offer a convenient way to survey

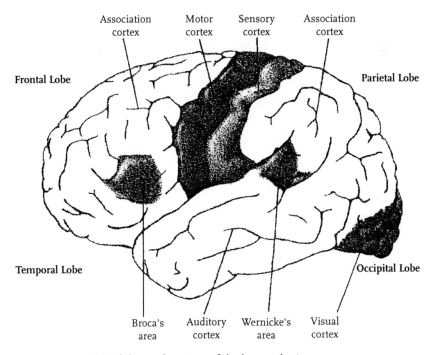

FIGURE 2.1. Major lobes and cortices of the human brain.

brain function. Each lobe carries out a variety of processing activities, and major neural systems can be localized within each lobe. This localization of specialized neuronal systems also allows brain structures to be linked with behaviors. Extensive study of healthy, diseased, and damaged brains has enabled researchers to map mental activities onto specific regions of the brain, though many processes, including memory, are associated with multiple areas of the brain.

The frontal lobe, the largest of the cortical regions, includes the area of tissue from roughly the midpoint of the head forward. The frontal lobe takes the lead in the planning and execution of movements, a specialization that is accented by the presence of the primary motor cortex and other neural areas dedicated to motor control. Further subdivisions of the frontal lobe contribute to higher-order human functions. The prefrontal cortex, for example, is involved in memory and behavioral processes. The frontal lobe is also the site of Broca's area, the part of the brain related to speech.

The parietal lobe, which abuts the central sulcus with the frontal lobe and extends toward the rear of the head, is mainly in charge of sensory processing. The major structure aiding in this task is the somatosensory cortex, which receives input from the thalamus and processes information about limb position, pain, body temperature, and touch. The occipital lobe, located at the back of the head, is devoted to vision. Here the primary visual cortex receives input originating in retina cells and transmitted along the primary visual pathway. This highly complex cortical region assembles visual images by coding features like brightness, color, and orientation. At the same time this information is shunted to other centers of the brain, which identify the "what" (form) and "where" (location) of each visual object. The temporal lobe, the region of the cerebrum along the side of the head, houses auditory processing areas. Sound waves received by the cochlea are routed to the primary auditory cortex via the thalamus, where perceptual qualities such as tone and volume are coded. The temporal lobe is also the location of Wernicke's area, the part of the brain related to language comprehension.

There are also large areas of the cerebral cortex that are not directly engaged in motor and sensory tasks. Found in each of the lobes, these neural areas are called association cortex because they receive and integrate input from more than one modality. The association cortices are thus sites of higher-order mental processes, where information from motor and sensory areas of the brain is used analytically and converted into complex responses. The work of the association cortices also highlights the presence and importance of connectivity throughout the brain. Despite distinctions of function, locale, and "higher" versus "lower" brain structures, the mind operates as a complex system with multiple components engaged in the processing of almost all forms of perception and thought.

The most striking physical feature of the brain as a whole is the longitudinal division of the cerebrum into two nearly symmetrical hemispheres that communicate with one another via a dense bundle of neural fibers called the corpus callosum. Although the two hemispheres appear similar, study of split-brain patients reveal that they are functionally dissimilar. In addition to receiving sensory signals from the opposite side of the body and sending motor responses contralaterally as well, each hemisphere is specialized for different kinds of mental activity. Research has shown a relationship between hemispheric dominance and whether a person is right or left-handed. In most right-handed people the left hemisphere is dominant in processing skills associated with language, math, logic, and speech. The right hemisphere dominates in judging spatial relationships, recognizing emotional expression, and processing complex imagery and music. In left-handed people the pattern of hemispheric specialization is more variable.

With the in utero completion of each of the brain's major structures comes the initiation of functional development. As early as the first trimester of a pregnancy, the fetus already possesses centers of balance and motion that respond to the mother's own movements. At the halfway point of gestation a fetus can hear. Sight remains severely muted, though; unlike for the sense of hearing, there are few external stimuli in the uterus. But by the seventh month the eyelids are open and the fetus can see by diffused light coming through the abdominal wall. Taste, too, is working as the fetus takes in amniotic fluid. In addition to these basic functions of sense and motor control, there is also clear evidence that the human brain is busy *learning* in the womb. One example utilizes the fetus's well-developed sense of hearing. Clever experiments that chart the rhythm with which a newborn sucks on a rubber nipple reveal preferences for a mother's voice and other patterns of sound heard while in the womb (DeCasper and Fifer 1980). Numerous similar experiments confirm that before birth individual brains are already attentive and actively engaged with the surrounding world, however limited.

This is a very good thing. The larger world into which babies are born is a buzzing, flickering, chaotic place. They need to be able to make sense of all this noise, light, and movement around them. Some skills, like language, can be put off until later, but others are foundational to both immediate functioning and further development. There is a three-dimensional world to be surveyed, spatial maps to be constructed, social connections to be made, objects to be identified, and so on—all the kinds of abilities that *enable* learning and which are themselves not learned in the usual sense. Each new human brain is not only comprised of the mental hardware it takes to execute these kinds of tasks, but also comes with the requisite operating system as well. Without this innate bundle of mental programs it would be impossible for newborns—or adults for that matter—to recognize or understand anything at all.

This is the surest sign that human knowledge is a biological phenomenon, and developmental psychologists continue to probe the true depth of the knowledge that is already present at birth. Babies are born with complex brains that do complex things, not least the assembly of mental representations and responsive behaviors that go well beyond the level of the input received. Babies can differentiate between people and objects. They act according to preferences, discriminating between familiar and unfamiliar faces, sounds, and smells. They recognize expressions of happiness, sadness, and anger. They know how people move. Babies possess social minds, which they use to place themselves in relation to others. Newborns imitate facial expressions, and they coordinate their own movements, gestures, and emotions to those who hold them. So wide is the range of mental abilities with which babies come equipped, and so skilled are babies at using them to analyze and predict the world, that Alison Gopnik, Andrew Meltzoff, and Patricia Kuhl like to speak of newborns as "scientists in the crib," pointing out that the cognitive capacities that even the most sophisticated lab-coated researcher brings to a question about the world have their origins in infancy:

> Babies and young children think, observe, and reason. They consider evidence, draw conclusions, do experiments, solve problems, and search for the truth. Of course, they don't do this in the self-conscious way that scientists do. And the problems they try to solve are everyday problems about what people and objects and words are like, rather than arcane problems about stars and atoms. But even the youngest babies know a great deal about the world and actively work to find out more. (2001: 13)

In short, humans are born doing human things. Such a statement sounds commonsensical, trivial, even foolish, especially to anyone who does not view the minds of human infants as blank slates. Unfortunately, that's precisely how philosophers and psychologists have characterized them for a very long time. For most of the past century it was assumed that babies arrived in the world as empty vessels that do little more than respond to external stimuli and acquire knowledge only as they are exposed to culture. Mental ability and content were assumed to be the products of rigorous social learning, not of innate programming. Of course learning from others *is* important, and adults as well as babies spend a good amount of time doing it. But what is crucial to see is that biology has bestowed both the functional mental abilities babies are born with *and* the powerful learning mechanisms they use to rapidly increase and restructure their knowledge. Nurturing takes place *via* nature. Throughout one's life the mind retains a plasticity that allows for learning—the continual acquisition, reshaping, and revising of information. The link between learning and hardwiring is even graphically expressed in the first year of life, when a baby's interactions with the world are directly reflected in the connectivity of the brain. During this period the number of synapses between neurons multiples rapidly, creating millions of new connections each day. It is unclear to what extent this neural development is dependent on external experiences as opposed to simply representing the final phase of mental construction, since, as with the maturation of key cognitive abilities, all children follow similar timetables. Nevertheless, the main point being expressed here is *that* we come to learn, as well as *what* we come to learn, are both grounded in biological inheritance. The human computer arrives packed with both the knowledge it takes to immediately begin interpreting the world and the mechanisms necessary for assimilating new information. Additionally, as we'll see later, much of what we do come to learn, regardless of when, is built on the same innate forms of knowledge with which we all begin life. As Gopnik, Meltzoff, and Kuhl conclude, adults, even adult scientists, are just "big children" (2001: 9; see also Harris 1994).

The final section of this chapter will return to the subject of what newborns know, for it is precisely in studying the minds of babies and young children that we can begin to circumscribe the content and application of innate human knowledge. But before moving from the hardware of the brain to a look at some of its central programs, there is another—a hidden—structural level to the brain that is crucial for understanding *how* we think. Exploring the various anatomical segments of the human brain, even identifying their areas of specialization, does not tell us how thought takes place, why the brain is so quick and efficient, or what about its particular design gives rise to such distinctly human capacities as imagination and creativity. Answering these types of questions requires models that describe the brain's *activity*, that attempt to map the mind in the way that neuroscientists map the brain itself. To be successful, such models cannot neglect the connection between the present and the prehistoric past, since the same forces that shaped the hardware of the brain would also have been at work on its selection of software. Enter evolutionary psychology.

Mental Modules and the Hidden Structures of Thought

When we see a mother holding her newborn it often sparks thoughts of the future rather than of the past. The life of this brand new person extends forward into tomorrow after all, and for the moment it represents the most recent, state-of-the-art version of *H. sapiens*. In reality, this baby's biological continuity lies not with the future, which does not yet exist, but with the past, with its mother, who came before, and then progressing backward through "mitochondrial Eve" and beyond. In canvassing the basic structures and functions of even the newest human brain it is important to bear in mind that our mental equipment has a long evolutionary history with clear links to the rest of the animal kingdom.

The common division of the human brain into forebrain, midbrain, and hindbrain helps to illuminate this process of cognitive development, which involved both the reorganization of old neural structures and the growth of new ones. The hindbrain, consisting of the brain stem and cerebellum, is often referred to as the "reptilian brain" because it is the evolutionarily oldest and most primitive part of the brain. As described above, the components of the hindbrain support the types of vital bodily functions, reflexes, and involuntary actions shared by all animals. The midbrain, including the tectum, tegmentum, and surrounding fibers, is the next oldest in evolutionary origin. The midbrain is functionally more central in nonmammals, where it serves as the main site of visual and auditory information. In mammals this data is handled by the forebrain, though the midbrain continues to help control eye movement and other motor activities. The structures of the midbrain, however, are crucial to our experience of self-awareness—an experience decidedly different from mere reflex. The forebrain, comprised of the cerebral cortex, limbic system, basal ganglia, and diencephalon, is a more recent evolutionary addition to the brain, with the bulky cerebral cortex, or "neocortex," representing the newest improvement, both with respect to brain size and computational power.

It is interesting to note that the prenatal development of the human brain within each individual (ontogenesis) corresponds to the evolutionary development of the brain within the species as a whole (phylogenesis). The brain of a human embryo starts out as a simple tube of tissue that, within weeks, begins reshaping itself into three circular enlargements that will become, in developmental order, the hindbrain, midbrain, and forebrain. Later the cortex of the forebrain divides into the two cerebral hemispheres and grows outward to cover much of the lower brain regions.

Internal shifts in brain function, such as the rerouting of visual and auditory information from the mid- to the forebrain, offer other direct evidence of the brain's evolutionary past. A frequently cited example is the limbic system, which, while taking the lead today in the experience and expression of emotions, originally evolved to evaluate smell. For animals with powerful olfactory senses, smell is a primary means for negotiating the world, such as deciding whether an object should be approached or avoided. In primates and humans the sense of smell has been greatly superceded by vision. As a result, the structures of the limbic system have largely lost their links to smell yet retain their job of generating emotional reactions ranging from fear to elation.

As a biological machine, then, the human central nervous system has much in common with those of other living organisms, designed, as all are, to control bodily function and to interpret and respond to signals received from the outside world. The human brain, however, is clearly different from that of any other creature on earth in displaying the higher-order mental activities we label with names like "intelligence" and "consciousness." Just what such terms mean, precisely, is widely debated by cognitive scientists and philosophers alike, but few would argue with the fact that humans, while anatomically similar to other kinds of animals, are functionally very different. It is often pointed out, for example, how alike certain members of the primate family are, but likeness at the level of genes or gross anatomy in no way translates into likeness of cognitive ability. What makes us humans so different is the kind of mind we have, which in turn is the result of our brain's specific evolutionary development.

Tracing humankind's cognitive evolution returns us once again to basic principles—how natural selection works, and how it would have gone about sculpting the minds of our ancestors. The first principle is elementary: nervous systems, like all body parts, evolve because improvements enhance an animal's chances to survive and reproduce. While not all animals require more than simple reflexes to succeed at the game of life, complex mental abilities bring other animals decided advantages. Brains enable active, voluntary behaviors rather than passive ones; a thinking animal can seek out food and avoid danger instead of waiting for them to come to it. Inevitably, natural selection moved some trajectories of mental development in the direction of improved cognition over basic life support. As brains get better, so do their problem-solving abilities and the benefits that accrue to their owners.

The second principle is more complicated. Just how does natural selection shape minds? How is thinking improved within the context of a particular environment? How are adaptations reflected in the brain? What does the modern mind owe to its evolutionary past? The discipline of evolutionary psychology brings a provocative set of suppositions to bear on these questions, overturning, in the process, some deeply entrenched ways of viewing the human mind, such as the claim that babies are blank slates. The central suppositions of evolutionary psychology have already been introduced on preceding pages, but now it is time to look more closely at how these ideas lead to clearer, more accurate models of the modern mind and also provide essential background for understanding contemporary thought and behavior.

We start with the idea that brains are computers—an insight borrowed from cognitive psychology. Conceiving of brains as computers has proven tremendously fruitful to research on artificial as well as biological intelligence. On the one hand, a computational theory of mind helps explain how organic tissue can process information and execute complex responses. On the other hand, this comparison points up the profound gap between the respective talents of neural and silicon circuitry and hints at what it takes to create "smarter" mechanical systems. Today's computers can crunch mathematical formulas at mind-numbing speed, but they are woefully stupid when it comes to basic human tasks like recognizing objects in the world, reading expressions, or finishing a sentence. Two of the most immediate differences between artificial and biological intelligence, then, are complexity and flexibility. Just as it is, without need of additional software or plug-ins, the human mind can complete an astounding array of functional, interpretive, and analytical jobs, moving freely from one to the next, doing many simultaneously, even combining inputs across modalities to create new and novel outputs. No computer made of plastic, wire, and silicon can yet *transpose* a rose through simile, *get* a joke, or *feel* the death of the machines that made it.

The present differences between artificial and biological intelligence throws up all kinds of challenges to the computer industry, which strives to design systems that increasingly emulate the complexity and flexibility of human thought, but they have also forced brain researchers to revise their understanding of how the mind itself works. When cognitive psychologists first began to investigate the mind, they envisioned it as a very powerful yet very simple program. This early model saw the mind as a kind of "general-purpose problem-solver" that operated according to a set of procedural rules that could be applied to all forms of information. Testing this model of the mind, however, led one directly to the quandaries faced in computer design. It is easy to create simple programs that master specific tasks, even abstract tasks, but such programs aren't much good at doing anything else, let alone at achieving the level of multi-tasking typical of human minds.

For example, one might suppose—and rightly—that a finite set of procedural rules can solve a wide range of mathematical equations. In this case, a brain and a computer could be precisely the same. So far so good. Yet it takes little thought to realize that this suite of procedural rules for doing math would be of little value to the task of language, or much else for that matter. Now what is required is one set of procedural rules for mathematics and other, completely different sets of procedural rules for the coding and decoding of speech. But of course there are a multitude of other unrelated operations that the mind can do, all of which require their own sets of procedural rules as well.

So the early general-purpose problem-solver model of the mind simply wasn't tenable. The evidence suggested that this model of the mind needed to be replaced with a model of the mind as a system of special-purpose programs. Thus cognitive scientists have come to view the brain not as one big machine capable of multiple tasks, but rather as a consortium of numerous small, independent machines, each of which specializes in a single task, and which, working together, lend the mind its obvious complexity of thought.

This perspective is known as the "modular" model of mind and was first earnestly proposed in Jerry Fodor's book *Modularity of Mind* (1983). The modular model of mind accounts for the complex, flexible nature of human thought by delegating specific processing tasks to discrete domains hardwired into the brain called "modules." For Fodor, each encapsulated module carries out its singular work quickly, automatically, and without access to the information found in other modules. In his groundbreaking work Fodor argued for a limited number of modules that corresponds to the sensory inputs of sight, sound, smell, taste, and touch, as well as one dedicated to language. After completing their specialized tasks, these input modules send their information on to centralized processing systems that, because they are not themselves modular, allow for the assimilation of lower-level perceptual knowledge into higher, integrative, problem-solving forms of cognition.

While responsible for setting the study of the mind on the right course, Fodor's seminal idea has since been extended by evolutionary psychologists like John Tooby and Leda Cosmides, who champion a widely accepted model of the mind known as "massive modularity" (1992). The main arguments anchoring the massive modularity model are that Fodor's modular model, while correct in principle, is still too limited and too cumbersome to account for the speed and tremendous variety of computational tasks of the brain, and that massive modularity better falls in line with the engineering methods of natural selection. The second argument, drawn from evolutionary biology, is even more compelling than the one from cognitive psychology.

Recall that natural selection works by solving successive adaptive problems posed by an organism's environment. As a result, adaptations accumulate over time, with each modification representing the best available solution to a specific pressure. In Tooby and Cosmides's view, the entire mind, even Fodor's general-purpose central processes, must be modularized because in the context of adaptation there are no *general* problems only *specific* ones. Lacking both the time and foresight necessary to organize parsimonious mechanisms—which would be impossible in any case since different adaptive problems likely require different solutions—natural selection instead addressed specific problems using specialized mental mechanisms. Such mental mechanisms, or modules, are effective, reliable, and fast because they are dedicated to a single task and, key to the discussion, because they are "content rich"; that is, each mental module is already pre-programmed with the set of procedural rules and knowledge about the world it needs to execute its specific task. In this way, natural selection slowly designed processes of thought, what Steven Pinker calls "Natural Computation," that not only successfully met adaptive problems but also did so in a way that achieved all the coveted goals of "Artificial Intelligence" (1994: 83).

The massive modularity model understands the human mind to be a bundle of hundreds, perhaps even thousands, of specialized devices, each applying itself to a single processing demand. Here the mind might best be envisioned as a Victorian mansion rather than as Fodor's mental apartment. In the massive modularity model, higher cognition does not take place in a single main living area supplied by input from a few side rooms; rather, the specific tasks of intelligence occur in a labyrinth of rooms, closets, and corners, all of which function smoothly together to generate the thought life of the typical human being.

What kinds of mental modules does the human mind contain? The current module hunt was actually initiated in the 1950s by the linguist Noam Chomsky, who was struck by the fact that children easily acquire language despite the fact that their exposure to it is grossly impoverished (1959). Children, Chomsky noted, receive nothing resembling formal grammatical instruction. Our everyday speech consists largely of improperly constructed, halting, unfinished strings of words, as every journalist knows. Yet children take this mess of syntax and speedily become competent language users. The reason, Chomsky suggested, is that language is not so much *learned* as naturally *developed*. This hardwired capacity shared by all people represents the first mental module, which Chomsky dubbed the "language acquisition device."

Another early modular approach to the mind was taken by David Marr, who was interested in how the visual system recognizes and constantly holds external objects in spite of the fact that visual information (color, shading, shapes, motion, and so on) is even more chaotic and underdetermined than is conversation. To account for the wizardry of sight—a feat involving a substantial amount of mental *interpretation*—Marr constructed a theory of vision in which the final images that we see are the result of different modules dedicated to detecting edges, motion, color, and depth (1982). A modular model has also been applied to auditory processing, showing that different mental mechanisms are engaged in the analysis of speech versus non-speech sound. (Liberman and Mattingly 1989). As already noted, Fodor agreed with this empirical work in the domains of language and sensory perception and used it to compose his original list of innate input modules.

For evolutionary psychologists, the complete slate of mental modules will only be uncovered as we place the modern mind against the backdrop of its ancestral past. If mental modules are evolved mechanisms constructed in response to adaptive problems, then we must consider the environment in which these problems were faced. That means looking again into the Pleistocene's evolutionary forge. It is wrong to attempt to explain the architecture of the mind in relation to contemporary times. The human mind evolved under the selective pressures confronted by our Stone Age relatives. Indeed, the post-Pleistocene period—a mere tick of time constituting only about 5,000 human generations—is largely irrelevant to the composition of the mind. Our minds remain adapted to a Pleistocene way of life; the mental modules we use today are the same ones our hunting and gathering ancestors used to survive in their own unforgiving Pleistocene world.

Cosmides and Tooby point out that many psychologists also erroneously attempt to describe the cognitive architecture of the mind based on the study of what it *can* do rather than of what it was *designed* to do (1994: 95). The evolutionary engineering of the past was completed without regard to present circumstances or with an eye to enabling cognitive skills beyond those necessary to solve problems within the Pleistocene environment. The novel ways we use our minds today, however impressive, are but secondary consequences, or by-products, of their functional design and cannot be used as an explanation for how that design came to be. "For humans, the situations our ancestors encountered as Pleistocene hunter-gatherers define the array of adaptive problems our cognitive mechanisms were *designed* to solve, although these do not, of course, exhaust the range of problems they are capable of solving" (Cosmides and Tooby 1994: 87).

By exploring the selective pressures our Pleistocene ancestors faced it is possible to predict and test for associated modular adaptations. For those who doubt the possibility of bridging the cognitive past and present, a well-known experiment employed by Cosmides demonstrates our ability to see ancient mental mechanisms in action (1989). A creative twist on a standard psychological test called the Wason selection task reveals how abstract reasoning capacities like deductive logic are by-products of mental modules designed for other, more practical purposes.

There is a deck of cards with numbers on one side and letters on the other. Four of these cards are placed on a table in front of you in the following arrangement:

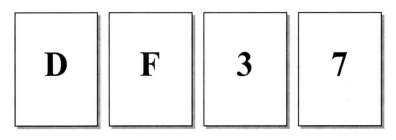

FIGURE 2.2. Wason selection task (deductive logic).

You are then told this single conditional rule: If a card has a "D" on one side, then it also has a "3" on the other side. The test of logic? Which cards do you need to turn over to determine whether or not this rule is true?

In point of fact, most people fail this test when it is presented in this way. The correct solution is to turn over the first and last cards, since the logically proper response for a rule of the form *If P then Q* is always *P and not-Q*. This form of reasoning is highly abstract, and it takes some time to arrive at the right answer. It is even hard for some people to see the logic of the solution after it is shown to them. What is intriguing, however, is that most people quickly and easily give the correct answer when the same test is presented to them in a completely different context. Cosmides (following Griggs and Cox 1982) set up the test like this:

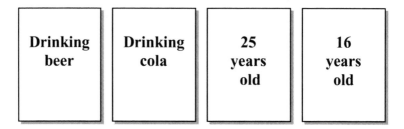

FIGURE 2.3. Wason selection task (cheater detection).

You are working at a local bar as a bouncer charged with policing under-age drinking. The four cards now represent four different people, with one side showing each person's age, the other side showing what each person is drinking. Now, which cards do you have to turn over in order to determine whether the drinking age is being violated?

Note that the logical structure of both versions of the test is exactly the same, and yet the solution to the second is obvious. The immediate explanation for this is that human reasoning skills change dramatically depending on the context of the problem. But it turns out that only *certain* contexts markedly enhance performance. Other versions of the Wason selection task confirm that people are not highly competent at spotting violations of descriptive or causal rules either. What people *are* good at, and what the drinking-age test isolates, is deductive reasoning that relates to social exchange.

As the last chapter pointed out, astute social intelligence is critical to group living. Successfully navigating through complex social arrangements requires the mental skills involved in mind reading, kin relations, alliance formation, and many other facets of group life. The ability to detect individuals who cheat on the social contracts that underpin personal relations is among the most important of these skills, and we should expect this selective pressure to have been met with an associated mental adaptation—a module with specialized procedures for reasoning about social exchange. The second version of the Wason selection task capitalizes on this cheater-detection module; the logical problem is simple precisely because it is all about detecting cheats.

This sort of empirical evidence strengthens the argument for the modularity model of mind. If the human mind truly works like a general-purpose problem-solver, then context should make little difference to the outcome. The fact that the same problem is easy in one context and difficult in another suggests instead that specialized, context-dependent cognitive processes are at work. This test also reveals a second significant feature of mental modules. In addition to being *content-rich*, already pre-programmed with the processing information they need to do their work, mental modules are also *domain specific*. This means that a given module is only activated by input relevant to its specialized task. It also means that the processing information in one module remains inaccessible to others. One of Cosmides and Tooby's conclusions from their study of Wason selection tasks is that deductive reasoning developed as part of the cognitive processes regulating social exchange (1992). The first version of the test proves difficult because it poses a logical problem in an abstract form rather than in a concrete social one. As a result, it fails to activate the mental module capable of solving the problem with ease. If Cosmides and Tooby are correct, it suggests that the varieties of abstract logical thought unique to humankind are secondary consequences, or by-products, of cognitive capacities evolved for more worldly purposes.

Just as we should expect natural selection to have designed a cheater-detection module to deal with the exigencies of group living, we should also expect the modern mind to be loaded with mental modules for solving a host of other adaptive problems. The massive modularity model of mind argues for thousands of mental modules at work in human cognition, all of which make perfect sense in light of evolutionary history. Though the possibilities remain speculative, the following short list of mental modules serves as a sample of some of the more widely accepted candidates and illustrates the range of thinking and behaviors related to them:

- *Predator detection*: Fundamental to daily survival, mental modules related to predator detection rapidly distinguish threats in the environment and trigger avoidance or defensive behaviors.
- *Food preference*: Also fundamental to daily survival, mental modules regulating food preferences promote a desire for safe, nutritious foods (especially those rich in sugar and fat) and dislike and disgust for harmful or poisonous items.
- *Mate selection*: Daily survival is the means to a gene's ultimate end—reproduction. Mental modules help to discern sexual partners who are genetically and developmentally robust based on subtle aspects of physical appearance, such as body shape and symmetry. Mate selection criteria also include characteristics that suggest individuals will be good mothers and fathers, markers (for example, age, resources, and loyalty) that are gender specific. Conversely, related mental modules work at advertising oneself as a good choice for others.
- *Child rearing and kinship*: In many species reproductive success necessitates a period of childcare after offspring are born. Likewise, non-reciprocal support of close relatives helps assure genetic propagation. Related mental modules support familial behaviors, including skills such as face recognition and estimating degrees of relatedness.
- *Alliances and friendship*: For highly social animals, the ability to form mutually beneficial partnerships with conspecifics is vital to gaining and maintaining access to basic resources (food, sex, and protection).

Related mental modules include the mechanisms involved in monitoring social exchange.

These mental modules are directly related to survival and reproduction within the ancestral environment (both ecological and social), and from an evolutionary standpoint this is indeed the functional raison d'être of all adaptations. But natural selection cannot focus solely on activities associated with food and sex since being good at living and reproducing requires a wide range of supporting skills. As Tooby and Cosmides argue, this requirement is responsible for the accumulation of distinct families of specialized information-gathering, inference, and decision-making modules that progressively increased the power and breadth of thought and, ultimately, gave rise to the polished cognitive capacities of the modern mind:

> By adding together a face recognition module, a spatial relations module, a rigid object mechanics module, a tool use module, a fear module, a social exchange module, an emotion perception module, a kin-oriented motivation module, an effort allocation and recalibration module, a childcare module, a social inference module, a sexual attraction module, a semantic inference module, a friendship module, a grammar acquisition module, a communication pragmatics module, a theory of mind module, and so on, an architecture gains a breadth of competences that allows it to solve a wider and wider array of problems, coming to resemble, more and more, a human mind. (1992: 113)

Tooby and Cosmides's massive modularity model is not the final word on the architecture of the mind; not all cognitivists are comfortable with it. Steven Mithen, for instance, argues that the only way to account for such unique and provocative human capacities as imagination, creativity, and analogical and metaphorical thought is to build into the mind processes capable of combining the many forms of thought in flexible, novel ways (1996). Dedicated, encapsulated mental modules like those proposed by Cosmides and Tooby should be inherently incapable of producing the variety of cross-domain reflection that appears to be the hallmark of modern intelligence. Resting his model of the mind on the classic idea that "ontogeny recapitulates phylogeny," and drawing evidence from the work of developmental psychologists like Patricia Greenfield (1991) and Annette Karmiloff-Smith (1992), Mithen argues that the mind of each person passes through three architectural phases of development resulting in what he calls "cognitive fluidity," the basis of our extraordinary mental abilities.

According to this model, babies are born with a "generalized mentality" very like the general-purpose problem-solver described above. The mind of the infant soaks up different types of information about the world using the same

cognitive processes as its neural wiring settles into place. The phylogenic connection here is that the mind of the human infant is similar to the mind of a
chimpanzee; both use general intelligence to interpret and interact with the
world. At about the age of two, children enter the second phase of mental
development, shifting from a generalized mentality to a "domain-specific mentality." This phase of mental development is characterized by precisely the kind
of modularization articulated by Cosmides and Tooby, and it is no coincidence,
Mithen argues, that much of the empirical evidence for modularized thought
comes from the study of children around the ages of two and three. As expected, this is the period when specialized, content-rich intelligences take
shape, such as language acquisition and an understanding of object perma-
nence. It is also an important period in that cultural context plays a role in
determining the range of domain intelligences that eventually develops. In this
phase of modularization the child's mind is like those of our Pleistocene ancestors, whose intellectual and technical abilities were clearly superior to
chimps and early hominids but who left little evidence that they were engaged
in more sophisticated forms of thinking. During the third and final phase of
mental development, marked by a shift from a domain-specific mentality to a
"cognitively fluid mentality," the mind's suite of modules begins to work together, building connections that facilitate information exchange. Rather than
remaining isolated in encapsulated domains, different forms of knowledge can
be linked and combined, allowing for the diverse, intricate, spontaneous, and
imaginative nature of truly *human* thought.

For Mithen, a developmental model of the mind explains both the unique
mental capacities of modern humans and the mysterious period of cultural
explosion evident in the archaeological record. As Mithen points out, the start
of intense cultural proliferation some 50,000 years ago does not coincide with
the appearance of the first modern humans around 100,000 years ago. While
scientists have long found it easy to herald brain size as the defining characteristic of human evolution, Mithen asserts that intelligence has more to do
with the design of the mind than with its dimensions. It was the later, final
development of cognitive fluidity that brought about the "emergence of the
modern mind—the same mentality that you and I possess today" (1996: 15)
and ignited the cultural explosion. The fundamental changes in lifestyle and
the many new artifacts that appear at this time were the result of nothing less
than a major alteration in the very nature of the mind.

Whereas Fodor's model of the mind (limited modularity) is like an urban
apartment consisting of a central living space and a few side rooms, and Tooby
and Cosmides's mind (massive modularity) is like an immense Victorian mansion where thought takes place in hundreds of private rooms, Mithen describes
the modern human mind (integrated intelligence) as a majestic cathedral,
whose construction takes place in three phases as individuals move from infancy to adulthood. The finished edifice is comprised of many classrooms,

offices, and chapels, each with doors opening to a grand central nave of general intelligence where knowledge and ideas flow freely and harmoniously between the domains of specialized intelligence and promote brand new forms of thinking and behavior.

There are other models of the mind that complement the ones presented here. Dan Sperber, for example, has proposed that the apparent gap between a massively modular mind and a creative one can be bridged with yet another specialized module, one that evolved to enable the forms of cognition described by Mithen and the developmental psychologists. Sperber calls this hypothetical mechanism or set of mechanisms the "metarepresentational module" and suggests that its job is to take the concrete mental representations produced by other modules and generate second-order "mental representations of mental representations" (1994: 60), precisely what takes place in instances of imaginative and metaphorical thought.

Regardless of the exact nature of mental modularity—limited, massive, or integrated—what ties these various models together is an understanding that all of the present structures and functions of the modern mind are selected adaptations accumulated over the course of evolutionary history. The mind did not develop all of a piece; rather, specific modules evolved to solve specific problems. The result is a complex assemblage of mental units that achieve rapid, efficient information processing, and which, either through generalized connections or thorough specialization, advance higher-order forms of cognition. Another commonality between all of these modular models is the recognition that the human mind comes loaded with lots of pre-programmed knowledge and hardwired cognitive skills. Reacting against the Standard Social Science Model, which views the neonate mind as essentially a blank slate and places a fundamental division between biology and culture, the models of mind put forth by cognitive, developmental, and evolutionary psychologists rightly include innate knowledge bases that facilitate computation in specialized domains. The rest of this chapter will describe three of these intuitive *kinds* of thinking as well as some *ways* of thinking, both because they help round out the survey of mental architecture provided in this chapter and because one of them, namely, intuitive psychology, is foundational to the discussion found throughout the rest of this book.

Some Programs and Processes of Human Thought

Already the cognitive scientist's preferred analogy for the human brain—the common computer—has provided a fruitful way to explore some of the structures and functions of this most outstanding biological organ. But there is one more likeness between the mind and the machine worth exploiting here. As the last paragraph affirmed, the newborn baby and a newly shipped Dell have something very important in common: they both arrive ready to hit the ground running.

Consider any infant and off-the-shelf PC. After jettisoning its protective sack of amniotic fluid, a baby leaves the safety of the womb and enters a bright, noisy, touchy world. It is poked and prodded, subjected to medical tests, and fondled incessantly by an array of people, only one of which is its mother. The computer arrives in a womb-like carton, ensconced in protective layers of cardboard and foam. There are no medical procedures to be completed and certainly no slap to be administered, but the ensuing set-up process, cable connections, and reference materials approximate the attention lavished on a newborn in the delivery room. Once this flurry of activity subsides and one steps back to observe the new baby and the new PC quietly doing what they were designed to do—being a human and being a computing machine—it becomes clear that each one already knows a great deal about what these respective tasks entail.

The innate abilities of mind and machine are not only intriguing but also essential. There is, of course, no mystery to the fact that the computer already has knowledge and can immediately begin its work, but thinking for a moment about this trivial fact helps to clarify the less obvious, and certainly less trivial nature of the newborn's mind. In short, computers work because they are programmed to do so. Every new computer comes complete with an operating system that contains instructions for how to be a computing machine as well as for how to recognize and process new input. Without this elaborate program the computer is nothing more than an inert sculpture. A computer that arrived at your doorstep as hardware only would be utterly useless. Even if you owned a library of software, the computer would understand none of it. It is the personal computer's operating system, call it PC 1.0, which enables the hardware to understand the meaning of any new input received from the outside world—from basic word processing programs to complicated flight simulation software—and to begin implementing it properly.

Living machines have the same operational requirements. From the moment of birth a baby is bombarded by input from its strange new world. Some sensations are random and incidental, others are deliberate and personally relevant. Some things in the environment are inanimate and insignificant; others are alive and intentional in their actions. Competency at the tasks of recognition and interpretation is crucial to survival and successful development, so it needs to begin immediately. Yet, if human brains were only hardware they would be functionally useless. All of that light, noise, motion, and touching, let alone the kaleidoscope of objects and people, would remain insensible. Without some rather crucial innate skills, newborns would be like new computers lacking operating systems.

So for mechanical reasons a blank-slate view of the mind is simply untenable. No mind could possibly understand, respond to, or use a piece of new information received from the environment unless it already possessed the equipment and knowledge that *enabled* it to understand, respond to, and use this new information. Nor can learning mechanisms alone account for the development of mental abilities. As Tom Lawson points out, though there are parents and other models for nurturing the growth of newborns, "from the child's point of view, the behavior of the parents and all the other things in the environment requires as much interpretation and explanation as all of the other things and events that the child encounters" (2000: 76). Newborns immediately begin the work of being human because they, too, come programmed to do so. The biological computer, model Modern Human Brain, arrives preinstalled with an operating system prepared by evolution that contains all the instructions for human computation as well as programs for processing new input. Like computer models whose operating systems are the same right out of the box, MHB 1000s run on MHB 1.0.

The efforts of developmental, evolutionary, and cognitive psychologists are rapidly adding to our understanding of how MHB 1.0 works and what some of its programs do. Because they were designed to help people successfully interact with their natural environment, the programs bundled into the human operating system work to organize, interpret, and predict objects and events in the world. One way that psychologists commonly refer to these types of crucial, innate programs is with the label "intuitive" or "folk" knowledge. The term "folk," coined by Daniel Dennett as part of the phrase "folk psychology" (1987), has come to denote the several systematic forms of knowledge and thinking that ordinary people use to explain the things, activities, and other individuals encountered in everyday life.

There are three categories of intuitive knowledge that are almost universally accepted and which illustrate well the nature of the operating system guiding human thought: intuitive biology, intuitive physics, and intuitive psychology. Developmental psychologists have come a long way in charting the innate foundations of these three knowledge bases as well as the astonishing speed and general timetables under which related interpretive skills mature. Such evidence strongly suggests an interactive understanding of cognitive development in which the experience of external stimuli interacting with innate cognitive mechanisms and predispositions results in the acquisition of new forms of knowledge (Groome 1999). What follows are general synopses covering the content and use of each of these important forms of tacit thought:

- *Intuitive biology*: Intuitive biology refers to the way minds categorize and reason about living things. The world is filled with all kinds of "stuff"—there's people, animals, plants, natural objects, and hand-made artifacts. Humans naturally sort the external environment ontologically. At the most basic level, we know that living things and inanimate objects are fundamentally different. Thinking about the class of living things also prompts a wide range of inferences that apply only to biological organisms, including organic composition, vital functioning, movement, and intentional behavior. Extensive research shows that very young children possess this knowledge, too, and they reason accordingly. One intriguing way that living things are understood is through "essentialism." What a plant or animal *is* is based on the attribution of a species-specific "essence" that cannot be changed despite appearances. For example, children will not call an animal shown to have gears inside its belly a living thing, or decide that a man who has lost his legs is no longer a person, or think that a mother hen will give birth to a hamster, or agree, as Frank Keil has playfully shown, that a horse fitted in a striped costume becomes a zebra (1989). Scott Atran has thoroughly demonstrated the universality and extent of intuitive biology, showing how people groups across the globe use the same systems of species exemplars and hierarchical taxonomy to identify and organize the natural world (1990).

- *Intuitive physics*: Intuitive physics refers to tacit knowledge about basic mechanical properties and principles that adhere in the world of physical objects, such as solidity, motion, and causality. Experiments with very young children confirm that they understand a set of rules that govern material objects—rules that differ from those that govern mental concepts and living things—and, like adults at a magic show, they are surprised when these rules are violated. Researchers such as Renée Baillargeon and Elizabeth Spelke have found that infants are capable of reasoning about the physical properties of objects involved in simple events (for example, Spelke 1991, Baillargeon 1995). Babies only a couple months old take into account the continuity and solidity of objects and have a range of expectations about how such qualities apply. For example, infants grasp the continuity of shape and make assumptions about partially occluded objects. They understand that solid objects collide with each other and do not normally pass through other solid obstacles. Additional expectations infants have are involved with cause and effect. Objects move when other objects push them; actions cannot be caused at a distance. Infants also grasp basic laws of motion. Moving objects must follow sensible, continuous trajectories. If a ball rolls behind a screen, for instance, then it ought to emerge again at a predictable spot and time. Spelke shows that children also count on the rules of gravity and inertia, though these physical concepts take more time to fully develop. Material objects are also recognized to be different in kind from the class of living things. The elaborate system of classification used to organize biological knowledge is not used in the world of objects. Most importantly, people do not employ the idea of essences when thinking about artifacts. Material objects can be put to new uses and therefore can be thought of in totally new ways. Things made of plastic blocks, for example, can be broken apart and remade into completely different objects with no sense of lost continuity. What a given object is, as opposed to what a living thing is, depends on context rather than on a sense of internal essence.

- *Intuitive psychology:* Intuitive psychology refers to the natural attribution of mental states to other people and the cognitive skills involved in the ongoing interpretation of those states. As the first chapter discussed, we are all consummate psychologists who spend large amounts of time and energy attempting to read the minds of others, especially as their beliefs and desires pertain to ourselves. But working from a theory of mind also helps to explain the causes of behaviors and events in the world more generally, particularly within the social networks that define human life. A large body of research in child development reveals the extent to which a mentalistic perception of the world is present at birth and the degree to which it matures in a few short years. In the crib babies favor social stimuli like faces and voices, and they soon begin to follow the gaze of eyes and check nearby people for clues about happenings. By the age of two children have mentally separated themselves from others, recognizing that those around them do not necessarily share their own beliefs and desires. They also grasp the difference between psychological and physical causality—in the realm of living things, actions can be caused at a distance after all! Pretend play, which begins in earnest, openly attests to the mentalistic world in which all humans live. By the age of four children reach a final milestone in the development of their psychological apparatus by coming to realize that other people can hold beliefs that they themselves know to be false. This ability opens the door to the full-blown theory of mind introduced earlier as well as to skills of deception and other mental strategies that comprise social intelligence.

As these three foundational domains of intuitive knowledge illustrate, there is an expansive bundle of programs hardwired into the human mind. These knowledge bases are species-specific and rooted in innate mental mechanisms. While some cognitive abilities require phases of maturation, it is impossible that these knowledge bases could be acquired, to such depth and with such speed, from infants' limited experience of the world. Rather, people possess minds designed to immediately begin recognizing relevant information about the environment. We are all intuitive biologists, physicists, and psychologists. From an evolutionary standpoint, these mental skills are crucial: intuitive biology provides detailed information about the natural world; intuitive physics makes it possible for us to count on a stable, lawful sphere of existence; intuitive psychology grounds the kind of intelligence it takes to interact with others. Natural selection has well equipped human beings with the mental tools necessary for life in the cognitive niche.

The presence of intuitive knowledge not only allows babies to hit the ground running but it also makes them (makes everyone, actually, regardless of age) ready learners. Because babies are born with foundational knowledge bases, they are able to assimilate a wide range of new information using these same intuitive systems. Young children are not confused when they encounter an unfamiliar animal for the first time because they already know what "animals" are like. Young children aren't shocked when a building made of blocks topples over because that's how "things" work. Some young children are shy around other people because they know that they are being watched, and that's normal too. The acquisition of a native language takes place in the absence of real grammatical instruction precisely because, as discussed earlier, it depends upon yet another domain of intuitive knowledge. Such intellectual feats in small children highlight the *noncultural* foundations of many forms of human knowledge. True, grasping the principles of Euclid geometry or Husserlian phenomenology may take a semester or two of intense formal instruction, but when it comes to new information about the world at large, "common sense" usually affords all the education that people need.

Talk of the noncultural foundations of knowledge, then, extends beyond natural *kinds* of thinking to natural *ways* of thinking; that is, to the cognitive mechanisms responsible for recognizing and organizing information received from the world. Think for a moment about the little considered but rather astounding process going on inside you at this very moment. All normal people see, hear, smell, taste, and feel the world "out there," but it's really amazing that they do. Sight, after all, is the result of nothing more than photons of light striking the retina. Hearing is the result of slight changes of air pressure that cause vibrations in the eardrum. In all areas of sensory perception the brain takes what are grossly impoverished stimuli and, through an intricate process of translation and transformation, literally constructs an accurate model of the world. The hidden nature of this mental construction project—and our wonderment at it—escalates as the level of complexity is extended. Why do you not only see the light reflected from a familiar face *as a face* but also know *to whom it belongs?* Why are you able to quickly recognize someone from behind as well as from the front? How can you picture someone who isn't in view? How, indeed, can you conceive of someone or something or some concept that doesn't even exist?

The starting point for the standard answer to questions about how we construct worlds of real and imagined objects and ideas is that our minds take the various forms of raw information—sensations, signals, communications, and so on—and turn them into mental "representations." A good definition of a "representation" is hard to come by, but essentially representations are internal pictures or models created by the mind that allow for beliefs, thoughts, and actions. The mind generates these pictures and models using cognitive procedures that are hardwired into the brain. Cognitive psychology is all about discovering the processes that stand behind our mental representations of the world. One of these complicated processes—pattern recognition—can be grossly simplified by imagining the mind as a kind of virtual workshop containing grids, gauges, and tools used to measure incoming information and produce the proper representations. In this capacity, the mind takes in a few clues about real things in the world and builds mental replicas of them based on patterns it already has on hand.

The subject of faces provides an excellent example of pattern recognition at work because, given humankind's gregarious past and present, our mental workshops are hypersensitive to patterns that resemble faces. We see them everywhere—in clouds, behind two blinking lights, on the surface of the moon, in the most arbitrary splotches of ink. In his charming book *Unweaving the Rainbow* (1998) Richard Dawkins describes a household experiment that illustrates the inexorable nature of pattern sensors like the ones responsible for representing faces. Dawkins urges readers to buy a rubber mask like those worn at Halloween. Set the mask up at the opposite end of a room and look at it. When faced toward you, the mask obviously looks solid, because it is. But when you turn the mask around so that the hollow side faces out, a remarkable illusion takes place. Despite your knowledge that the mask is hollow, and in spite of direct visual evidence reaching your retina that confirms that the mask is hollow, your pattern sensor for faces is so powerful that it trumps all other stimuli. The mental workshop naturally goes about its work of finishing the job and produces a complete image. You cannot help but perceive the empty mask as a haunting, solid face.

The same kind of cognitive process is at work in the internal representation of objects and ideas. Pascal Boyer speaks of another important supply of patterns found in our mental workshops as "templates," which help minds identify and organize what is observed and learned (2001). Boyer refers to these templates as "ontological categories," which align nicely with one of the intuitive knowledge bases. These templates work like folders in a mental file cabinet, with one folder for each kind of thing that exists in the world: *Animal, Plant, Person, Natural Object, Artifact,* and so on. These templates make concept building easy because they allow us to file new information rapidly and accurately. A young girl who encounters a giraffe for the first time may find its figure comical and quite unlike anything she's ever seen before, but she has little trouble placing it in the correct folder: *Animal.* Her mind simply draws out the template for *Animal* and creates a new concept, *Giraffe.*

What is particularly important about this system of ontological templates is that each one already contains lots of information about the kind of thing it represents. The *Animal* template, for example, includes general descriptions that apply to all animals: natural, living, eats, moves, and so on. These general descriptions are very different from those found on the *Artifact* template, for instance, which includes the information: not natural, inanimate, doesn't eat, doesn't move. Having generalized knowledge like this allows the mind to spontaneously infer a host of additional information when building new concepts. As the young girl sees the giraffe for the first time, much more takes place in the creation of her *Giraffe* concept than the acquisition of a new name. She also automatically adds to her new concept all of the information that applies to *Animal* in general. She may not know what a giraffe eats specifically, but she is quite sure that it does.

Conceptualization can also work backward from the generalized information to the proper template. If Boyer tells you, as he does in his book, that "Zygoons are predators of hyenas" and that "Thricklers are expensive" (2001: 58–59), you will likely infer that in the first statement he is talking about an *Animal* and in the second about an *Artifact*. These inference connections are made because the knowledge that predators eat other animals automatically activated the *Animal* template, and the knowledge that things are purchased automatically activated the *Artifact* template. Furthermore, after you activate the proper template, additional inferences will automatically be added to the original information, such as expectations about the Zygoon's other animal characteristics. This process of inference is also revealed through the ease with which we create concepts of unreal or imaginary things. The idea of a *Ghost* is easy to assimilate because it automatically activates all of the inferences that apply to the category *Person*, save for the one that makes it unnatural: not living.

Boyer refers to the networks of automatic connections that foster thought as "inference systems" and shifts from the metaphor of templates to the reality of cognitive inferences. Of course the mind doesn't literally contain file cabinets and templates, but it does think by utilizing complex inference systems. Through a process of intuitive leaps and systematic generalizations the mind is able to go beyond fragmentary information and build up rich representations. In fact, "the way people generalize is perhaps the most telltale sign that the mind uses mental representations, and lots of them" (Pinker 1997: 86). The employment of inferences and generalizations is one of the hallmarks of human cognition, accounting for the speed, efficiency, and flexibility of thought.

Yet it is also important to see that inferences and generalizations proceed along specific paths depending on the information given. The concept of an animal does not naturally activate inferences about an object. Thinking about a person does not naturally activate inferences that apply to a plant. This means that thought is not random but constrained in various ways. Two helpful terms for describing mental activities like pattern recognition and inference are "bias" and "predisposition." The human mind has a disposition to process information along particular channels that lead to predictable ends. This assures that representations remain constant—that when you see a face it's always a face rather than a cat or a rock and that if you encounter a tiger in the wild you won't assume it doesn't eat. Randomness in the generation of representations would be dangerous, not to mention utter madness. Among the notable features of MHB 1.0, then, are default settings that guide reasoning processes unless conscious effort is taken to override them.

Intuitive knowledge, pattern sensors, and inference systems are just some of the programs and processes of thought, but they sufficiently demonstrate aspects of human cognition that will be featured prominently in the next stage of this discussion. First, having minds that are predisposed to think in consistent, predictable ways means that all people everywhere build concepts using the same procedures and, ultimately, represent the world of things and ideas in very similar ways. This has important implications for the study of culture and the ideas that people share. A standardized mental operating system should result in, and consequently explain, a wide range of common and persistent representations.

Second, even a cursory look at the programs and processes of thought reveals how the finished products of the mind owe their existence to hidden cognitive mechanisms. One of the most significant findings of cognitive psychology is how much of our thinking takes place below the level of awareness. Representations are constructed in mental workshops outfitted with specialized machinery of all sorts, each contributing to the project at hand. Most of this work is automatic, rapid, and incorrigible; only the finished product is made available, by means of a mental dumbwaiter, to conscious inspection. Normally this process runs so smoothly that we experience a perfect constancy of thought and perception. Only clever experiments or tragic events like brain damage disclose how truly complex the simplest task can be.

Finally, the constructive nature of human cognition makes it clear that what we often refer to as imaginative, abstract, or even sublime ideas rest on banal, garden-variety forms of thought. We need not search for special cognitive processes to account for "special" kinds of thinking. *What* people think is explained by *how* they think. We can account for a great range of human ideas by connecting them to the kinds of hardwired programs and processes described above. Many of the marvelous thoughts we humans entertain rise well above the level of brute existence, but they can nevertheless be understood as by-products of cognitive skills and tacit forms of knowledge designed to accomplish more mundane calculations. This book, of course, is concerned with explaining *religious* thought, a mode of thinking long deemed "special." Yet the cognitive science of religion is demonstrating that religious ideas and behaviors—some of the most sublime uses of the human mind—are eminently tractable.

3

Minds, Other Minds, and the Minds of Gods

What Do Gods Have to Do with the Brain?

Most people dissociate scientific inquiry and daily life. Science is interesting, to be sure: natural history piques curiosity; anatomy and psychology intrigue; the animal world stirs wonder and the physical world respect; speculation about human origins draws attention from every quarter. Nevertheless, science is largely viewed as something done in labs and universities by people who look peculiar and speak more peculiarly still. While many people acknowledge that science leads to amazing achievements like medicines and moonwalks, fewer readily agree that it informs the deeper questions of human existence—how we live and move and have our being.

In one respect this is understandable. After all, should plate tectonics be factored into your travel plans? Could knowledge of mental modularity save a flagging dinner date? Would imitating macaque behavior help to secure a raise at work? Might a hominid genealogy enrich your next family reunion? Or, for the philosophically inclined, does mentation truly relate to metaphysics, science to spirituality? Yet the reason science works—what those who consider it to be an oblique, detached enterprise miss—is that its subject matter is *precisely* the stuff of daily life. Science seeks to explain the nature of and relationships between real things in the real world. Uncovering correct and complete explanations might well require forays into some rather arcane territory—realms ranging from the subatomic to the galactic, processes governing everything from the Krebs cycle to black holes—but the various disciplines of science have arisen with the express purpose of illuminating the character and conditions of everyday life. In the process, science frequently reveals how mysterious is the ordinary, and, how ordinary is the mysterious.

In the same way, this book aspires to throw back a bit of the mystery surrounding the origins of religious thought—namely, ideas regarding the reality of gods and the systems of belief, behavior, and community they support. At first glance there may seem to be little point of contact between evolutionary history and the thoughts you are entertaining at this very moment. Even if the ins and outs of natural selection are accepted, it remains hard to see how ideas we humans ponder here in the twenty-first century have anything to do with the thoughts of strange hominids eking out a living millions of years ago. Likewise, it is difficult to clearly relate the physical structures and functions of the brains that we carry around inside our heads with the amorphous ideas that spring so naturally from them. Yet the connections between ancient past and present day, and between gray matter and invisible thought, are direct and paramount. A central tenet of cognitive science is that we cannot understand *what* we think until we understand *how* we think. And how we think is the result of mental mechanisms molded by selective adaptation over many millennia. Intriguingly, it is possible to speak of the "history of ideas" in biological terms.

Having explored some of the phylogenetic and ontogenetic background of human cognition in general, it is time to begin looking at features of thought that play a role in the generation of specifically religious ideas. It should be clear by now that an explanation for mental concepts like gods requires no appeal to unusual causes or categories of thought. Religious ideas, like all other kinds of ideas, owe their existence to a raft of specialized tools used in the brain's mental workshop to interpret and organize the world. Ideas, even when they are communicated to us whole, are made (or remade) by the mind each time they are entertained. Whatever the content of a given idea, it exists because of our mental workshop's prowess at quickly and consistently constructing concepts. Religious ideas are simply one of many products that come down the assembly line. "People are equipped to create and employ religious ideas, Tom Lawson writes, "because they are equipped to create and employ ideas" (2000: 81).

What does require further investigation, however, is the actual set of mental tools needed to build religious concepts. Gods, after all, are quite different things from cows or computers or mathematical equations. We should expect different mental tools to be involved in the representation of each of these things, though it is important to keep in mind that, like the ubiquitous hammer and screwdriver, the same mental tools often contribute to the construction of similar kinds of concepts. Also, the number of patterns and tools found in the mental workshop is not all that large, so many seemingly unrelated concepts in fact share underlying similarities. We'll see that in some significant respects cows and gods aren't so different after all.

It turns out that thinking about gods, while requiring the complete brain system, actually pivots on just a handful of quite ordinary mental tools that are present at birth and mature in the first years of life. The two most important of these mental tools are the Agency Detection Device (ADD), which recognizes the presence and activities of other beings around us, and the Theory of Mind Mechanism (ToMM), which ascribes sentience to agents and tries to interpret their intentions. Working in conjunction with each other, these two mental tools account for some of the most critical, as well as some of the most creative, operations of human intelligence—from the attention needed to survive in hostile and competitive environments to the sensitivity and cunning involved in interpersonal intercourse to the conceptual framework behind lots of imaginative thought.

But there is much more to gods than being and mind, and this chapter charts a number of other features of human cognition that inform and promote representations of gods. In doing so, a detailed picture of what gods are like begins to emerge. Of course, religious people (and the nonreligious too) already have a good idea about what their gods are like, and they can usually describe them with precision and confidence, but viewed from the perspective of cognition, the real attributes of gods are not necessarily those long-discussed and defended by theologians. Indeed, theology is just the sort of activity that results in formally expressed *differences* between god concepts. Attention to cognition accounts both for the striking *similarities* of gods found around the world and why these kinds of gods are so easily—so *naturally*—rendered by the types of minds that all humans possess.

Seeing Agents (ADD) and Reading Minds (ToMM)

Life today can be tough. Depending on where people live, they face tensions and challenges ranging from family strife, traffic, and tax bills to illness, crime, and armed conflict. Yet the exigencies of modern human society pale in comparison to those faced daily by even the simplest animals. The stakes are rather higher for creatures trying to stay alive than for those attempting to make more money. People who are poor understand this better than people who are privileged, yet even the poor can usually find assistance. Nature is brutal and cold. It offers little by way of welfare or social aid. Boardrooms may be cut-throat, metaphorically speaking, but the African plains are literal killing fields. So are the oceans, the skies, the soil, and every other ecosystem. To you and me the natural world may be filled with beauty, but beauty is indeed in the eye of the beholder. While a resplendent sunset often stirs the human heart, in the animal kingdom it signals the arrival of a whole new set of dangers.

Our ancestors shared this less romantic view of the natural world. For a large part of evolutionary history, our ancestors were the hunted as well as developing hunters. Possessed of bodies woefully unprotected and significantly weaker than any of the apes, the earliest humans would have been acutely aware of their vulnerability and the many threats of injury or outright attack waiting at every turn. Even as they traveled far down the road of intelligence and began to capitalize on the new forms of defense it enabled, the first humans continued to depend on many of the same cognitive skills that all other animals use to navigate foreboding landscapes filled with enemies, foes, and friends.

It makes sense, then, that one of the most basic and powerful activities of the brain involves the ability to quickly detect other agents in the environment. *Agents* are not to be confused with *objects*, which, from the perspectives of both ontology and cognition, are very different things. Objects are all the things that exist but can only respond to the world, if they respond at all, in purely mechanistic ways. Objects include everything from natural things like rocks and sticks to common animate things like plants and trees to human-made artifacts like clothes and catapults. Agents, on the other hand, are beings capable of independently and intentionally initiating action on the basis of internal mental states like beliefs and desires. The most obvious intentional agents are animals and people. Lions take down wildebeests because they *feel* hungry. Women adorn their bodies because they *believe* it makes them more appealing.

The capacity to quickly and accurately distinguish between objects and agents in the environment is clearly crucial to survival. An animal that fails to recognize a spotted form as a cheetah or a buzzing coil as a snake is unlikely to fare well or long. An animal that preys on rodents but habitually attacks trees is equally unfit for life. Even though the world of objects is important, agents deserve special attention. Objects are predictable and generally harmless once understood. Agents are unpredictable and capable of dangerous and exploitive behaviors, or of offering personal benefits like food, sex, and protection. Anticipating and reacting to the behaviors of agents requires the initial step of discerning them amid the ambiguous mass of objects that fill the world.

Because agents are the most relevant things in the environment, evolution has tuned the brain to quickly spot them, or to suspect their presence based on signs and traces. As the previous chapter's discussion of modularity pointed out, a mental device that operates simply, automatically, and nonconsciously would best carry out this task. When you need to know immediately whether that big brown thing beside the path is a bear or a rock, complex analysis could be costly. Not all agents are dangerous, nor is every agent potentially beneficent, but it's imperative to first see them; you can then determine their significance.

Cognitive psychologists have begun to call the mental mechanism responsible for recognizing agents the Agency Detection Device, or ADD. As part of the core architecture of brains, the operation of ADD is evident in infancy (for example, Stern 1985; Poulin-Dubois and Shultz 1988). In addition to employing ADD to meet their immediate needs, such as distinguishing mothers from bedposts, infants pay greater attention to the presence of agents than to objects, as well as to objects and events that mysteriously behave like agents, such as a chair that moves under its own power or causal sequences that lack animate agents (Golinkoff and Kerr 1978; Leslie 1984).

ADD is everything a device designed for its purpose should be: rapid, effortless, and intent. ADD constantly scans the environment for agents, and it is eager to find them. The power and tenacity of ADD make frequent appearances in daily life. In addition to instantaneously identifying the people and creatures that cross our paths, we are also prone to make up agents based on minimal input from any of our senses. We sense things in the night, glance anxiously at shadows, and start at the sound of rustling leaves. Note that neither shadows nor rustling leaves are the *source* of our anxious or jumpy reaction; rather, shadows and sounds are merely signs of agents that might be lurking behind them. Similarly, if you reach for the light switch in a strange room and your hand instead brushes a fur coat hanging on a nearby hook, it's a safe beat you'll quickly pull away. Despite characterizing ourselves as something more than bundles of instincts, the human brain is still governed by many incorrigible responses like those produced by ADD.

As these examples show, though, ADD is not perfect. There is always a trade-off between speed and accuracy, and it inevitably results in misidentifications of agency. The bear beside the path may in fact turn out to be a rock and the coiled snake may be, on closer inspection, just a discarded rope. Yet when survival is at stake, false alarms are ultimately advantageous. The surge of emotion caused by a false alarm may be disorienting and the energy spent running away wasted, but such mistakes are harmless. Failing to perceive an actual agent is not. So ADD's default interpretive strategy—namely, when in doubt about whether something is an agent, assume that it is—is worth the errors in judgment. It's better to have a fast device that occasionally gets it wrong than a slow device that is always accurate.

The tendency of ADD to *over*-attribute agency to objects is graphically illustrated in famous experiments by Fritz Heider and colleagues (Heider and Simmel 1944; Michotte 1963). Heider showed adult subjects two-dimensional geometric shapes moving randomly across a flat surface. While these experiments were intended to test thinking about physical causality, subjects also reported their perceptions that the shapes were chasing each other around in space and displaying other intentional behaviors. Because an identifying feature of agents is that they are self-propelled, motion is one of ADD's natural triggers. Subjects went so far as to attribute desires, emotions, and even gender to the shapes. People understand that objects like geometric shapes cannot really be agents, but they also cannot help seeing objects as agents given the proper circumstances. Almost any object that shows spontaneous movement or goal-directed change will activate ADD.

The propensity of ADD to attribute agency at the slightest provocation has led psychologist Justin Barrett to describe this mental system as "hyperactive" and to refer to it instead as the *Hypersensitive* Agency Detection Device, or HADD (2000). Barrett's work, like his adjective, highlights the centrality of ADD in human cognition and extends the reach of this foundational mental system. As Barrett points out, ADD is activated not just when agents or oddly behaving objects are present, but it also pushes its way into interpretations of everyday actions and events.

Though the world is overwhelmingly comprised of objects, it is hardly a quiet, static place. There is activity everywhere: noise, movement, action, happenings set in motion whose causes escape our notice. All of these things matter because they are signs or traces of agents. Objects are capable of generating sound, but we most often attribute sudden sounds to agents (creaks in the night prompt us to first wonder *who* rather than *what*). Objects can only be *caused* to move (the wind bends branches; gravity rolls rocks downhill) whereas agents control their own movements and are frequently responsible for causing it (animals bend branches and roll rocks, too). Objects can play roles in actions, but, as Lawson and McCauley have shown, each of us possesses an "action representation system" that naturally links actions to the activity of agents (1990). Events can be loosely defined as occurrences involving change, but again, events beg explanations, particularly if they are personally relevant. The consequence of having a hyperactive detection system is that our minds are prone to attribute agency in each of these cases.

ADD's effectiveness and speed are due to the application of ready inferences and expectations about what agents are like. Just as movements that seem purposeful can cause ADD to override compelling visual evidence and see geometric shapes as agents, so ambiguous actions and events can lead ADD to postulate agents where none are immediately present. In an updated version of Heider's two-dimensional experiments, Barrett and Amanda Johnson asked adult subjects to comment on the movement of marbles rolled around in unexpected ways by hidden magnets (2003). As in Heider's tests, subjects who merely observed the movement of the marbles tended to think of them as agents. However, subjects who played a role in controlling the movement of the marbles never did. Barrett interprets these results by suggesting that once ADD is activated by a stimulus like motion, it searches for an agent and settles on the candidate that best accounts for the action. When the subjects controlled the movement of the marbles, they were identified as the obvious agent. But when the subjects were not responsible for the motion of the marbles, the marbles themselves became the best candidates for agency.

Agent searches like this constantly take place as we move through the day. Almost all searches end instantly. We see other people as agents and recognize that their behaviors account for many of the sounds, movement, actions, and events that occur. We also frequently encounter animals doing things, especially pets, and ADD quickly tags them as agents as well. But some sounds, movements, actions, and events are inchoate and demand more intensive agent searches. A bush moves as you walk by then suddenly stops when you stop. Why? And does it matter? Of course, the environment in which you live can make a world of difference to your need to locate agents, as well as your response to inconclusive searches. In rural Iowa a moving bush may provoke curiosity, but failing to find a satisfying candidate agent is little cause for anxiety. At night in New York's Central Park, a moving bush will likely be a bit more disconcerting. For the cow-herding Masai of Kenya and Tanzania, the agency behind a moving bush, if indeed there is any, is a pressing concern.

In all ambiguous situations ADD tries its best to attribute agency because agents are what matter most to us. Identifying agents is crucial not only for making sense of the natural environment but also of the social one. As intensely social animals, humans need to identify the sources of social events in the course of interpreting their import. In typical natural and social encounters, agent searches rapidly seize upon known agents. When dealing with ambiguous information, though, agent searches may come up inconclusive and simply terminate, or, they may lead to counterintuitive candidates, as in the marble experiment. In the absence of other known agents, cues such as motion can implicate objects—though everyone recognizes that this is problematic.

A third alternative for ADD in ambiguous situations lacking obvious agents is to consider novel or imaginative candidates, particularly those already believed in or seriously entertained by others. Examples of this sort of attribution of agency are numerous and, interestingly, quite common from society to society. For instance, the idea of ghosts is ubiquitous the world over, and because it is everywhere, in the air, so to speak, it can easily become the candidate of an agent search in an ambiguous situation. Recall again that creak in the night: If the sound cannot be attributed to another known agent, then a person who has the idea of a ghost in his or her head may well find ADD entertaining "ghost" as a possible candidate. A personal belief in ghosts is not necessary here; ADD is simply intent on its goal of finding the agent behind an event. For people who do believe in ghosts, though, this *possible* candidate may easily be accepted as the *real* one.

Regardless of the veracity of such a conclusion, this example illustrates the obstinate operation of ADD and its consequential role in our interpretations of the world. ADD finds agents everywhere, and its attributions of agency underpin many of our behaviors and beliefs. A great deal of human reasoning—from judgments while driving to daydreaming to crafting and following literature—involves the mental representation of agents who are both present and absent, both real and unreal.

Recognizing an agent *as* an agent is only the first part of this essential cognitive process, however. The reason why the attribution of agency to objects is problematic and ultimately unsatisfying, and why, conversely, imaginary agents like ghosts manage to endure, is that agents are looked upon as much more than things that can move and instigate actions. Our knowledge of agents links physical causality to *mental* causality. Agents, we intuitively assume, have minds. They are beings that think. Agents have feelings, intentions, and an array of private beliefs and desires. Their behaviors, we also assume, are motivated by these beliefs and desires. Unlike objects, agents are understood primarily in mentalistic terms, and this perception requires a mental mechanism different from one like ADD, which simply sorts the world of objects.

Our personal belief that agents operate mentalistically is referred to as "theory of mind," and the mental tool responsible for this perception is called the Theory of Mind Mechanism, or ToMM. A complete picture of the nature and significance of agents is the result of ADD working together with ToMM. As ADD examines the objects we encounter, those displaying characteristics of agents activate ToMM, which in turn initiates a rich array of inferences about what agents are like. It also engages some powerful cognitive skills for interacting with them. As with ADD, ToMM functions rapidly, effortlessly, automatically, and mostly nonconsciously.

Theory of mind is called a "theory" because ToMM appears to operate on the basis of internal assumptions about how minds work (Wellman 1990), assumptions described in the previous chapter as "intuitive psychology." In reality, there is no way to directly access or experience the mental life of another, let alone to prove empirically that minds even exist. Yet everyone—save for a few principled philosophers—believes that they do. Our natural, if unsubstantiated, belief in the existence of minds is yet another result of evolutionary development within the sort of environment in which humans live. As discussed in the first chapter, our mentalistic perception of the world was shaped not just by the basic need to differentiate objects and agents (something many kinds of animals do) but also, indeed primarily, by selective pressures particular to life in large, tightly knit social groups. A robust theory of mind allows us to make sense of the agents that matter most: other people.

Human beings are complex systems. At the same time, cohabitation requires some means for explaining and predicting human behavior. Evolution's solution is theory of mind. Attributing mental states to others is the best way to understand their actions. Theory of mind doesn't just ascribe desires, intentions, thoughts, and motives to others; it also assumes that mental states *cause* their activities. As a result, we all naturally *interpret* the behaviors of others, as well as lots of events that occur around us, in terms of mental states. Consider the following tableau:

A woman wearing a coat and carrying a purse walks into a kitchen. After scanning the countertops and even the floor, she quickly opens several drawers, riffles through their contents, and then closes them again. Finally, she throws her hands up into the air and walks out.

Almost everyone would explain the actions of the woman and the event itself using mentalistic terms. There are a number of possible reasons for why the woman behaved as she did—the most obvious being that she was looking for something, say, her car keys—but nearly everyone's explanation would include mentalistic notions: "She *wanted* something that she *believed* was in the kitchen and was *frustrated* when she couldn't find it." Notice that while this train of thought may be obvious, it is hardly trivial; only humans and (probably) apes are capable of it. A dog observing the same scene would register nothing more than movement. Nor do mere events necessarily yield mentalistic interpretations. If a robot were designed to mimic the woman's activities, we would be inclined to chalk up the motions of the robot to mindless programming rather than to internally generated mental states. A robot might cause uncertainty in ADD, but ToMM is much less likely to ascribe mind to an object than to a person.

Theory of mind, then, is another powerful tool that the adapted human brain uses to organize and interpret the world, in this case the commonly inhabited social world. Granting feelings, intentions, memories, beliefs, and desires to others makes them intelligible. This interpretive strategy, which Daniel Dennett calls the "Intentional Stance" (1987), evolved as a requisite for life balanced between cooperation and competition. Success in understanding and anticipating a constantly changing world requires persistently adopting an intentional stance. Our mentalistic orientation is so well calibrated, in fact, that it is difficult for us to make sense of the world in any other way. As Robin Dunbar highlights, ToMM's functioning, like ADD's, is profound and promiscuous:

> The human mind seems to have been built in such a way that it assumes other individuals are trying to communicate with it. . . . We assume that everyone else behaves with conscious purpose, and we spend much of our time trying to think our way into their minds so as to divine their intentions. We are so imbued with this way of viewing the world that we easily transpose it on to other animals, and even occasionally on to the inanimate world. (1997: 81)

Theory of mind is not only the basis for explaining a world like ours but also for interacting with it. If we can make sense of other individuals and, consequently, the social networks they form, then we can locate ourselves in relation to other individuals and, hopefully, benefit from their networks (Brothers 1990). Theorizing about the existence and causal powers of minds allows us to directly engage with those minds, and perhaps to influence them. In short, theory of mind lets humans communicate. But moving back and forth between comprehension and communication calls for some extraordinary analytical work. We cannot truly understand the behaviors of others, or effectively interact with them, unless we know with some precision what their mental states happen to be. It's not enough to know that someone can be angry; you need to know what makes them that way. It's not enough to know that someone is capable of a caring gesture or a deceitful feign; you need to know what their intention is at the moment. When you speak to someone, it's important to know not only that they hear what you are saying but also that they grasp what you are trying to communicate.

This sort of running mental analysis is the foundation of interpersonal relations and the lifeblood of social intelligence (Humphrey 1984). As discussed in the first chapter, the advantages afforded by community life rest on sophisticated cognitive skills—detecting cheaters, tabulating social exchange, monitoring alliances and mate loyalty, and so forth—none of which would be possible without ToMM. As Dunbar has noted above, we do not just assume that people have minds; we also invest a great deal of time in trying to divine their thoughts.

The ability to discern the thoughts of others is commonly referred to as "mind reading." Contrary to inevitable connotations of the term, mind reading has nothing to do with telepathy or direct contact with people's thoughts. Thoughts, like minds themselves, are invisible. Mind reading actually amounts to highly skilled guesswork about what is going on inside people's heads. All normal humans are adept mind readers, and each of us spends a large part of the day trying to decipher other people's thoughts and intentions. *Does he really mean what he said? Why did she do that? What is he thinking right now? Does she know the truth?* Of course, these kinds of queries may require calculated reflection, and our final impressions might turn out to be wrong, but most mind reading occurs instantaneously and with certainty. We have little difficulty inferring the thinking behind most of the behaviors we witness around us. When we converse with others, we constantly monitor their reactions, tailoring our speech to facial expressions and other responsive clues. Amazingly, mind reading effectively takes place in the absence of words. Physical gestures can impart volumes of information, as the earlier example of the woman in the kitchen illustrates, or the smile of a stranger from across a bar.

How the impressive feat of mind reading is achieved is the subject of intense study. Indeed, the centrality of both ToMM and mind reading to human life has made for a dynamic field of psychological investigation. While ToMM is presented here as a single working unit, several influential researchers parse it into discrete subsystems or attribute mind reading to a suite of innate mental mechanisms supported by ToMM (for example, Leslie 1994; Baron-Cohen 1995). Simon Baron-Cohen has proposed one of the most interesting procedural accounts of mind reading, suggesting that the skill is the outcome of a "mind-reading system" comprised of four separate but connected mechanisms—an Intentionality Detector (which could easily be associated with ADD), an Eye-Direction Detector, a Shared-Attention Mechanism, and

ToMM itself (1995). Though each component is critical to the system, the real interpretative work of mind reading pivots on the evolutionary ancient Eye-Direction Detector. In animals, EDD monitors the gaze of other animals. In humans, EDD also contributes a rich assessment of the mind behind the gaze, reading eye-contact signals like staring and averted gaze in terms of mental states. According to Baron-Cohen, a mutually intelligible "language of the eyes" is responsible for bringing two human minds into alignment. This is why poets immortalize the eyes as the windows to the soul and poker players often wear sunglasses.

Like ADD, ToMM is part of the core architecture of the brain, though its functioning clearly matures over the first years of life. Developmental psychologists like Alison Gopnik, Andrew Meltzoff, and Patricia Kuhl affirm that from their earliest moments infants not only distinguish objects from agents (and favor the later) but also see people *as persons*; that is, as beings that "have a mind as well as a body" (2001: 24). Infants openly interact with others: they capably read facial expressions and imitate them (Meltzoff and Gopnik 1993). By the end of their first year, infants know that actions are usually goal-driven, understand the mental link created by shared attention, and use the reactions of other people to make judgments about objects and occurrences. Between the ages of 18 and 24 months toddlers begin to pretend and to recognize pretense (Leslie 1987). Pretending marks a significant new phase in child development, demonstrating both a rich appreciation for other minds and the recognition of how they actually work. A mind, this invisible entity that can drive teddy bears as well as mommies, thinks things, feels things, and wants things.

From roughly the ages of 2 to 3 years children are grappling with what is called "belief/desire psychology," the understanding that other individuals have their own opinions and desires, and that personal ideas and preferences stand behind behavior. Eventually working this out, often through perverse experimentation with their parents, heralds a qualitative shift in a child's way of thinking. Despite their early awareness of other minds, young children are essentially self-centered, believing that other people believe and desire as they themselves do. At about the age of two, children start to acknowledge the thoughts and emotions of others and can—if they chose—empathize with them. This new view of minds is key to effectively entering the social world, since human interaction turns on the ability to assume another individual's perspective.

The accepted benchmark for a fully developed theory of mind is successfully passing a "false belief" test. This test affirms whether or not a child is aware that other people hold opinions and beliefs that the child knows to be incorrect. This standard test can be administered in many ways, but the classic version incorporates two dolls named Sally and Ann. During the test, Ann (and the child) watches as Sally places candy under a cushion and then leaves the room. While Sally is out of the room, Ann takes the candy from under the cushion and hides it in her pocket. Sally then comes back into the room, unaware of Ann's deceptive antics. For the child who observed this scene, the question is simple yet telling: "Where does Sally think the candy is?" Before the age of four, children will usually say that Sally thinks the candy is in Ann's pocket. They do not yet recognize that other people can have beliefs different from their own. They assume that everyone sees things as they see them. So Sally, too, must share their information. After the age of four, however, the responses usually change. Children will now say that Sally thinks the candy is still under the cushion.

As noted in the first chapter, a full-blown theory of mind not only enables children to begin properly assessing the mental life of those around them but also to engage the challenging social world armed with the tools of strategic thinking. One of the consequences of recognizing false beliefs, for example, is the ability to deceive. Without an understanding of false beliefs children cannot lie—or at least they have a hard time carrying it off. There is little subtlety in their denying having eaten all the candy because they have little grasp of alternative perceptions. To them, other people are still like Sally; never mind their candy-colored tongues. Other methods of mental manipulation and persuasion also hinge on an understanding of false beliefs.

Though our theorizing about minds undoubtedly undergoes a process of maturation, there are compelling reasons for viewing ToMM as an innate biological endowment. The first is that ToMM, like other core mental mechanisms, is localized in the brain and can be impaired by birth defects or brain damage. Baron-Cohen, for instance, distributes the components of his mind-reading system throughout a three-node brain circuit including the amygdala, superior temporal sulcus, and the orbito-frontal cortex, associating ToMM specifically with the latter structure. Neuroimaging studies confirm that thinking about mental-state terms activates cells in the orbito-frontal cortex, and neurologists have also discovered that injury to this brain region results in impairment of social judgment and other cognitive skills requiring ToMM (Eslinger and Damasio 1985; Baron-Cohen, et al. 1994). Perhaps the most famous example of the loss of social skills as a result of brain damage is the case of Phineas Gage. While blasting rock to lay track for the Rutland & Burlington Railroad, an accidental explosion drove a metal rod through Cage's left cheek and out the top of his head. Though Gage survived the trauma, the damage to his frontal cortex left his personality wrecked, most markedly his ability to interact with others. Relatedly, ADD appears to be localized in the brain, too. Patients with focal brain damage have lost their ability to recognize objects and to categorize things as either animate or inanimate (Warrington and Shallice 1984).

The most-talked-about and revealing relationship between ToMM, theory of mind development, and brain function arises from the study of autism. This mental disorder, which affects about ten in ten thousand children, strikingly manifests itself in the domain of social cognition. While individuals with autism often have additional mental disorders, many autistic people possess normal, even high intelligence. Yet their autism clearly marks them as different. Generally speaking, autistic individuals are detached from others, sometimes unreachably remote. They often prefer things to people, typically fail to distinguish facial expressions or to pretend, display abnormal communication skills, and are incapable of recognizing or expressing the full range of mental states. Autism, it seems, is characterized by an inability to properly perceive other minds.

Again, Baron-Cohen and his colleagues have provided much of the seminal research in this area (for example, Baron-Cohen, et al. 1985, Baron-Cohen 1990). Baron-Cohen refers to the plight of autism as "mindblindness" because autistics cannot truly see other minds. According to Baron-Cohen, while parts of the mind-reading system still function in autistic individuals (specifically ID and EDD), there is massive impairment to both SAM and ToMM (1995). As a result, autistics fail to achieve joint attention with others and virtually every aspect of a normally functioning theory of mind is missing or impaired. Autistics generally fail to pass false-belief tests and miss the connection that seeing leads to knowing. They cannot follow or instigate tactical deception such as lying or recognize the causes of emotions. They cannot easily distinguish appearance from reality or step outside of the present moment. Perhaps most catastrophic of all is the autistic's impaired ability to grasp the ontological distinction between mental and physical entities. This suggests that autistics do not share the mentalistic perception that is a hallmark of human thought. This is a tremendous deficit that renders other people unintelligible, unpredictable, and very likely frightening. In the social world—the most important world for humans—autistics are effectively "blind."

To summarize the discussion to this point, the human brain is endowed with an array of tools for organizing and interpreting the world. Given our natural environment, the presence of agents is much more relevant than objects. Agents can injure and agents can nurture. Agents can attack and agents can protect. Agents can be good to eat and agents can be good at eating. So evolution has designed a mental mechanism, ADD, to quickly detect and respond to agents. Of the kinds of agents that exist in the world, other humans are of special importance. As species-dependent animals, humans rely heavily on one another throughout the course of their lives. But constant interaction with others carries challenges and risks as well as opportunities and benefits. Social life is give and take, cooperation and competition, and it is crucial that individuals have a way to understand and predict the complex behaviors of those with whom they have contact. Nature's provision in this case is ToMM, which allows us to safely view our surroundings in mentalistic terms, to make sense of other people, to effectively communicate, and to pursue our own needs and desires within the human community.

The question, however, is what ADD and ToMM have to do with gods. The promise was not simply to introduce new mental mechanisms but to directly link them with religious thought and behavior. Thoroughly building the connections between minds and gods will require other explorations into human cognition on pages still to come, but the operation of ADD and ToMM provides the foundation needed to get started. First, of all the objects in the environment, agents matter most. The connection?—*gods are agents*. Second, humans understand the world, and particularly agents, in light of minds. The connection?—*gods have minds*. These facts are exceedingly trivial, but they are also exceedingly explicative. They tell us exactly what kind of things gods are and how we think about them.

Counterintuitive Concepts and Gods

Whether or not they believe in the existence of gods, almost everyone has a basic idea of what gods are and what they are supposed to be like. It's hard not to. Given the prominence of religion in public life, talk of gods is commonplace. Of course, talk of gods is not a feature of religious discourse alone. Secular language, too, is filled with references to supernatural beings. Gods are common not only because they are important to many people and are therefore widely communicated but also because gods are intriguing ideas in themselves. One need not be "religious" to think about gods or even to spend a lifetime studying them. The academic discipline of religious studies explores the subject of religion in all of its aspects, yet it owes its existence to the human compulsion to think about gods.

But while almost everyone has a basic idea of what gods are, few people have taken the time to dissect the concept "god" and to consider how it is represented by the mind. This is part of the work of the *cognitive* branch of religious studies, and what this work reveals goes a long way toward explaining the preponderance, persistence, and persuasiveness of gods. Contrary to the assumption that ideas are interesting because they are colorful or somehow clever, cognitive science shows that widespread, enduring, and engaging concepts are usually the result of how their properties link up with the brain's thinking processes. What typically makes a concept work in people's minds is not its clever properties but, rather, its more common ones.

A word of warning is in order. In describing the nature of god concepts, our language has to become more precise. Throughout this book terms like "gods" and "supernatural beings" are used to keep the discussion general and accessible. Again, almost everyone understands what labels like these signify.

In this section, however, a more technical terminology for gods will emerge. This new terminology is important because in correctly isolating and naming the properties of god concepts three major features of religious thought are illuminated. First, we discover the structure of god concepts, and this structure in turns tells us how gods are processed by the human mind. Second, the fact that similar mental machines similarly form god concepts explains why ideas about supernatural beings are remarkably alike the world over. Third, understanding the way god concepts are constructed reveals that they closely resemble other kinds of ideas that people entertain. Though those who believe in them treat gods as unique beings, "gods," as concepts go, are not unique at all.

Day in and day out, people encounter ideas best described as fantastical. The fiction we read is often full of imaginative and abnormal characters. Many of the movies we watch feature otherworldly landscapes populated by creatures with improbable skills. Our holidays and festivals open up mundane time and space to unearthly beings ranging from the charming to the monstrous. And we hardly need to create special opportunities to entertain the fanciful. As every parent knows, the minds of children are playgrounds for fabulous ideas, and the human penchant for the strange and peculiar is retained in the thought life of adults. As a result the public square is alive with unnatural, preternatural, and supernatural concepts—ghosts haunt homes, witches cast spells, animals act like people, aliens keep watch, robots feel emotions, spirits inhabit rocks and trees, and so on.

Cognitive scientists refer to the kinds of imaginative concepts featured in fantasy, folklore, and faith as "counterintuitive" concepts (for example, Boyer 1994a, Pyysiäinen 2001b). The term counterintuitive means that, taken as a whole, concepts such as ghosts, goblins, and gods cut against the grain of our natural expectations about how things work in the real world. When living things die they are supposed to stay dead, so the concept of an animated spirit is counterintuitive. A statue is understood to be an inanimate, man-made object, so when reports are heard of a stone Madonna weeping, this concept is counterintuitive to everyday thought.

When we look hard at counterintuitive concepts, however, we find that they are structurally more complex than meets the eye. Counterintuitive concepts, at least those that become popular, are not simply outlandish. As we'll see in chapter 5, ideas that are truly incredible don't seem to captivate. Widespread counterintuitive concepts, on the other hand, turn out to share a specific, well-balanced structure. In counterintuitive concepts, properties that, from a cognitive perspective, are actually quite ordinary are matched with the properties that make them extraordinary. This structural combination of ordinary and extraordinary properties is key to the attraction of counterintuitive concepts, so we need to examine both aspects in some detail.

Perhaps the best way to demonstrate the structure of a counterintuitive concept is to build one, something that is exceedingly easy to do. The first step is to think about any ordinary object—a human, a horse, a house. Forming a mental concept of objects like these is simple not only because they are real things but also because we know *intuitively* what such things are like. As discussed in the previous chapter, objects like humans, horses, and houses match up with the mind's natural ontological categories. Consequently, inference systems are automatically activated that construct robust mental concepts. Horses, like all animals, are alive, eat, move, and so forth. Humans are like this, too, but they also come under the scrutiny of ToMM and other mental tools used for thinking expressly about people. Houses, being inanimate artifacts, are hardly like animals or humans at all, so few of their inferences overlap. The point here is that because our minds naturally form concepts in accord with intuitive expectations about ontological categories, there is nothing unusual or surprising about concepts that behave as expected.

But counterintuitive concepts are precisely that—unusual and surprising. So the second step in building a counterintuitive concept is to *contravene* one or more of the expectations about the way an otherwise ordinary concept ought to be. This too is simply done. Take a horse and make it invisible. Imagine a house that speaks. Talk about people who cannot die. The way intuitive expectations come together to form ordinary concepts under normal circumstances makes it easy to re-make them into extraordinary, counterintuitive ones. And the effect ranges from some really silly ideas to the handful of concepts that have proven extremely provocative. Cartoon animals and many Disney characters are familiar counterintuitive concepts. Santa Claus, HAL the computer, and genies are counterintuitive also. So are kami, Kalki, Quan Yin, and Yahweh.

There are two principal ways to render a counterintuitive concept. The first way is to *violate* intuitive expectations associated with a given ontological category. For instance, the primary counterintuitive property of vampires is that they live forever (unless killed in a special way). This is counterintuitive, of course, because vampires are people and people, like all living things, are expected to die. The concept of a vampire violates a major intuitive expectation associated with the ontological category *Person*. This particular violation is used in many common counterintuitive concepts. The second way to make a counterintuitive concept is to *transfer* the expected properties of one ontological category to another. Animals are not expected to speak, at least not in English or Portuguese, so the idea of an animal that speaks like a human involves the transfer of a particular expectation about people onto the ontological category *Animal*. Counterintuitive transfers of this sort are prevalent as well.

In addition to the two *ways* in which intuitive expectations can be contravened in counterintuitive concepts—violations and transfers—the *kind* of intuitive expectation that is contravened can also be specified as either biological, physical, or psychological. This makes sense given the fact that our mental inference systems work on the basis of default assumptions generated by these three categories of intuitive knowledge. So in the example of vampires, the intuitive expectation being violated, death, is biological in nature. Other instances of counterintuitive biology include natural and man-made objects that are said to be alive, volcanoes that must be fed, bodies containing immaterial souls, and women, like Queen Maya and the Virgin Mary, who conceive without first having sex. Counterintuitive concepts that feature counterintuitive physics include ghost and spirits, which are capable of passing through solid objects. Other instances of counterintuitive physics include beings that can influence other objects at a distance, levitation, and omnipresence.

Of the three kinds of intuitive expectations that can be violated or transferred, the most common and consequential are psychological in nature. In such cases various objects in the world are given mental properties not normally expected of them, or else ordinary mental abilities are made extraordinary. Instances of counterintuitive psychology abound: statues that hear and answer prayers, plants and animals that think and feel, natural and man-made objects with likes and dislikes, people using telepathy and omniscient deities. Counterintuitive concepts involving psychological violations and transfers are particularly pervasive because, as discussed above, mentalistic explanations of the world are central to human thought and the hyperactivity of ADD and ToMM predispose us to take special note of this set of counterintuitive ideas. As Pascal Boyer affirms, "the mind-concept is such a rich source of inferences that we use it spontaneously even in cases where some of its usual assumptions are challenged" (2001: 70).

Most of the examples of counterintuitive concepts used here are clearly imaginative, fictive, or religious, but it is important to point out that just because something is counterintuitive does not mean that it is unreal or even unnatural. Nature contains numerous examples of real yet counterintuitive objects. For example, the idea of a plant that moves and eats meat is counterintuitive because our intuitive expectations for the ontological category *Plant* preclude self-propulsion and carnivorous behavior. These are expectations we normally have about animals and people. Botanists, though, can show us a number of plants that capture and eat insects and other organisms, and some, like the Venus's-flytrap, do so with visible aggression. Likewise, mammals such

TABLE 3.1 Sources and examples of counterintuitive properties.

Expectation	Violation	Transfer
Biological	immortality, souls, asexual conception, etc.	animacy, language, atypical skills, etc.
Physical	invisibility, omnipresence, levitation, etc.	metamorphosis, atypical skills, etc.
Psychological	omniscience, telepathy, telekinesis, etc.	awareness, desire, emotions, etc.

as bats, whales, and platypuses are counterintuitive owing to their atypical appearances, abilities, and lifestyles. What the present discussion of "counterintuitiveness" primarily intends to show is not that counterintuitive ideas are unreal or untrue (though that is often the case) but, rather, the specific conceptual structure of such ideas and how they gain their unusual qualities. It also helps to clarify the link between extraordinary ideas and ordinary mental mechanisms. Religion is all about claims concerning extraordinary ideas, but such ideas, truth claims aside, are the creation of the same garden-variety cognitive processes that stand behind nonreligious ideas too.

In fact, it is the other side of counterintuitive concepts, their *ordinary* properties, that make them possible and, potentially, believable. While what is unusual about counterintuitive concepts eclipses what is familiar, it is the familiar that makes them intelligible in the first place. The idea of an invisible horse means nothing unless the underlying concept of the horse itself stays firm. The idea of ancestral spirits makes no sense unless one's basic expectations about people remain operative. In other words, counterintuitive concepts must conform in most respects to our intuitive ontology. Counterintuitive properties only work because they are grounded in standard ontological categories and supported by other, quite normal expectations that remain true. As a rule, then, counterintuitive concepts contravene one or more intuitive expectations associated with an ontological category while at the same time preserving others.

While this combination of intuitive and counterintuitive properties is essential to well-formed counterintuitive concepts, so too is the balance between them—it makes a difference just *how* counterintuitive a concept is. Concepts with too many counterintuitive properties, though perhaps recognized as highly creative, will nevertheless be rejected as nonsense. A successful counterintuitive concept must remain sufficiently familiar to be intelligible and generate further inferences. Boyer calls the delicate balance between intuitive and counterintuitive properties the "cognitive optimum" position, and, through experiments conducted with Barrett and other colleagues, has isolated the general parameters of cognitively optimal counterintuitive concepts (Barrett and Nyhof 2001, Boyer and Ramble 2001). Barrett refers to concepts with this right mix of intuitive and counterintuitive properties as "minimally counterintuitive" (MCI) concepts because it is now clear that the most widespread counterintuitive ideas are those with a small number of violations (2000). It also turns out that MCIs have several advantages in the marketplace of ideas. Well-formed counterintuitive concepts garner more attention and are more memorable than are either ordinary or bizarre concepts. The unusual qualities of MCIs also make them useful candidates for explaining certain kinds of experiences.

An interesting consequence of the conceptual structure of counterintuitive concepts is that this family of ideas can be quantified as well as qualified. While it might seem that the range of counterintuitive concepts is unlimited—having two ways to contravene three kinds of intuitive expectations results in lots of creative options—there are in fact recognizable restraints on the kinds of ideas, ordinary as well as extraordinary, that our minds produce. As discussed in the last chapter, the human brain is a marvelous craftsman, able to take fragmented stimuli like photons, sound waves, and the feel of textures and sculpt them into full-color images, majestic symphonies, and the sleek sensation of silk. But the patterns and tools that this craftsman has to use are limited. The brain is a genius at making the kinds of things it already knows, but it is literally unequipped to construct the unknown.

In his acclaimed book and television series *Cosmos* (1980), which brilliantly introduced the workings of the universe, the late Carl Sagan paused to consider the limitations of the inner cosmos that is the human mind. He asked his audience to ponder whether or not there might be a fourth dimension to space instead of the three we move through daily. It is, of course, impossible for us to imagine what a fourth dimension would entail. What dimension, after all, is not already covered by height, width, and depth? But Sagan points out that our failure to grasp the measure of a fourth dimension does not negate its possibility, and he demonstrates this claim by asking us to follow a thought experiment in the opposite direction, to imagine a world that only has two dimensions rather than three, a world named "Flatland."

Flatland has width and depth but not height. Its habitants, infinitely thin Flatlanders, go about their business without any idea of height, incapable of imagining a third dimension covering "up" and "down." Such words do not even exist, since to Flatlanders they signify nothing. Then, one day, adventurers from another world land on Flatland, their ship descending out of the sky and settling amid a gathering of terrified natives. To the Flatlanders who observe this event, the ship—or the slice of it that they can see—has suddenly appeared out of nowhere. Though they hear the roaring of its engines, the ship itself simply winks into existence at the dimensions of width and depth. Even after learning from the intrepid travelers about the dimension of "up" and their having come "down," the Flatlanders are still incapable of imagining height because their minds, the products of two-dimensional existence, still lack the tools to grasp it.

Sagan's point is that we humans might well be Flatlanders ourselves, living three-dimensional lives in what is really a four-dimensional universe, our minds unable to fathom its full measure. This thought experiment is instructive because our minds have limitations right here on our own plane of existence. There are boundaries to human thought set by the mechanics of thought itself. Cognitive scientists refer to these restrictions and their ramifications as "cognitive constraint." The conceptual range of the human mind is constrained by its own processing methods and by the patterns and tools it uses to interpret and organize the world. There are only so many ways we can think about things. Animals come in specific forms, for example, as do people and the other categories of objects. The effect of cognitive constraint on the production of novel ideas is easily observed. School children asked to draw "aliens" from other planets will yield predictable category similarities. Psychologist Thomas Ward describes the same result within more formal settings, examining the products of adults asked to create imaginary, otherworldly animals (1994). Our mind's natural design makes it rather difficult for us to "think outside of the box."

Maintaining the analogy of the mind as a workshop filled with patterns and tools makes it possible to identify the cognitive constraint imposed on the construction of counterintuitive concepts. As we've already seen, the most important patterns and tools in the mental workshop are the ontological templates used to categorize things as *Animal, Plant, Person, Natural Object,* and *Artifact.* Once the mind selects an ontological template, inference systems are activated that quickly and automatically build them up with category-specific expectations. It is only at *this point* that counterintuitive violations and transfers can be introduced. The basic ontological category, therefore, remains intact, which is good because it needs to if the resulting concept is to continue to make sense. But this also means that all counterintuitive concepts share common templates, rendering them both similar in design and limited in scope. The recurrent features of counterintuitive concepts—recurrent not just within people groups but also around the world—are not due to the concepts themselves but to the ontological templates used to construct them. Boyer has gone so far as to present a small "catalog" showing the limited conceptual options available for building culturally successful counterintuitive ideas, including supernatural concepts (2000a, 2003). Combining the five primary ontological categories with the three kinds of intuitive expectations that can be violated or transferred produces a surprisingly short list of conceptual possibilities (see Table 3.2).

Obviously, gods are included in the broad class of counterintuitive concepts. Gods are prime examples of the kinds of concepts that are both highly unusual and universally distributed. Indeed, from the standpoints of longevity and influence, god concepts are among the most culturally successful ideas ever produced. For most people, though, particularly those for whom gods actually exist, the ordinary properties that constitute god concepts are either not recognized or, being recognized, are explained away as an unfortunate consequence of language or the feeble attempt of finite brains to grasp inscrutable beings. This, of course, is to enter into the realm of theology—an interesting enterprise but one wholly irrelevant to understanding the way minds think. God concepts have the same cognitive foundations as every other kind of idea. If they are special it is only in that they are counterintuitive rather than intuitive, extraordinary rather than ordinary. But then, so are lots of ideas.

The coarseness of god concepts is revealed as we deconstruct them in the same way that we took apart the structure of counterintuitive concepts in general. As we'll see, god concepts display the same balance of intuitive and counterintuitive properties: specific intuitive expectations associated with an onto-

TABLE 3.2 Boyer's "catalog of supernatural templates."

Natural Ontological Category		Counterintuitive Property
Person	+	violation/transfer of intuitive biology
Person	+	violation/transfer of intuitive physics
Person	+	violation/transfer of intuitive psychology
Animal	+	violation/transfer of intuitive biology
Animal	+	violation/transfer of intuitive physics
Animal	+	violation/transfer of intuitive psychology
Plant	+	violation/transfer of intuitive biology
Plant	+	violation/transfer of intuitive physics
Plant	+	violation/transfer of intuitive psychology
Natural object	+	violation/transfer of intuitive biology
Natural object	+	violation/transfer of intuitive physics
Natural object	+	violation/transfer of intuitive psychology
Artifact	+	violation/transfer of intuitive biology
Artifact	+	violation/transfer of intuitive physics
Artifact	+	violation/transfer of intuitive psychology

logical category are contravened while others are preserved. Supernatural beings are amazingly popular not because they are mysterious but because they are understood *so well*. In seeking examples of well-formed counterintuitive concepts that at once stimulate and produce rich inferences for further thought, god concepts are nearly perfect. The rest of this chapter exposes the conceptual structure of gods by looking at their ordinary, intuitive properties; what makes them extraordinary and counterintuitive will be treated in the next. Ironically, it turns out that in both cases theology *can* play a role in explaining religious concepts after all. Theological reflection makes an ideal foil for intuitive forms of thought.

The *Real* Attributes of Gods

Theologians, people whose vocation it is to think long and hard about what gods are like and to explain them to others, are virtuosos of imaginative reasoning. Over the course of intellectual history, it is safe to say that theologians are responsible for some of the most profound and influential reflections ever produced. Theologians have elucidated the creation of the universe and the origins of humankind. They have helped to launch wars and to secure peace. They have outlined the nature of morality and defined the very meaning of life. Usually working from a body of sacred texts or teachings and employing a mixture of logic and subjective experience, theologians craft remarkably detailed statements about their deities and how these beings intersect with the material world.

In monotheistic religions like Christianity—though *all* forms of religion have their theologians and theologies—systematic explanations of divinity often begin with a discussion of the "attributes" of god. One cannot ponder the activities and ramifications of a particular god until one is clear about what that god is like. For theologians, the attributes of god represent those distinguishing characteristics of divinity that are inseparable from the very idea of god. As an example, among the attributes of god described by Christian theologians as absolute and incommunicable are omnipresence, omnipotence, omniscience, immutability, impassibility, simplicity, infinity, and spirituality. The relative and communicable attributes of god include holiness, perfection, fealty, wisdom, mercy, justice, and love (see Table 3.3). Religious specialists from other faith traditions define the nature of divinity in similar terms. All three Abrahamic faiths speak of deity using virtually the same language. The Eastern faiths show more variability but make few additions or subtractions. Some religions include separate gods representing each different expression of divinity.

Students of religion have noticed something very interesting about theological definitions of gods, however. These abstract concepts may certainly provide sublime insights into the nature of an invisible, inscrutable being, but they seem to lie a bit beyond the way that ordinary believers think about the objects of their faith. Consider the following comment on the divine attribute of perfection by the German theologian Wolfhart Pannenberg, widely regarded to be one of today's most significant Christian thinkers:

> Even reflection on perfection—an idea that is connoted by the concept of the Infinite when it is thematized as such—is not sufficient to derive the concept of God, unless the idea has been derived from another source, namely, from the religious tradition. Of course, given this concept, we can maintain correctly that Infinity and highest perfection befit only the one God. Hence we can also say that the confused intuition of the Infinite, which lies, prethematically, at the basis of all human consciousness, is already in truth a mode of the presence of God, even though in it God is not yet explicitly known as God. (1990: 29)

Now consider an alternative description of the same god, this time from a decidedly less "theological" source, the novelist Milan Kundera:

> Agnes recalled that once as a child she was dazzled by the thought that God sees her and that he was seeing her all the time. Her mother, who was a believer, told her, "God sees you," and this is how she wanted to teach her to stop lying, biting her nails, and pick-

ing her nose, but something else happened: precisely at those times when she was indulging in her bad habits, or during physically intimate moments, Agnes imagined God and performed for his benefit. (1990: 31)

To some, this pericope from Kundera's novel *Immortality* is in poor taste. Nevertheless, it makes the significant point that gods are often conceived of and put to use in ways that have little resemblance to formal theological statements. For a professional like Pannenberg, even a rigorous grammar of divinity is obscure and inadequate if we are to think rightly about god. For Agnes, the essence of god is no mystery at all: god is a seeing, thinking being with likes and dislikes, who might even be affected by the revelries of an impious young lady.

Without doubt, the supernatural beings that people come to believe in are much more noteworthy than everyday agents like animals and people. The beings that become the focus of both personal lives and complex social systems are spoken of as possessing rather unusual personalities, powers, and principalities. The methods of manipulating concepts may be limited, yet it is still large enough to create some diverse and creative ideas. What is important to recognize, though, is that while the colorful variety of gods is interesting, it is also conceptual window dressing. Theologically developed ideas about gods are stretched over a cognitive framework well worn with use. And the composite nature of mental concepts should no longer be surprising. As discussed above, human thought is constrained by the patterns and tools found in our mental workshops. Applying the process of concept construction to the representation of gods reveals not only that they too are composite ideas, but also which patterns and tools the mind is using to make them.

What gods are, at bottom, can be approached from several directions. Intuition provides one vista, since intuition is now understood as something more significant than mere "gut feeling." It's quite easy to reach the conclusion that, of the available ontological categories, a god is best understood as *Person*. Evidence drawn from comparative religion strongly supports this supposition. Gods are never merely *Animals, Plants, Natural Objects*, or *Artifacts*. These kinds of things may be closely associated with supernatural beings and figure prominently in religion, but, as will become clear later, something quite different is taking place when animals, plants, and objects are imbued with divinity. The basic design for building a god is based on the mental blueprint for building a person. And because *Person* is the mind's ontological starting point, inference systems spontaneously add default assumptions about what persons are like.

Studies from comparative religion also confirm that basing supernatural beings on the *Person* template makes it very difficult to talk meaningfully about gods without drawing on *Person* terms: personality traits, physical attributes, even gender. In various religious systems gods eat, drink, marry, produce children, take bodily forms, display emotions, and die, just as humans do. Likewise, it is very difficult to gather anything relevant from a description of a god that avoids *Person* terms. Processing gods as persons is simply the best way to make sense of them. Gods have minds, feelings, and, most important of all, interact with the human social world. *Person* is the only natural ontological category that the mind possesses for comprehending the type of entities that gods are said to be. For ordinary people, gods and humans are very much alike. It is only theologians and religious specialists who present them as radically "Other." But people who present gods as radically different from the category *Person* make them incomprehensible and irrelevant as well. Mel Gibson's portrait of the "Passion of Christ" will always be more compelling than Paul Tillich's obtuse depiction of god as the "Ground of Being" (1973).

As with creative renderings of aliens and imaginary animals, the conceptual limitations associated with gods can also be graphically captured. The psychiatrist Robert Coles, who has probed in detail the religious thought of children, frequently asks them to draw pictures as a means of expressing themselves. As his collections of pictures demonstrate, children of all ages and places cannot avoid depicting their gods in human form, complete with human habitations, even when they are aware of crucial theological attributes (1996).

The claim that, to the mind's eye at least, a god is essentially a person is rather bold, not to mention naive from the standpoint of believers in gods. Is there other evidence besides intuition and the drawings of children? There is—and the most compelling comes from believers themselves. Justin Barrett, whose finely tailored experiments have provided a wealth of empirical data for the cognitive science of religion, has produced groundbreaking insights into the way people think about non-natural concepts like gods. Employing variations on the well-known narrative recall task, Barrett has been able to move beyond individuals' professed beliefs about gods to the kinds of ideas about gods they use in daily life. A more complete and technical description of Barrett's work will be given in chapter 6, but an outline of his findings is instructive here.

Curious to see how minds represent entities that, in their formal guises, do not conform to existing ontological knowledge, Barrett and his colleague Frank Keil ran a series of experiments on adult subjects from the United States and India whose religious affiliations included Bahaism, Buddhism, Christianity, Hinduism, and Judaism (Barrett and Keil 1996; Barrett 1998). In these experiments, the participants were read short stories in which "God" was an active agent. The typical narrative went like this:

> A boy was swimming alone in a swift and rocky river. The boy got his left leg caught between two large, gray rocks and couldn't get out. Branches of trees kept bumping into him as they hurried passed. He thought he was going to drown and so he began to

struggle and pray. Though God was answering another prayer in another part of the world when the boy started praying, before long God responded by pushing one of the rocks so the boy could get his leg out. The boy struggled to the riverbank and fell over exhausted.

Using stories like this one to query the way minds work is especially effective because they place people in real time, or what psychologists call "on-line" thinking situations that simulate day-to-day life. When people are simply asked about what they think or believe they tend to respond using learned concepts that they feel are correct but which may or may not be part of their actual on-line thinking process. After hearing each story, the participants were asked to recall if particular pieces of information had been included in the story or to make judgments based on the information provided. The principle behind the narrative recall task is that subjects' prior beliefs distort their recollection of information and are also drawn on to interpret ambiguous information (Bransford and McCarrell 1974). The question for Barrett and Keil was, which "prior beliefs" crop up most frequently, professed theological attributes of gods or more natural, *Person*-like ones?

In keeping with the mind's natural categories of thought, Barrett and Keil found an overwhelming tendency for subjects to think of "God" as exhibiting *Person*-like characteristics rather than theological attributes. Though questionnaires revealed that the participants shared similar theological ideas about what gods are supposed to be like, these theological ideas were not used in their on-line reasoning. For example, the participants agreed that God is all knowing, omnipresent, and atemporal, yet when reasoning about situations within individual stories they represented God with physical and psychological limitations. Participants readily characterized God as having to accomplish one task at a time, having a limited focus of attention, having fallible perception, and having a single location in space and time. The boy in the river needed to wait for God to finish answering one prayer in a distant place before turning his attention to the boy's plight.

Similar results come from observations of how people pray to divine beings. Barrett speculated that if people really do represent gods as *Person*-like, then it should be detectable in their actions as well as their thinking. In a series of experiments that included questionnaires, prayer journals, and spontaneous tests, Barrett charted the ways that Christian subjects appealed to god during

TABLE 3.3 Common theological attributes of the Christian god.

Categories	Attributes
Absolute (immanent), Incommunicable	omnipresence, omnipotence, omniscience, immutability, impassibility, simplicity, infinity, spirituality
Relative (transitive), Communicable	holiness, perfection, fealty, wisdom, mercy, justice, love

petitionary prayer (2001). In Christianity, as in other faith traditions, believers can ask god to act in the natural world in several ways. Being omnipotent and omnipresent, god can conceivably and with equal ease intervene biologically (such as healing a disease) physically (such as preventing an automobile accident), or psychologically (such as changing someone's mind). What Barrett discovered, however, is that his subjects preferred to ask god to act psychologically. Because god is implicitly conceptualized as *Person*-like, the mechanistic limitations that define personhood incline those who pray to ask god to act in the same way that people get things done—by influencing psychological states.

Of course religious adherents typically side with theologians and say that they know full well the special attributes of their gods and that any language that likens gods to humans is merely metaphorical. But the issue here is not whether religious people understand the language of theology—whether during times of careful consideration they display "theological correctness" (Barrett 1999)—but what gods are in the language of cognition. These experiments demonstrate how ordinary cognition informs thinking about gods as well as the distance that exists between explicit, theological concepts of gods and the implicit, intuitive representations of gods that people bring to on-line tasks. Religious people may be quite capable of reflection on their tradition's official concept of god, but when they are thinking on the go, they default to a concept with few "god-like" properties. As Barrett points out, this is because people represent both gods and humans with the same cognitive resources:

> Christians, Jews, Hindus, atheists, and agnostics use strikingly similar concepts of gods. Regardless of theological tradition, in non-reflective contexts, concepts of gods conform to intuitive expectations people hold about all intentional beings: that they have fallible beliefs, desires that motivate purposeful action, limited attention, limited sensory-perceptual systems for gathering information about the world, a particular physical location in space and time, and so forth. In short, when rapidly generating inferences about religious agents, people automatically attribute to them many human properties—even when they are inconsistent with explicitly endorsed theology. (2002: 95)

This all sounds very anthropomorphic, and it is certainly no new idea to link thoughts about gods to thoughts about people. Anthropomorphic explanations of religion are legion, employed by figures ranging from Xenophanes to Feuerbach to Freud. But from the perspective of cognition, there is more going on here than unconscious "projection" or symbolic expressions of psychological need. Nor is the making of gods in our own image simply a requirement of language. Metaphors might aid limitations of expression but they can also reveal limitations of thought. With the representation of gods, Barrett and

Keil suggest, it may be the case that the use of anthropomorphic metaphors "actually expresses the underlying conception" (1996: 221).

A cognition-based account of religious concepts advances the idea that anthropomorphizing gods inevitably follows from parsimonious ontological kinds. The basic assumptions needed to understand supernatural beings are supplied by intuitive knowledge about quite natural ones. Apart from theological discourse, which tends to produce representations incompatible with tacit thought, gods are processed by the mind according to the ontological category that most closely matches their perceived properties. Gods are said to be entities that think, desire, and communicate—a slate of properties characteristic of sentient beings. So it is likely that the forms of anthropomorphism reported in Barrett and Keil's experiments, such as spatio-temporal limitations, are indicative of cognitive constraints pressuring god concepts into their most natural ontological category: "This gives rise to a sentient being which looks very much like a human being, the most salient example of this specific ontology" (Barrett and Keil 1996: 242). Contra traditional understandings of anthropomorphism, we do not project human-like qualities onto gods but god-like qualities onto humans.

The anthropologist Stewart Guthrie, one of the individuals responsible for launching the cognitive science of religion, argues that the mind's propensity to cast intentional agents as human is the result of an even more rigorous and overarching strategy of perception (1980, 1993). Guthrie believes that survival in our evolutionary past (as well as in the present) required that we interpret ambiguous objects and events firstly as those possibilities that matter most. These possibilities include living things, but especially humans. The result is a perceptual system strongly biased to anthropomorphism. We automatically and involuntarily perceive the world as alive and *Person*-like, interpreting even the faintest cues in terms of human traits. That anthropomorphism is so often mistaken does not negate its role or power as the fundamental default assumption, nor does knowing about it make it go away. Designed to extract the safest and most relevant information from every encounter, our minds inevitably gamble on the most significant interpretation.

Though the tendency to anthropomorphize is familiar to all—think of our pets, our festivals, our visual arts—Guthrie has amassed a large body of evidence illustrating the extent to which anthropomorphism pervades human thought and action. His examples drawn from cognitive science, developmental psychology, and ethnography are revealing; those taken from daily life, pop culture, and marketing are down right enjoyable. Because perception is itself an interpretive activity (seeing is "seeing as"), people cannot help finding apparent instances of human-like objects and activity everywhere they turn. We see faces on mountains and on the surface of Mars; we hear voices in the wind and divine friendly and fiendish images from inkblots; we construe accidents as meaningful, read messages in natural formations, and suspect purpose in happenstance. People also find the human being to be a useful and dramatic model for imposing their own order on the world. We anthropomorphize in literature and architecture; we dream up human-like entities to both entertain and explain; we find cartoons and monsters credible and advertisements featuring talking geckos and sexy bottles compelling. As Guthrie notes, "such illusory perceptions tell us more about ourselves than about the world" (1993: viii).

It is a small step for Guthrie to move from the many "secular" experiences of anthropomorphism to the anthropomorphism of religion. In fact, assuming that these two forms of anthropomorphism are somehow different is to miss the thrust of his argument. Like previous writers, Guthrie sees anthropomorphism as basic to religion, but he also claims forthrightly that anthropomorphism *explains* religion. The most pressing need from a cognitive standpoint is to explain anthropomorphism itself. With that done, religion can be understood for what it is, *systematized anthropomorphism*:

> Religious anthropomorphism typically is elaborate, shared, and enduring; secular anthropomorphism typically is ad hoc, idiosyncratic, and fleeting. The anthropomorphism we call religion also is relatively systematic, and addresses relatively powerful and important entities, such as gods, which have a key human capacity, that for symbolic interaction. However, the continuity of religious and non-religious spheres means there is no break either between our conceptions of gods and our conceptions of ordinary humans or between religious anthropomorphism and secular anthropomorphism. Demeter and Chiquita Banana, Thor and Jack Frost are of one piece. (1993: 112)

For Guthrie, then, what makes religion possible is what makes it plausible, and what makes religion plausible is that its central objects and concerns mesh closely with our central cognitive strategy for understanding the environment. Religious thought, like secular modes of thought, is a means of interpreting and influencing the world. Religious thought, also like secular modes of thought, achieves this goal by animating and anthropomorphizing, by positing beings that are *Person*-like, capable, at the very least, of interacting symbolically with humans. Religious thought differs from secular thought mainly in forming enduring systems of belief, practice, and community around these beings. This evolutionary argument works in both directions: the cultural fact that all religions have a god or gods corresponds well with the psychological fact that all people anthropomorphize. As Robert Wright points out, "one good reason to suspect an evolutionary explanation for something—some mental trait or mechanism of mental development—is that it's universal, found everywhere, even in cultures that are as far apart as two cultures can be" (1994: 45).

Despite the obvious strength of Guthrie's hypothesis, some cognitivists suggest that it must be nuanced to properly account for what is most crucial and most common about religious concepts. Barrett and Boyer both point out that a rigorous application of the anthropomorphism argument can be misleading in two important respects. First, though anthropomorphism implies that supernatural beings are represented has having human features and displaying human characteristics, the only absolutely critical and unquestionably ubiquitous human-like attribute ascribed to gods is that they have *minds*. Of course, many gods are described in broadly human terms—some eat, have bodies, live only in specific locations, are quick to anger, and so on—but the slate of human attributes given to gods are either as diverse as people themselves or, in some religious traditions, wholly absent. Theologians especially seek to do away with inevitable but unfortunate anthropomorphic ideas by distancing gods from humans. Yet no matter how different theologians make gods, they never abandon the idea that gods have minds. "Anthropologists know that the *only* feature of humans that is *always* projected onto supernatural beings is the mind" (Boyer 2001: 144).

Second, though possessing a mind that perceives, plans, desires, remembers, and communicates is certainly something that can be said of humans, the concept of a mind is not *exclusively* human. The operation of intuitive psychology is much more robust than that. As the studies of human perception noted earlier discovered, people are naturally prone to attribute minds to every known agent, to phenomena without an immediately definable source, even to peculiarly behaving objects. Such findings suggest, as Barrett noted some time ago, that people are not necessarily biased to interpret ambiguous objects and events as "human-like" but that the attribution of mind might best be explained "in terms of a more general intuitive-generator that operates on all intentional agents" (1998: 617).

Both critiques of the anthropomorphism argument are insightful and, as we'll see, indispensable for circumscribing the various forms that religious ideas take. It is worth noting, though, that anthropomorphism is still at play even when we attribute minds to nonhuman sources. Mind is not a generic concept. We know of only one kind of mind—a *human* mind—and it's this sort that we attribute to other agents. We imagine that our pets understand us because we give them human understanding. Geometric shapes "chase" each other because that is the kind of action human minds instigate. Gods know as humans know, they just know *more*. If intuitive psychology does indeed track along a "theory" of how minds work, then it is instructive to consider the model used to produce this theory. If we can know only what the human mind is like, then it would seem that theory of mind is necessarily anthropomorphic and the attribution of minds an inherently anthropomorphic exercise.

In any case, Boyer and Barrett's observations advance our understanding of religious concepts in two decisive ways. First, they make specific both the core structure of god concepts and the principle mental mechanisms used to process them. Gods are first and foremost intentional agents, *beings with minds*. There are plenty of ways to dress up this core structure—a god may look and act like a bawdy warrior or exist as an all-pervasive immaterial spirit; a god may be endowed with cosmic powers or be seen as relatively innocuous—but the core structure is always there. And representing gods as beings with minds in turn shapes the way people think about and respond to them. ADD and ToMM, which recognize and understand agents in terms of mental states, effortlessly process god concepts, generating rich inferences that make gods readily intelligible and, for many people, entirely plausible. Theological language notwithstanding, gods can be seen as perfectly "natural" ideas in the sense that they come easily to minds like ours (Boyer 1994a). As concepts go, gods have all the qualities and salience as real agents in the world.

Second, in directly implicating ADD and ToMM in religious thought, Boyer and Barrett's work helps to explain why so many different kinds of things end up imbued with religious significance. As discussed above, ADD and ToMM are intrusive mental mechanisms. The human mind is prone to suspect agency given the slightest excuse, and it is most interested in objects and events that appear mentalistic in origin. This is revealed not only by the determined agent searches we constantly conduct and the readiness with which we connect traces of agency to actual agents—a bird's nest suggests a nest maker; tire tracks suggest a driver—but also by the degree with which we seek out "usefulness" and "purposefulness" behind so many of our encounters with both living and nonliving things (Keil 1994; Bloom 1998).

It is tantalizing that here too cognitive science can borrow the language of theology to describe a natural propensity of the human mind. The psychologist Deborah Kelemen is currently pursuing research showing that, from an early age, the brain appears to be already turned to reason "teleologically" about the world (1999a, 1999b, 1999c, 1999d). We seem to want to see things as being the way they are for specific reasons rather than as the result of random chance. Just as an animal's horns are useful for deterring adversaries, so young children will say that pointy rocks are pointy to keep people from sitting on them. Intuitively, humans create purposes for things, and things for purposes. And because useful designs and apparent purposefulness make the most sense in relation to intentional agents, teleological reasoning evokes inferences provocative to both Christian apologists like Paley and cognitive scientists like Kelemen, who asks if, as children, humans might not be "intuitive theists" (2004).

Barrett points out that teleological reasoning is naturally extended to events and personal experiences as well as to objects. While many common explanations for daily happenings are ascribed unproblematically to agents that are never actually present, Barrett shows how more confusing experiences can be resolved, at least tentatively, by postulating agents that are both unnatural and supernatural. In his book *Why Would Anyone Believe in God?* (2004), Barrett offers two examples. The first is the phenomenon of crop circles, which, while assumed by most people to be jokes perpetrated by quite human agents, are actually looked on by a few as traces of extraterrestrial beings. Similarly, when inexplicable personal events take place, such as a man's miraculous escape from an exploding gain silo, some people comfortably see the intervention of a divine agent, while others see no need to attribute agency to the event at all. What is relevant about such explanations from the standpoint of cognition, Barrett maintains, is not whether they are true but their fit with the normal operation of ADD.

So ADD is eager to plot agents in the world, even in cases where agents are not physically present and their actions cannot be directly observed as events. This promiscuous feature of human cognition is true of ToMM as well. While ToMM normally operates in concert with ADD, applying theory of mind to the agents ADD identifies, ToMM is also quite capable of working on its own, positing minds even in the absence of input from ADD. In the same way that ADD is prone to suspect agents on the basis of traces, ToMM readily implements theory of mind without first having to literally see an agent or its signature.

The independent operation of ToMM can be demonstrated in several ways, but one that is both striking and pertinent to religion comes from experiments that test people's thinking about death performed by psychologist Jesse Bering (2001, 2002). Working with child and adult subjects holding differing views on the nature of death, Bering examined how people represented agents who are no longer alive. As Bering discovered, while neither children nor adults have difficulty recognizing that the physical and biological functioning of agents disappear with death, both continue to think of deceased agents using theory of mind. Regardless of their explicit beliefs about personal consciousness after death, people implicitly represent dead agents' minds in the same way: psychobiological and perceptual states cease while emotions, desires, and epistemic states continue. The ongoing activity of ToMM in the absence of a real agent—even the known death of an agent—provides, Bering reasons, a "natural foundation for afterlife beliefs," including the universally recurrent belief in ghosts and spirits (2002).

This practical demonstration of ToMM's independent operation is mirrored by the more general human capacity for imaginative thought, which owes its existence, in large part, to the autonomous work of ToMM. Indeed, Robin Dunbar has called theory of mind humankind's "most important asset" because it not only allows us to make sense of the world but also enables the forms of higher-order cognition that are the hallmarks of human thought (1997: 101). In order for theory of mind to operate effectively, we must be able to step back from ourselves and look at the world reflectively. This level of reflection takes place when you wonder what someone else is thinking or feeling, when you assess the source of your own thoughts or feelings, or when you attempt to evaluate the consequence of an action. The watershed comes with third-order intentionality, which is what it takes to represent the content of the mind of someone who does not actually exist. At increasing orders of intentionality, this ability deepens and the range of cognitive skills broadens. The uniquely human capacity for detached, creative thought, which includes the ability to conceive of imaginary beings and alternative worlds, stands behind literature, art, science, and, of course, religion.

The centrality of theory of mind to such systematic modes of thought is clarified further by considering again those for whom theory of mind is deficient or absent. Earlier in this chapter autism was used as an example of what life is like for those with impaired mind-reading systems. Though autism comes in different forms and intensities, it follows from Dunbar's argument that this mental disorder would inhibit religious thought and behavior. Because autistics are incapable of functioning with high-level intentionality, they fail to appreciate metaphor, grasp humor, engage in fictive thought, or imagine that the world could be other than it appears. This is particularly detrimental to religious thought because religion not only requires the ability to conceive of imaginary beings and alternative worlds but, more specifically, the ability to conceive of imaginary beings as thinking, interactive minds. Baron-Cohen's finding that autism is in part a failure to develop a full-blown theory of mind suggests that autistics lack the mental tools to represent god concepts in the same way as people with normally functioning ToMMs.

The independent operation of ToMM suggests as well that Barrett and Boyer's mind-only explanation of religious concepts, while correct, ought to be finessed a bit. There is no reason to lessen the force of Guthrie's anthropomorphic argument simply because additional human-like features are so often excluded from religious representations. Not only is mind itself already an anthropomorphic property but also it is likely that in situations where ToMM freely functions without the aid of ADD—as happens especially in imaginative thought—"mind" is the *only* anthropomorphic property that remains. Common examples of the personification of ambiguous "causal forces" seem to support such a claim. Jason Slone pursues this line of thinking in his investigation of how people tend to conceptualize culturally recurrent notions like "fortune," "misfortune," "chance," and "luck" as psychological agents (2004). Because psychological agents engage ToMM, and in the face of profound conceptual ambiguity, our mental apparatus is prone to bracket such ideas into its nearest ontological category. As a result, we find widespread representations akin to "Lady Luck" as well as more highly developed and systematized examples of personification: the goddesses Lakshmi, Benzaiten, and Fortuna, and so on. "Like other forms of supernatural belief," Slone writes, "such thinking is a natural by-product of human cognition" (2004: 120).

Regardless of the ways in which ToMM functions, it is clear that the concept of mind is an extremely portable one. It is flexible to context, richly explanatory, and easily transferred across ontological categories. This makes sense given our evolved mentalistic perception and the informational value that accrues from ascribing mind to objects and events. All of this is highly relevant to the subject of religion because, returning to Barrett and Boyer's contributions, it explains why almost any feature of the world or any personal experience can be given religious significance. Because the salient feature of gods is that they are thinking, acting minds, practically everything can become part of a religious worldview. Boyer's work draws the blueprint for the varieties of religious thought; Barrett's identifies the mental machinery.

As reflection on human evolutionary history has brought to light, what matters most as we negotiate our environment is the presence and activity of intentional agents, particularly as they relate to ourselves. In response, natural selection has equipped our brains with mechanisms that enable us to deal effectively with a world filled with "others." We employ ADD and ToMM to identify, explain, predict, and possibly control the people and events that surround us as well as to guide and gauge our own beliefs and behaviors. These critical cognitive systems have resulted in strong mental biases that speed our ability to see agents and read minds. As we face the day, we assume an intentional stance, perceiving and interpreting the world primarily in mentalistic terms.

Yet strong mental biases have inherent side effects. One already raised is the tendency of ADD and ToMM to overestimate the stimuli that they were designed to detect. On balance this is beneficial. In a competitive environment it is far better that these cognitive systems be fast rather than slow, wrong rather than uncertain. The activity of intentional agents is simply too important to ignore or overlook, so having cognitive systems that operate with a certain level of hyperactivity helps insure that this does not happen. A more intriguing side effect of mental biases is that they make our minds susceptible to ideas that align with them, even if these ideas are highly unusual. Mental biases don't just color our perceptions; they also shape our conceptions. So it should not be surprising that our preoccupation with intentional agents extends to imaginative versions, especially when they are represented in ways that give them immediate importance. The fact that humans are so strongly predisposed to ordinary notions of agency "opens the gates to conceptualizing agents with some extraordinary qualities" (Lawson 2001: 147).

This is the other half of the picture when it comes to explaining the structure of god concepts and, ultimately, people's responses to them. On the one hand, supernatural beings can be viewed as "natural" agents in that their conceptual structure matches the way our minds conceptualize agents in general. In most respects god concepts conform to an ordinary ontological category and the intuitive expectations we associate with it. Thus for many on-line tasks, thinking of a god as a *Person* with biological, physical, and psychological properties gets the job done. That this process is automatic, quick, and nonconscious means it typically takes place in spite of professed theological beliefs, which are parasitic on normal conceptual tools in any case.

But of course gods *are* much more than ordinary, intuitive agents. If gods were merely ordinary they would garner no special attention, let alone the level of systematic concern they in fact enjoy. Gods are represented as agents possessed of remarkable abilities that make them extraordinary. Gods are invisible, super-knowing, and super-powerful. Gods are creators and destroyers, saviors and tormentors. Gods are timeless, limitless, formless, and so many other things. So when it comes to gods, we are not simply talking about intentional agents but—to finally settle on a proper definition—*counterintuitive intentional agents* (Pyysiäinen 2002). Gods belong to that class of ideas that, by variously violating normal expectations about how things work in the real world, grab our fancy, and sometimes our fealty, in dramatic ways.

The next chapter explores the unexpected properties of god concepts— with unexpected results. Once again it turns out that, from the perspective of cognition, the characteristics that make gods noteworthy are not necessarily the same characteristics that have been so rigorously detailed by theologians. Just as the properties that make god concepts plausible are the ordinary rather than the extraordinary ones, so the counterintuitive properties that make gods salient to people are not found in any primer of theology. Gods, like religions, are practical concerns. Gods matter, we'll see, primarily because they hold personal, not cosmic significance.

4

Gods and Why They Matter

What Does the Brain Have to Do with Gods?

Though mountain gorillas bend foliage into comfortable sleeping mats, human beings build luxurious beds for elegant homes and five-star hotels. Though chimpanzees recognize the utility of wadded leaves for drinking water, humans bore wells to underground aquifers and construct plumbing systems extensive enough to service cities. When compared with even the most intelligent animals on the planet, the ingenuity of humans speaks for itself. Our creative powers and our ability to exploit natural resources certainly have their negative sides, yet it is truly amazing how, over the long process of earth's evolutionary development, just one form of life emerged capable of agriculture and industry, of splitting atoms and of interplanetary travel. One animal—a relatively slow, weak, and vulnerable animal at that—arose with a mental organ that, while able to be held in one hand, can in many ways out think the largest of supercomputers, which of course it also designed.

This same small mass of nerve cells is equally possessed of remarkable imaginative powers, as prone to delirious flights of fancy and sublime speculation as it is to vacant musing and mundane instinct. Modes of cognition that recognize "beauty," "tragedy," "metaphor," "harmony," and similar concepts unknown to the rest of the animal kingdom have led to less pragmatic forms of self-expression that make up art, drama, literature, and music. And again, a moment's reflection on the emergence of such unusual activities out of natural selective processes ought to yield as least a small measure of awe. Hubris is another negative side of unrivaled skill, but humans can be justifiably proud of their mental abilities and achievements.

As the previous chapters have made clear, though, many uniquely human thoughts and behaviors rest on more general mental processes, a lot of which are shared by other animal species. One of the reasons that some people reject evolutionary theory is that it appears that we have nothing in common with animal society, let alone with our would-be ancestors. Modern humans play baseball, wear makeup, and build airplanes. Did our Pleistocene forbearers do these things too? The answer, of course, is "no," but they did have rotating shoulder joints, select mates using visual cues, and possess the dexterity and foresight to craft stone tools. Playing baseball, wearing makeup, and building airplanes are by-products of the same adaptations that made these seemingly more "natural" behaviors possible. Indeed, all the things that we do today are doable only because of past adaptations, however ancient. A very large number of our thoughts and behaviors are not themselves adaptive or even advantageous, but they are nevertheless side effects—what Stephen Jay Gould and Richard Lewontin call "spandrels" (1979)—of physical and cognitive adaptations designed for other purposes.

This book puts forth the same argument for the phenomenon we call religion. Religious thought is a by-product of similar, seemingly more "natural" forms of thinking. The cognitivist approach to religion is not that humans evolved to think religiously or that religious thought is somehow adaptive, but that religious thought rests on normal mental structures and processes designed for different though functionally related purposes. ADD and ToMM, two mental mechanisms already highlighted as key components of human cognition, are perfectly suited to thought about supernatural agents because they are already perfectly suited to thought about agents. Yet ADD and ToMM are not the only mental mechanisms that underpin religious thought. Numerous other mental modules are involved in understanding agents and guiding social interaction. The first part of this chapter explores some features of social cognition that also support thinking about gods and enhance their significance. Once again it turns out that it is careful attention to the intuitive activities of the brain rather than to theological depictions that tells us what gods are really like and why they matter.

What makes religious thought particularly interesting is not just that humans are capable of it but also that so many take it literally. A tremendous number of people across place and time have assented to religious truth claims—the most basic of which is the belief that gods actually exist—and have shaped their behaviors and relationships in accord with these claims. So it is not enough to explain the cognitive foundations of gods; something must also be said about why such ideas are believed, about how gods move from being concepts that are merely plausible to ones that are accepted as entirely real. And this explanation, too, needs to be cognitive in nature, for "in one sense or another, the beliefs people subscribe to should be explicable in terms of the evolved human mind" (Wright 1994: 366).

In route to a cognitive explanation for belief in gods, this chapter outlines some additional psychological and social factors that contribute to commitments to supernatural beings. Gods are represented in such a way that they not only fit the description of agents that might actually exist but also align with other interesting tendencies of human thought that lend them increased salience. There are all kinds of counterintuitive concepts adrift in cultural currents, but gods clearly hold a special power to provoke human commitment. As intentional agents—and really important ones at that—gods evoke intense feelings and emotional experiences, and these too help to spur, enhance, and harden religious belief. Such emotive experiences often take place in the context of public gatherings, so one cannot neglect the importance of religious communities and regular participation in religious practices as factors promoting personal belief in gods.

But the topic of religious belief is a jump too far forward. As counterintuitive concepts, representations of supernatural beings feature a balanced combination of ordinary, intuitive properties and extraordinary, counterintuitive ones. The previous chapter explored the ordinary properties of gods—their fit with natural ontological categories, their conformity to intuitive reasoning. Now it is time to consider the properties that make gods so extraordinary, so attention grabbing, and so often faith provoking.

Social Minds, Social Gods

Quite a lot has been written on the fact that human beings are an intensely social species. The several isolating forces of contemporary urban life may obscure the interconnections between people, even cause individuals to feel crowded, but as John Donne's famous mediation puts it, "No man is an island." Humans are as dependent on one another for their psychological and emotional well being as they are for their physical needs. We naturally group up, as many other species do, but we are far more sophisticated in our interactions, and we reap a broader range of benefits. Matt Ridley suggests that sociality is the flipside of humankind's evolutionary success. It's not simply high intelligence that sets humans apart but a specific kind of intelligence:

> The human brain is not just better than that of other animals, it is different. And it is different in a fascinating way: it is equipped with special faculties to enable it to exploit reciprocity, to trade favors, and to reap the benefits of social living. (1996: 131)

It is appropriate, then, to speak of the human mind as a "social mind" and our specialized brand of intelligence as "social intelligence." As Ridley here also points out, there are immediate advantages that accrue to a species with keen social minds—mutual aid, returned favors, and so on—yet almost every facet of human existence involves social intelligence, from family life and friendship to commerce and armed conflict. This complex web of social interaction can be simplified, however, by recognizing that all beneficial social activities require two basic resources: cooperation and information. In order to live as we live, we need to help one another. In order to help one another, we need information. Of course, social intelligence is all about improving and fine-tuning these resources. For example, we tend to cooperate in tasks and relationships that are mutually beneficial with individuals we trust to contribute their part, and we decide which tasks and relationships are beneficial and which individuals are trustworthy by constantly gathering and updating information. These two resources are obviously connected in the opposite direction as well; each of us is largely dependent on other people to supply us with our own database of information.

Focusing on cooperation and information, the currency of animals that exist together in the cognitive niche, both usefully defines the range of activities that constitute human interaction—mind reading, monitoring social exchange, detecting cheaters, sharing gossip, trading favors, building coalitions, and so on—and helps to explain how the human brain has become such a sensitive and powerful instrument of social cognition. Much of the brain's computational energy, in accord with much of the body's daily behavior, is directed toward the work of social cognition. A suite of mental mechanisms designed for complex social interaction carries out this work. These mental mechanisms include ADD and ToMM, which do the fieldwork of identifying and interpreting the minds of agents, but numerous other mechanisms are involved in instigating and overseeing the complicated tasks of social interaction.

The central role played by social cognition in human life, as well as some of the mental mechanisms that facilitate it, has already been discussed in previous chapters. We return to it here, however, because social cognition has a direct bearing on religious thought and behavior. Because we humans are intensely social beings, and because, as intensely social beings, we navigate our ecological niche using a hypertrophied social intelligence, we are particularly sensitive to anything in the environment salient to social cognition. Objects, events, and even mental concepts related to intentional agents automatically activate the mental mechanisms involved in social cognition and cause us to take note. Natural selection has shaped a mind for which intentional agents are of vital importance. This biological predisposition means that ideas that naturally recruit the mind's systems of social intelligence are, at least tentatively, of personal interest. They also prove advantaged in cultural transmission, since all intentional agents are of interest to all people.

Summarily put, religious thought *is* social thought. This does not simply mean that religion is a social activity, though it typically is, but that, in the first place, gods and supernatural beings, the concepts around which religion forms, are represented and processed by the human mind as social agents. Through the activity of ADD and ToMM gods are conceptualized as beings with minds, and as a result, other inference systems and mental mechanisms involved in social cognition are activated as well. In the same way that we automatically evaluate the import, intentions, and utility of all intentional agents, and especially other humans, we also process god concepts using the suite of mental mechanisms involved in social intelligence.

The fact that gods engage our social mind is the key to explaining both what gods are like and why they matter. In the last chapter we looked to theologians and religious specialists to tell us how gods are special and why they deserve our attention. What theologians have to say is important because they contribute to the spread of religious ideas in two significant ways. The most obvious way religious specialists help to spread religious concepts is by talking about them. Preaching, teaching, ritual performances, books, billboards, and broadcasting are all highly effective means of disseminating ideas, and religious specialists employ them to great effect. The other, less obvious way that theologians help to spread ideas is by providing god concepts with their extraordinary, attention-grabbing counterintuitive properties.

Recall that counterintuitive concepts feature two crucial characteristics. On the one hand, counterintuitive concepts include enough ordinary, intuitive properties to give them intelligibility and inference potential. They conform in most respects to natural ontological categories and to the intuitive expectations associated with them. A woman provides the basis for a perfectly viable god because our minds are filled with intuitive knowledge about what women are like. On the other hand, counterintuitive concepts contravene, either through violations or transfers, some of those same intuitive expectations, thereby rendering the final representation strikingly extraordinary. A woman who controls death and dances out the destruction of the universe makes the basic concept a good deal more interesting and memorable.

At the same time, theologians and other religious specialists should not be overrated. While some of the counterintuitive properties that theologians proclaim are clearly important to the transmission of god concepts, others—including many that theologians themselves favor—contribute little either to mental representations of gods or to their relevance. Christian theologians, for example, are fond of saying that god is "impassible." But just how useful or meaningful is such a counterintuitive property? You cannot infer anything from the knowledge that god is impassible other than that god is impassible; nor is it of any immediate relevance. By paying attention to the intuitive activities of the brain rather than to theological depictions, we learn that the counterintuitive properties of gods that actually matter to people are social in orientation, practical in nature, and a little less grandiose than those that are spectacularly theological in presentation.

Pascal Boyer has provided the most thoroughgoing and insightful description of what we are referring to here as the *real* attributes of gods; that is, the qualities of supernatural agents that not only make them superlative but also cause people to take them seriously (2000a, 2001, 2003). As a starting point, Boyer, like other astute anthropologists and students of religion, highlights two crucial facts about everyday religious thought that many scholars in the field, and certainly many standard textbooks, gloss over. The first is that while popular cultural myths, folktales, legends, and lore are filled with all kinds of counterintuitive objects, creatures, and deeds, when it comes to religion—to those systems of belief that people seriously hold, live by, and die for—the counterintuitive concepts that predominate are decidedly human-like. Trees that speak, specters that haunt, and trolls that live under bridges make for good yarns, but even if they are taken seriously, they usually represent local anomalies, ones to be avoided rather than engaged.

The second common feature of religious thought and behavior that is clear to those who keep their noses to the ground is that religion is a manifestly practical enterprise. Contrary to long-standing explanations for religion—that it provides answers to existential questions, that it staves off psychological trauma, that it holds society together—the most central role that religion plays in people's lives is to get things done, to make things right, and to keep them that way. Religious people participate in effective rituals, carry amulets, live in step with norms said to bring blessings rather than curses, make vows and commitments that merit heaven rather than hell, and pray intently when needs or fears arise. Shamans, priests, and pastors are well aware of the practical utility of religion, spending, as they do, much of their time listening to people's immediate problems or prescribing gestures that help to solve them. Here, again, is another way in which theologians and philosophers of religion are fundamentally irrelevant: their profundity and their abstract, tightly reasoned statements of the properties and logic of gods are of little practical value to us common folk.

> Many people seem to feel no need for a general, theoretically consistent expression of the qualities and powers of supernatural agents. What all people do have are precise descriptions of how these agents can influence their own lives, and what to do about that. (Boyer 2001: 140)

Both of these general features of religion are in keeping with the findings of cognitive research explored in the last chapter. People represent supernatural agents as human-like because the kinds of beings that gods are said to be are only intelligible in relation to the natural ontological category *Person*. This incorrigible effect of cognitive constraint dramatically shapes the way people intuitively think about gods. Supernatural beings not only feature many of the ordinary properties of *Person*-like agents but, important to the present context, are also naturally represented as agents with whom we can *interact*. Gods think and know. They have beliefs, feelings, and concerns. They see, hear, and communicate. They act in ways that cause effects in the world. In short, supernatural agents are understood to be social agents, members of the human social network, residents of the cognitive niche. This is the only reason why religious activities like prayer, sacrifice, rituals, and good behavior make sense. Gods and humans interact as humans interact, and human interaction takes the form of social exchange. Not surprisingly, then, the interactions between gods and people are characterized by giving and receiving, by promises and protection, by reward and punishment, by activities of entreaty and supplication, and by attention to the inner workings of status, relationships, and reciprocity.

Herein lies the quality of Boyer's work: he presents a convincing case that, theologians notwithstanding, the special properties of supernatural agents that make them matter to people are those special properties that directly activate "mental systems geared to describing and managing social interaction with other human agents" (2002: 77). Thus when honing in on what matters most about gods, the place to begin is with what matters most about other humans. With gods, as with humans, social interaction turns on the twin resources of cooperation and information. The great similarity, and the great difference, between gods and humans can be framed in these same terms. What make gods simultaneously important and extraordinary is *what they know* and *how much they know*. The quality and degree of gods' knowledge, in turn, have consequences for human cooperative behavior.

As Boyer explains, the crux of social interaction between agents is "strategic information," the various sources of input that the social mind uses to evaluate a particular individual or situation and to regulate ongoing social interaction (2000a). Defining what constitutes strategic information is difficult because the mental mechanisms of social intelligence are largely nonconscious and the cues they use are complex, frequently subtle, and context specific. This is why the social minds of humans are so highly developed; establishing and maintaining relationships with other people requires powerful, sensitive, flexible mental abilities.

For example, when it comes to mating in animal society, willingness and desire is rarely subtle. Females openly display and reject; males actively court or insist. In some cases cunning and deception is involved, but these are the exceptions rather than the rules. In human society mating is usually much more involved. Humans flirt, act coy, and present every face in between. Correctly interpreting the signals and behaving accordingly can be a complicated business. And the same is true for many forms of daily interaction, from reading the minds of others to choosing sides in a dispute to determining what to do when a friend feels hurt.

What is and is not strategic information also relates to the situation at hand and to what is important at a given time. If you notice that a coworker is enjoying a ham and rye bread sandwich at lunch, this information will likely not be strategic in nature. However, if you notice a coworker eating a ham and rye bread sandwich after discovering that one was missing from your lunch box, this information probably will be deemed strategic. Two other significant features of strategic information are that it is often obtained through indirect sources, such as gossip, and that it retains lasting value. If a certain individual has cheated you in the past or is generally known to be dishonest, you will likely take this piece of strategic information into account when evaluating their future words and deeds.

Strategic information is critical to our social interactions. We use it to judge other people, to read social situations, and to gauge our own appropriate responses. But strategic information is not a one-way street. Other people also evaluate us and the social situations we are a part of, and they do this by gathering strategic information that tells them about us. In a cooperative environment, the information we *project* is as important as the information we *acquire*. Does she realize I'm a loyal person? Does he know I lied to him? Will my past work merit a promotion? Humans are deeply concerned about the strategic information other people possess, and shaping and maintaining personal reputations and public perceptions are an integral part of our social activities. Friendships and dinner invitations often evade individuals known to be unscrupulous.

We are likewise interested in strategic information held by others that may not be specifically about ourselves but which might be detrimental or useful to us in some way. Could someone else know about my lie and blow my cover? Does my colleague at work know yet about the boss's plan to promote someone in our department? Should I act now to get the advantage? Humans are as actively involved in the manipulation and exploitation of strategic information as they are in its propagation and interpretation. Obviously, intuitive psychology plays a key role in social cognition, and ToMM is one of the mental mechanisms hard at work in the acquisition and assessment of strategic information. Our every interaction with other people, in fact, involves a large array of mental processes intently calculating the impressions and exchanges that undergird social engagement. It should also be obvious that strategic information—both what you yourself hold, and what you know other people to hold—directly shapes behavior. If you know that he doesn't know you lied, then you can continue in your deception. But if you are sure that he knows you lied, then this knowledge will change the way you act.

This is precisely where the subject of strategic information gets interesting. One of the reasons that social interaction can be difficult and requires such sensitive mental equipment is that it is seldom clear what strategic information other people possess. We are frequently poker players trading in gaffs rather than in chips. Nevertheless, the game itself continues because it is clear that none of the players are infallible. One of our intuitive expectations about other minds is that they have limited, incomplete, and imperfect access to information. Everyone has false beliefs. No one knows everything. No one possesses all of the available strategic information in a given situation—that would require the ability to read minds in the literal sense. It's because people are naturally represented as having fallible, limited minds that social exchange is both possible and necessary. As a result, we spend a lot of time limning the boundaries of other people's knowledge.

That is not the case, however, when it comes to the supernatural agents that matter. Gods are treated as social agents and therefore activate the same cognitive systems that guide social interaction with other humans. This is, in part, why gods are so easily and so naturally conceptualized. But whereas human agents are assumed to have *limited* access to strategic information, supernatural agents are represented as possessing *full* access to strategic information. In Boyer's nomenclature, supernatural beings that matter are "full-access strategic agents" (2000a). Because gods are usually represented with various counterintuitive properties that give them easy access to information—they can be invisible, everywhere, clairvoyant, omniscient—gods are presumed to already have or of being capable of acquiring complete and accurate information, say the breadth of the universe, the needs of the sparrows, the direction to big game, or the cause of misfortune. But the knowledge of full-access strategic agents also extends to the kinds of strategic information that we mere mortals seek out and often protect: what we've done and what's going on in our hearts and heads.

The claim that important supernatural beings are full-access strategic agents may not be obvious—certainly gods around the world have diverse characteristics—but studies in comparative religion reveal that god concepts are not so different after all. As the previous chapter showed, there are only a few ways to design a counterintuitive religious concept and even fewer templates with which to begin. Nevertheless, one of the *recurrent* attributes of the supernatural beings that people pay attention to is a supernatural epistemology. In every culture the gods that matter know the truth, keep watch, witness what is done in private, divine the causes of events, and see inside people's minds. This does not mean that gods are necessarily wise, powerful, or good. Many gods are neither smart, nor strong, nor loving, and some are downright fearsome and vindictive. But this observation only contributes to the point. In spite of a plethora of traits attractive and not, what makes gods, ancestors, spirits, and other supernatural agents salient is that they know things—socially strategic things—and this causes many people to think about supernatural agents, to talk about them with others, and, potentially, to treat them as real and important.

Why, if real, would full-access strategic agents matter so much? First, consider what it would be like if another person had full and complete access to strategic information about you—your past deeds and misdeeds, your motivations and ambitions, your desires and dislikes, your charities and sins. Like it or not, such a person would immediately become profoundly relevant to your life. They would know all your secrets, both good and ill. They would have, in a very real sense, the advantage in all personal engagements. They would also hold the ability to disrupt and probably damage your social interactions with others. In the cognitive niche knowledge is power, and this is particularly true in the social domain. Of course, many of us do have people in our lives who enjoy intimate access to strategic information—spouses, close friends, confidants—but notice how rare such people are and how incomplete even their knowledge remains. Also notice what your relationships with such people are like. Access to strategic information comes only with trust, mutual support, and loyalty. What people know about us has a significant impact on how we relate to them. The people with whom we share substantial strategic information are the closest relationships we keep, for sharing requires commitment and cooperation. Disloyalty, breaches of trust, and outright breaks with such people are especially devastating and potentially dangerous.

The argument being employed here is one of *relevance*, the same argument used throughout this book. Many of the things that are important to people—like many of the causes behind common thoughts and behaviors—are important because of their role in our evolutionary past, which in turn has shaped our cognitive present. Just as agents are more relevant than objects, and humans are the most relevant agents, so people with extensive access to strategic information are more relevant than people with little. Given that humans are intensely social beings who rely on strategic information to navigate their environment, questions like *Who knows and who doesn't? Who's cooperating with whom?* and *Who knows what about me?* are of paramount importance. This information (strategic information about strategic information) significantly influences our behavior and determines the nature of our relationships with others. If limited-access strategic agents are this relevant, then full-access strategic agents, if they really are around, should be exceedingly so.

Considering the nature of strategic information itself reveals another aspect of human cognition that further heightens the relevance of agents said to have full access to it. As explained above, it is difficult to say what is and what is not strategic information. According to Boyer, strategic information is the subset of all available information that "activates social mind systems" (2002: 78), but specifying further which pieces of information are strategic is impossible because it depends on the context of the situation and the concerns of the person involved. Additionally, strategic information can be like general information in that it is often values-neutral. From a purely informational perspective, knowing that a business competitor has become financially insolvent (possibly strategic information) and knowing that a variety of mushroom is poisonous (probably general information) are identical kinds of data. They each say something useful about the world. Very often, however, strategic information takes on a *moral* tenor. Better put, what strategic information frequently has in common is that in activating the social mind systems of the brain it also activates mental mechanisms that contribute to personal value judgments about other people and events.

Now, concepts like "values" and "morality" are used very loosely here because they do not intend to signify some set of divinely endowed ideas of right and wrong described by moral theologians as the "natural law" or culturally contrived codes of behavior. As discussed in chapter 1, human beings are indeed endowed with moral instincts but our moral instincts are precisely that—instincts—naturally selected attitudes and behaviors related to the demands of group living and species-typical. The brain's systems of social cognition include specialized mental mechanisms that monitor social interaction—who is cheating, who consistently cooperates, who is trustworthy, who is my friend, who is a threat, and so on—and a biologically endowed grasp of the rules of social exchange aids in our evaluation of others. These rules also make explicit moral prescriptions easy to acquire because the ethical injunctions that are recurrent mirror our intuitive moral understandings. Lots of religions in lots of cultures warn against lying and extramarital sex, but everyone already realizes the social consequences of being branded a liar or an adulterer. It is common but quite unnecessary for gods and penal codes to decree that it is wrong to kill another person because few people want to associate with those who do.

So strategic information is not only important as a means of social interaction but also as input for human moral concerns. This is why it is such a valuable commodity to have and so important to protect. Again, other people use strategic information to understand us and to evaluate our own moral qualities. We know this implicitly and take care how we behave, straighten the cloth we present to the world, and cautiously select those with whom we openly share our idiosyncrasies and misdemeanors. We can manage these social demands to a considerable degree because we tacitly recognize that people are limited-access strategic agents, only partly informed, always fallible, and often fooled.

The same things cannot be said of gods. As full-access strategic agents, supernatural beings are represented not only as knowing everything that is important but also as maintaining a moral perspective on human behavior. Around the world, gods are consistently represented as concerned with the morally relevant aspects of social interaction, attentive to people's inner attitudes and outward behaviors. Ancestors know a hidden source of pollution in the village and who is responsible for it. The Buddha is aware of the subtle abuses of monks. The biblical god sees the sins of the heart as well as those committed in public. Such claims are often contained in religious writings or are part of oral instruction—many scholars have used this point to argue that religion itself is the principle source or enforcer of human morality—but people do not need to be taught that supernatural beings care about ethical concerns or that they ought to behave properly *because* gods care. In fact, nobody bothers to ask if or why gods care about moral issues; they simply assume that they do. The knowledge that a strategically relevant agent is also a morally relevant one is a natural inference made by social minds.

Once gods are represented as agents that are both strategically and morally important, other significant—and quite natural—inferences follow that shape how we think about these concepts and further enhance their relevance. Our implicit understandings of social exchange include assumptions concerning the proper conditions of exchange, reciprocity, fairness, and the identity of interested parties. It makes sense, then, that religious life, like secular life, should be so clearly construed in terms of exchange relations:

- *Conditions of exchange*: Social exchange involves interaction between at least two active agents. Supernatural agents, like human agents, are not just attentive to our thoughts, actions, and moral qualities but are also represented as being affected by and responsive to them. We naturally expect ancestors, spirits, and gods to be involved in social affairs and not merely to observe them. Gods become angered or pleased by the things that we think and do, and they behave accordingly. Social exchange may also entail a single, momentary interaction or be extended indefinitely. Religion is usually a form of long-term social exchange, requiring that proper social relations be maintained.
- *Reciprocity*: Social exchange involves forms of cooperation, including the giving and receiving of goods and services. It is important to recognize that less tangible possessions like promises, commitment, friendship, and faith are also valuable commodities of exchange. Another expectation of social exchange is that value passes in both directions, either simultaneously or paid up at some point in the future. Interaction with supernatural agents is based on such expectations. Disruptive ancestors and spirits are contented by a good meal now and then. Gods protect and fertilize in exchange for sacrifices. Faith merits heaven and eternal life. Covenant keeping brings land and nationhood.
- *Fairness*: Implicit expectations about social exchange include rules of fairness. People tacitly acknowledge that right and wrong behaviors are, or at least ought to be, followed by corresponding consequences. They also expect the proper response to be doled out by the affected party. With limited-access strategic agents, injustices may go undetected, but gods see the whole picture. As a result, gods reward moral behavior and punish wrongdoing. They are easily connected with the bounties and blessings (rich harvests, victorious battles, healed diseases, pay hikes, and so on) as well as with the curses and calamities (droughts, famine, foiled plans, sickness, death, and so forth) that befall individuals and groups. Interestingly, having extraordinary powers

does not absolve gods of the necessity of fair play. We expect our gods to follow the rules of social exchange. Many people learn to accept faceless misfortune and chance events, but like Job and modern arguers of theodicy, they remain troubled by seeming injustices perpetrated even by gods.

- *Identity of interested parties*: Mental capacities for monitoring social exchange also work to identify the interested parties in specific social interactions. This ability is connected to mental capacities that recognize kin and ethnic distinctions and regulate group identity. An act of social exchange can include just two people, but it may also bring in many more. Because full-access strategic agents are equally relevant to all people, their presence extends the boundary of interested parties to an entire community of believers. Through their link with general moral intuitions but especially with local conventions, gods can easily serve as rallying points for group identity, where shared commitments quickly broaden social contacts and strengthen social cohesion. And social transmission of god concepts heightens their relevance still further. If lots of people in a community include supernatural beings in their social interactions, then there is pressure for others to do so as well.

Again, no one needs explicit religious instruction to understand that gods are not indifferent to what we do, that interaction with gods entails give and take, that behaviors have consequences in which gods play a role, or that gods figure into the thoughts and actions of others. These general principles are already a part of our tacit understanding of social exchange. People have a wide range of strategic capacities that monitor and regulate social interaction, and these adhere in perceived interactions with supernatural agents as much as with human agents. It is also worth reiterating the point, better clarified now, that religion does not support morality. Instead, the moral intuitions and emotions that humans, as a species of cooperators, already possess support religion. In this as in many other respects, "religious concepts are *parasitic* upon intuitive understandings and inferences that would be there, religion or not" (Boyer 2002: 90).

The natural mental connections between god concepts, social cognition, and intuitive moral understandings go a long way toward explaining what gods are really like and why they matter. In both cases, the way that people intuitively process and employ god concepts has little in common with the portraits and apologies for gods provided by theologians and religious specialists. What matters most about gods is not some rehearsed list of abstract, theological properties but the unusual—though still implicitly understood—properties and powers that activate the mind's inference systems directing daily social interaction.

So from the perspective of cognition, the *real* attributes of gods turn out to be rather different from those provided by theology, such as the list of divine properties drawn from Christianity in the last chapter (see Table 3.3). A cognitive perspective on the connections between god concepts and intuitive knowledge reveals that the properties that make supernatural agents important are social in orientation, practical in nature, and less dramatic than the divine characteristics that are so often dogmatic.

Whereas theologians work to place ontological distance between gods and finite beings, our minds cannot avoid the use of natural ontological categories. Thus in everyday, on-line thought, gods are represented as human-like agents. Theologians would also like us to think of gods as anything but ordinary; they accept mundane or anthropomorphic ideas about divinity only as metaphors. But because we naturally think of gods as human-like social beings, our minds generate rich inferences about them. Intuitive psychology and the mental mechanisms of social cognition tell us everything we need to know to successfully interact with these concepts. Despite the lengthy list of divine attributes contrived by theologians, the counterintuitive property that makes supernatural beings immediately salient and especially relevant to human life (see Table 4.1) is that they have unique access to what matters most to minds like ours—strategic information and personal moral qualities. Other theological attributes of gods contribute little to on-line thought and are important only to the degree that they enhance the cultural transmission of full-access strategic agents. Finally, none of these cognitive processes, unlike theological reflection, require explicit instruction or careful consideration. The mental capacities that facilitate the representation of supernatural agents are automatic, quick, nonconscious, and common to everyone.

It is a trivial act to point out that because we have social minds we also have social gods. Yet the study of cognition has made a science of the trivial in

TABLE 4.1 Theological versus cognitive perspectives on god concepts.

Attribute	Theological Perspective	Cognitive Perspective
1. Ontology	Wholly "Other"	Intuitive ontology (*Person* template)
2. Ordinary properties	None	Intuitive psychology, adhere to rules governing social exchange
3. Extraordinary properties	Omnipresence, omnipotence, omniscience, immutability, impassibility, simplicity, infinity, etc.	Full-access strategic knowledge, direct moral virsion
4. Source of human knowledge	Divine revelation, natural law	Intuitive inference systems, social cognition

as much as what is trivial is both often overlooked and frequently a key to explanation. The cognitive science of religion rests on the claim that religious concepts take their form, function, and plausibility from mental capacities that people already have by virtue of their evolutionary development. The natural connections between supernatural agent concepts, intuitive ontology, and social cognition are prime examples of the cognitive foundation of gods and religion.

To summarize, god concepts have proven so resilient because they capitalize on some of the human mind's most powerful cognitive systems. Supernatural agents are represented in such a way that they naturally activate the mental mechanisms of social cognition. As social agents, gods are implicitly viewed as exchange partners and our interactions with them are automatically processed by the mind in terms of exchange relations. The counterintuitive properties of gods—that they know strategic information that has consequences for social interaction—renders gods immediately salient. Gods know what matters to human interaction, so gods matter to humans. The further connection between concepts of full-access strategic agents and our intuitive moral understandings gives gods and supernatural beings even greater relevance. As a result, god concepts are extremely easy to acquire and transmit, likely to be construed as real, and capable of generating sincere personal and social commitment—the basis of religion.

Emotions, Rituals, and Other Reasons Why Gods Matter

There is a debate among participants in the cognitive science of religion that focuses, quite literally, on the difference between Mickey Mouse and God (Atran 2002; Tremlin 2003). This juxtaposition seems silly, but it actually highlights some important questions inherent to the cognitive approach. The line of inquiry runs something like this: As one considers the persistence and preponderance of counterintuitive concepts like gods, one cannot help but note that people everywhere entertain a large variety of extraordinary concepts that, though they are not thought of as "gods," still seem very much like them. Pop culture is rife with examples: the personable animals and objects of animation; the pixies and elves of fairy tales; the vampires and zombies of horror films; the specters and apparitions of festivals and holidays. Like gods, these imaginative agents are easy to represent, attention grabbing, and memorable. So why aren't *these* kinds of concepts, which share all the hallmarks of successful minimally counterintuitive concepts, "religious"? How is it that non-natural agents like Santa Claus and the boogey man remain the stuff of whimsy rather than taken as reality? Or, if other imaginative agents are believed to exist—say, the ghosts and witches so common to many cultures—why are they treated differently than gods? Why do only *certain* counterintuitive representations provoke intense personal commitment and wind up the focus of psychologically and economically costly religious thought and practice?

These questions certainly deserve careful investigation, but if the so-called "Mickey Mouse problem" is really a debate about the proper definition of religion, about the function or necessity of supernatural agents, or about some quality of "counterintuitiveness" itself, then it is a red herring. As the foregoing discussion of supernatural agent concepts should at least suggest, there are some rather big differences between gods, monsters, and talking mice, between the MCI concepts that really matter to people and those that merely intrigue, scare, or entertain. At the risk of repetition or foundering on minutiae, here are three observations:

First, while gods are indeed MCI concepts, their unusual conceptual structure is not the only thing that makes them notable. As noted above, many of the counterintuitive attributes given to gods are irrelevant to people and do not contribute to the way the human mind represents them. Simply being counterintuitive is not enough to make a concept either plausible or convincing. Chapter 5 will discuss how counterintuitiveness markedly aids the processes of mental recall and cultural transmission, yet it does not follow that counterintuitiveness necessarily enhances believability or motivates commitment. In fact, it rarely does. Humans are flexible and creative thinkers but they are not all that naïve about how the real world behaves or what it contains. Again, our minds are filled with fictitious and imaginary concepts—from unicorns to space aliens, from literary characters to invisible friends—that, though each in its own way is perhaps plausible, never merit inclusion in our active belief systems.

Second, not all MCI concepts are created equal. While all successful MCI concepts display a balance of ordinary, intuitive properties and extraordinary, counterintuitive properties, it makes a difference to issues of plausibility and commitment which natural ontological categories and intuitive inference systems a representation activates. A car that can fly and a plant that devours insects are both MCI concepts but, given their respective ontological templates, they remain objects of interest rather than of personal importance. MCI concepts that are intentional agents are better because they belong to the natural ontological categories that matter and that generate rich inferences, particularly those represented as *Person*-like. Ghosts, witches, and similar representations go so far as to activate our social mind systems, including the mental mechanisms of social exchange. As a result, these kinds of representations hold a special salience the world over. Usually, though, they are treated as agents that need to be dealt with as one deals with other humans. What these concepts ultimately lack is the counterintuitive property that makes gods the focus of serious religious commitment: full access to strategic information, including people's moral qualities. Only god concepts capitalize on the mind's most powerful cognitive systems *and* have the counterintuitive properties capable of generating serious personal and social commitment.

Third, it should be obvious that not just any concept can garner serious commitment, let alone become the focus of costly religious devotion. Only representations that connect with specific ontological templates and activate specific inference systems make good candidates. Supernatural beings that matter must, at a minimum, be represented as social agents with whom humans can and ought to interact. These properties are the selected result of the evolved nature of human cognition. It's true that in many religions natural objects, man-made artifacts, and animals play important roles and are even considered divine, but in actuality sacred objects and animals owe their status to direct connections—as a proxy, as an incarnation, through the transfer of qualities, or some other means—with gods. Claims that a statue of the Virgin Mary has begun to weep and that its tears heal disease lead believers to venerate the statue not for its intrinsic value but because of its supposed connection with the supernatural agent it depicts. It's telling, too, that in religions that teach the existence of some ultimate power or impersonal divinity—the forces of Tao, Brahman, and Buddha-nature, the creator gods of many African tribes and of early American deists—such ideas are almost completely ignored in favor of more personal and practical deities.

The point here is that Mickey Mouse, monsters, ghosts, witches, and other widespread counterintuitive concepts can be nothing more than cultural icons or worldly problems because they are not represented and processed by the mind in the way that gods are. Gods are salient and evoke commitment not because they are novel or because they serve some social function but because their conceptual structure makes them credible and highly relevant to minds like ours (hence the need for a Tylorian rather than a Durkheimian definition of religion). Simply put, concepts of magical humans, intelligent mice, and the like make poor gods, so we should not expect them to become the focus of serious or costly religious commitment. It turns out, as we'll see in chapter 6, that the cognitive constraints that shape "good" god concepts work *against* official religion as well as for it. As Justin Barrett's experiments with theological correctness show, when it comes to thinking about gods, "not just anything goes" (1998: 617). God concepts themselves must stay within specific representational parameters if they are to remain relevant to believers. Abstract, theological descriptions of gods are largely ignored in on-line thought, have little staying power in the minds of people, and may not substantially impact how believers think and behave:

> Theologians and religious leaders cannot simply teach any ideas
> they want and expect those ideas to be remembered, spread, and be-
> lieved; rather, the way human minds operate gradually selects only
> those with the best fit to become widespread. (Barrett 2004: 30)

So gods demand attention due to particular cognitive propensities of the human mind. Yet there are a number of other factors, both psychological and social, that enhance the plausibility and relevance of god concepts, and two of these additional factors need to be mentioned, however briefly, before connecting notions like "plausibility" and "relevance" with actual religious "belief." The first and perhaps most powerful additional factor influencing religious thought and behavior is emotion. Discussing human emotion summarily and separately here is awkward because emotional responses play a more crucial role in human thought and action than typical treatments of cognition would suggest and because emotions are not independent from the mind's other processes of thought. Neurologically speaking, emotional and cognitive processes may comprise different brain systems but psychologists insist on the complex interrelations of emotional responses and cognition. Humans have what Daniel Goleman calls "emotional intelligence" (1995). Thought and emotion are *both* expressions of normal brain activity.

The most recent discussion of the role of emotion and experiential states in religious thought comes from Illka Pyysiäinen, who argues correctly that "the cognitivist, or functionalist, account of the nature of the human mind focuses on symbolic thought processes alone, leaving little room for emotions as a necessary concomitant to all sane cognition" (2001b: 78). Pyysiäinen certainly subscribes to the current cognitivist perspective on religious representation, but he also reminds those working in the field that human thought, despite its computational nature, is not a dispassionate, machine-like crunching of data. Human reasoning always includes "emotional coloring" that exerts a substantial influence on perception, decision-making, and behavior (2001a). Pyysiäinen's work represents only a first, tentative foray into an elusive aspect of human psychology, but it merits attention because it largely bypasses the language of "mystical minds" and "neurotheology" (for example, d'Aquili and Newberg 1999) and attempts to map the neurological links between emotions, cognition, and religious concepts.

Primary dialogue partners in this investigation are Antonio Damasio and Joseph LeDoux, whose work on the neurobiology of emotion shows that "emotion and cognition are separate but interacting mental functions mediated by separate but interacting brain systems" (Pyysiäinen 2001b: 98). As an example, LeDoux describes how the emotion of fear—perhaps the most basic of emotions, one designed to prepare animals to flee from predators or freeze to avoid being seen—is subserved by two distinct neural pathways (1996). One, a short, fast pathway between emotional stimulus (received by the sensory thalamus) and emotional response (produced by the amygdala), results in an immediate, intense, and involuntary reaction: the release of adrenaline, rapid heartbeat, heightened senses. This "dirty" pathway equates to the "better safe than sorry" principle that drives the Agency Detection Device; its operation activates disconcerting false alarms, but the need to avoid danger trumps inconvenience. By contrast, a long, slower pathway includes the sensory cortex, allowing cognitive processes to evaluate the source of the stimulus and decide whether or not the immediate response was truly necessary.

As discussed in chapter 2, the seat of emotional activities in the brain is the limbic system, frequently referred to as the "emotional brain." When naturally active or electrically stimulated, normal limbic systems produce the full range of human emotions: delight, disgust, panic, rage, remorse, and so forth. People with damaged limbic systems experience a loss of normal emotional behavior. But the production of emotions, like emotions themselves, is extremely complex and can involve many brain areas. Researchers point out how emotions, as mental states, even defy classification (Rorty 1980). Not only are emotions unlike each other in cause or tone but they can also be contrasted as active or passive, as thought-generated or instinctual, as voluntary or involuntary, as developed or spontaneous. Yet emotions *are* tractable because they can be described in relation to the structures and processes of the human brain—the same adapted, species-specific brain that thinks as well as feels. So in many ways emotional responses are like the cognitive processes described in this book: incorrigible, automatic, and constructive. Perhaps the most important similarity for our purposes is the one LeDoux himself highlights: "One of the major conclusions about cognition and emotion is that both seem to operate unconsciously, with only the outcome of cognitive or emotional processing entering awareness and occupying our conscious minds, and only in some instances" (1996: 21).

For Pyysiäinen, the answer to the "Mickey Mouse problem" lies precisely at the intersection of cognition and emotion: it is emotional variables that produce the crucial difference between ordinary counterintuitive representations and explicitly *religious* ones. Pyysiäinen argues that counterintuitive agents evoke strong emotions because they are represented in such a way that thinking about them triggers hardwired emotions like fear, sadness, happiness, and anger. These representations therefore acquire "somatic markers" (Damasio's term) and are ascribed lasting existential importance. Moreover, Pyysiäinen cautiously accepts Michael Persinger's (1987) identification of a specific neural mechanism in the temporal lobe capable of producing what are interpreted to be "religious" or "mystical experiences," like those commonly reported by epileptics. For Pyysiäinen, then, religious belief is not just a consequence of the cognitive inference potential religious representations possess, as it is for Boyer, but also of the engagement of neural systems that process emotional and experiential states.

Pyysiäinen's study provides one perspective on how emotions help god concepts acquire plausibility and relevance, but a more direct link lies in the connection between emotion and the cognitive processes that contribute to decision-making. As LeDoux's explanation of fear demonstrates, neural pathways run from the limbic system to cortical structures of the brain in charge of higher-order cognition, including the frontal lobes. The vital admixture of emotional intelligence is revealed when these connections are damaged. In such cases individuals retain normal reasoning abilities but find it very difficult to reach conclusions, resolve problems, or make firm decisions. Emotions both guide the decision-making process and provide the needed "feeling" that a particular choice is correct or that a specific action is right.

Such findings have obvious implications for descriptions of human thought that see the mind only in terms of information processing. But they also suggest that emotion is a constituent part of cognitive processes and not merely an addition or a response to them. On the one hand, many of our intuitive mental capacities, including several mentioned above, owe their successful operation to emotion. The moral underpinnings of social exchange, for example, are maintained by emotional reactions such as guilt, gratitude, and indignation. On the other hand, the feelings that the emotional brain provides are themselves descriptive and may directly shape perception. As Amélie Rorty points out, "having an emotion can not only be functional but also informative" (1980: 5). In both these respects, the factors that make a physical stimulus or mental concept salient and relevant to an individual are as much emotional as cognitive. Additionally, the emotional feelings that color private reflection and help to motivate personal commitment to religious concepts also encourage their public distribution.

However the neurobiology of emotion is configured, it should hardly be surprising that thinking about supernatural beings would stir powerful emotional links. While humans share a number of "basic" emotions with other animals, a rich repertoire of feelings is original to our species. The mind's emotional systems, like the mind's cognitive systems, were selectively designed to aid social interaction. The majority of our emotions are responses to the presence and activities of other people. The very variety and shadings of human feelings attest to the depth and complexity of gregarious life. "Emotional intelligence" and "social intelligence" are simply the two sides of the modern human mind.

God concepts engage emotional intelligence as actively as social intelligence. Gods are represented in relational terms, as beings that are personal, subjective, interactive, and involved. What is more, they are represented with extraordinary properties that make them uniquely important social agents. As a result, god concepts are capable of evoking exceptionally strong emotional responses that provoke and sustain religious belief and behavior.

The affective power of god concepts also opens the door to discussions about their natural ability to engage the mind's relational mechanisms, and thus to see religion as "relationship"—a perspective insisted upon by believers themselves. Lee Kirkpatrick, for example, offers the compelling argument that the human attachment system—another biologically endowed mental mechanism—is easily recruited by religious belief systems: "As a consequence, people often perceive their relationships with deities functionally in terms of attachment relationships, monitoring their sense of felt security and acting toward these deities accordingly" (2005:236). If gods can become attachment figures, then certainly their counterintuitive properties make them the best possible attachment figures, for what other figure could surpass the level of protection, security, and comfort provided by a god?

The role of emotion in religious thought is particularly visible in the context of religious practices, especially publicly performed rituals. Rituals have enjoyed special attention in the study of religion because of their social functions, but rituals and religious actions in general constitute a second significant factor enhancing the plausibility and relevance of god concepts *in the minds of individuals*.

Religious rituals and actions are as ubiquitous as religious ideas. Prescribed religious activities are found in all human groups and take many forms. Religious practices may be as passive as calming meditation; as solitary as prayer and dream quests; as demanding as recitation, pilgrimage, and fasting; as emotive as baptism, communion, and funerals; as dramatic as ordinations, dances, and sacrifices; as colorful as pujas, parades, and group worship; and as intense, terrifying, and painful as circumcision and initiation rites. Some religious rituals require specific procedures, elements, places, and times while others are general in production. Some religious activities are costly, flamboyant affairs while others are quietly and simply carried out. Some religious practices can be done by anyone while others require religious specialists like priests and shamans.

The subject of religious rituals is an extremely interesting area of study given its academic history. Anthropologists and sociologists have traditionally focused on the social effects of religious rituals—how they help to generate group identity, social cohesion, a common moral ethos, and so forth. Psychologists discuss the shaping influences of religious rituals on the mental and emotional lives of individuals. Students of religion understand religious rituals to be the necessary concomitant of religious belief, the means through which people commune with gods or express their awe. While these perspectives have often been overwrought, they endure because they capture important functions of religious rituals. Less discussed, however, are the ways these same functions also increase the credibility and importance of god concepts in public and private life.

Cognitive science aids in this task because knowing how minds work doesn't just help us to describe the social and psychological effects of religious actions but also to *explain* those effects. Linking religious rituals and practices to the features of human thought and behavior makes sense both of the forms that religious actions take and the influences they have on the people who witness or participate in them. For instance, the social effects of publicly performed religious rituals have been well noted. Emile Durkheim, who championed the view that religion serves the maintenance of society, argued that religious rituals work by fostering a "collective effervescence" (1912). Whether or not this lively statement is true, is can hardly be taken as an explanation—or at least we now need an explanation of the explanation.

A firmer, cognitive explanation of the effectiveness of religious rituals lies in the links between the social nature of religious practice and the social mechanisms of the human mind. Scholars of religion have long noted that religious practice has two social dimensions: one, vertically drawn, connects the community of practitioners with the supernatural agents believed to have inspired, shaped, or validated the religious practice; the other, horizontally drawn, connects the practitioners themselves. Many cognitively oriented scholars of religion recognize these twin dimensions of religious rituals, yet they find the second dimension much more provocative. They wonder: If religious concepts are parasitic on general mental capacities, then perhaps religious rituals are parasitic on general behavioral strategies.

Part of the difficulty associated with traditional studies of religious rituals has been a conflicted understanding of rituals themselves. As we'll see in chapter 5, Tom Lawson and Bob McCauley have good reasons to link religious rituals directly with gods, but ritualized behavior is hardly confined to the domain of religion. Secular life is filled with actions that are structured and repetitious. For Catherine Bell, rituals are natural fixtures of social life, best understood as shifting modes of action that help define "ordered relationships between human beings and their place in the larger world" (1997: xi). Anthropologist Alan Fiske has cataloged the many themes and concerns that religious and nonreligious rituals share in common, from special interests in numbers and patterns to ideas about purity, pollution, and boundaries, and he speculates on the development of "cultural complements" to natural social capacities (2000). Fiske also points out how normal, everyday behaviors become automatic and compulsive, even going so far as to relate compulsory gestures, concerns, and the emotional states that accompany them to pathological behaviors like obsessive-compulsive disorder (Fiske and Haslam 1997). Construed in such dispositional terms, ritualistic behavior perhaps ought not be viewed as unique to humans. Other animal species interact using procedural and consistent displays and performances. Anthropologist Chris Knight, however, argues that rituals began as a mechanism for coordinating human groups and necessarily coincides with the development of human language and culture (1990).

The message here is not that "religious" rituals are only ostensibly about religion and gods—though scholars like Durkheim would certainly fight that battle—but that religious behavior, like religious thinking, rest on biological foundations. Boyer, for example, argues that ideas about gods likely follow from rituals, not the other way around. Because the performance of rituals visibly precedes the acquisition of explicit notions of supernatural beings, "it may well be the case that rituals are not so much a *result* of people's representations of gods' powers as one of its many *causes*" (2001: 237). Boyer suggests that gods get added to rituals because they successfully, and quite naturally, fill the causal gap that exists between a ritual action and its supposed effect.

In any case, recognizing that ritualized behavior is also about what matters most to human life, the ordering of social relations, allows us to better understand the effects of religious rituals across their vertical and horizontal dimensions. In both aspects the psychological influences of religious rituals on participants have less to do with official religious claims than with the central concerns of nonreligious human behavior. Consider, as an instance, religious explanations for some of our most universal and extravagant rituals—those that surround births, the arrival of puberty, marriages, and deaths. In cultures around the world these "rites of passage" are in general expensive, elaborate, and public. These occasions are also usually colored with religious symbolism and assume or directly acknowledge the presence of supernatural beings. From a religious perspective, all of these elements are connected: (1) births, puberty, marriages, and deaths are events in which gods are keenly interested; (2) gods play a central role in the transformations that these events are believed to bring; hence, (3) these events require levels of sensory pageantry and participation equal to their import.

From a cognitive perspective, this line of reasoning is an illusion that covers what rituals like these are really all about. First, though gods are said to be interested in these singular events, few people could say why that is the case. Well-developed theologies have answers, but for most people the idea that gods care about their wedding is merely assumed. (Of course, lots of people don't hold even this basic assumption and dispense with religious symbolism altogether.) Second, while gods are implicated as agents in these life-changing events, they are in fact incidental to them. Children are born, become adults, marry, and die quite apart from supernatural intervention, and everyone knows it. Religious rituals play up the role of gods in rites of passages, but these claims amount to theological interpretations of naturally occurring biological and social events. Third, though the participation of the gods suggests the need for spectacular public ceremonies, any of these occasions could in fact be marked in private, or not at all.

An alternative understanding of these "religious" rituals is that they are really "social" rituals, behaviors related to intuitive beliefs about natural relations rather than to theological beliefs about supernatural ones. Seen from this angle, the pomp and circumstance surrounding rites of passage takes on new meaning and purpose. These events become ritualized because they entail the ordering, or re-ordering, of social relations, and they are publicized and performed publicly because they are of consequence to people besides those immediately involved. Births, maturations, marriages, and deaths directly impact social dynamics—sexually, economically, and politically. Puberty rites, for example, herald the appearance of new sexual partners, while marriages remove others from the pool and, additionally, create new family alliances. All of these major events are accompanied by ceremonies because they signal a recalibration of standing social relations, and these ceremonies are especially loud and elaborate not because the gods need to know but because others in the community do.

Other powerful dynamics of social relations are at work in the context of ritual practices and settings, even those that are more clearly *religious* in nature, such as baptisms, bar mitzvahs, and communion. As social actions, religious rituals are collective activities performed by groups of participants. While some religious groups are ecumenically minded, most exist as locally bounded communities. (Interestingly, Robin Dunbar's estimate that socially manageable groups consist of 150 members closely mirrors the average size of many religious communities, such as Christian congregations in the United States.) In the context of religious communities, rituals help to foster group identity by activating intuitions governing social exchange. Religious rituals often call for the sharing of resources, for significant intellectual and emotional commitments, and for other hard-to-fake signs of cooperation. As a result, natural coalitional behaviors like trust, solidarity, and mutual defense rise over time, as does the cost of defection. Thus rituals themselves are extremely important, whether they are truly efficacious or not, because *not* participating in them provokes distrust. Note that all of these social responses lie below the level of belief in gods or religious doctrines. Religious ideas merely provide a focus for social capacities that are already operative.

It might appear, then, that god concepts are extraneous to religious practice or that the vertical dimension of religious rituals is no longer relevant. Yet neither impression is true. Religious rituals are "religious" precisely because they assume the participation of gods in the ritual action, and it is this dimension that occupies people's minds. Ritual participants do not see gods merely as add-ons to actions that would work in any case. In religious rituals gods are believed to be causal agents in salient human actions, without which such actions would be empty. During rites of passage gods institute or sanction the physical and social changes. During ordinations and initiations gods empower and validate new religious and political roles. Gods forgive and protect in response to sacrifice and praise. Gods heal and bless in accord with chants and prayers. In short, people have expectations about the mechanisms and efficacy of religious actions, and these expectations are based on causal assumptions regarding supernatural agency and intuitive understandings of social exchange. Gods gain plausibility and relevance simply by virtue of their place in the structure of socially oriented religious rituals. God concepts and ritual behaviors may not necessarily be two sides of the same coin, but once gods are closely connected to salient human activities, it strengthens the idea that gods are present and involved in our lives.

Another way that participation in religious practices contributes to the success of god concepts is through the creation and resolution of what Leon Festinger calls "cognitive dissonance" (1957). According to Festinger, all of us hold in our minds a multitude of "cognitions," which can be thought of as individual pieces of knowledge. Festinger's theory of cognitive dissonance is specifically concerned with the mental relationships between these cognitions. The relationships between a great many of our cognitions are irrelevant because they have no or only slight connections with one another. Consonant relationships occur between cognitions when one cognition follows from or fits with another. Festinger argues that people naturally prefer consonance among their cognitions since it leads to a stable sense of the world. Some of our cognitions, however, exist in a relationship of dissonance because they conflict. The recognition of dissonant cognitions creates a state of psychological tension that, according to Festinger, people are driven to reduce. The principle way this is achieved is by changing or altering cognitions to bring them into alignment.

Many people find themselves participating in religious rituals even though they have no personal commitments to the ideas behind them. It may seem that these events would have no effects whatsoever on such individuals, and if they occur only occasionally then this assumption will probably remain true. However, psychologists have long been aware of the fact that people's thinking is affected by their behaviors as much as their behaviors are determined by their thinking. Festinger's theory suggests that sufficient exposure to discordance ideas, and in the case of religious practices actually behaving in ways that affirm those ideas, can cause individuals to adjust previous beliefs. Acting *as if* we believe something promotes belief itself. Religious rituals are particularly successful in this respect because they feature highly emotive practices that influence participants in less rational though equally powerful ways. The effects of cognitive dissonance also continue to work on those already religiously committed. As people invest greater levels of time and resources into religious practices—regular attendance, personal relationships, mission work, financial support, and so on—their commitment to the gods that motivate such behaviors is proportionately reinforced and strengthened.

Similar psychological forces are at work as we encounter religious ideas in the environment and interact with people who believe in gods. Throughout the whole of this discussion of cognition the focus has been on individual minds. The natural propensities of human thought make religious ideas attractive to us even in the absence of input from others. But other people do find religious ideas compelling, and this fact is not incidental to the content of your own mind. Social pressures exert a strong influence on all of our thoughts and behaviors. Conformity is a powerful if unattractive social behavior. We cannot enter into serious or lasting social relations unless we bring our thoughts and behaviors into alignment with those of others. Coalitions form between "like-minded" people. Public religious practices encourage belief in supernatural agents because they advertise the commitments of others. If those "others" include in-group individuals or people we admire or trust, then the plausibility and relevance of religious ideas increases. Previous chapters have attempted to show that god concepts are actually "reasonable" given the make up of our minds, but it is also true that we accept ideas simply because others do. Knowing that gods matter to other people helps to make them matter to us. As Barrett argues, "belief in gods in human groups may be an inevitable consequence of the sorts of minds we are born with in the sort of world we are born into" (2004: 91).

So gods matter largely for reasons that are biological rather than theological in origin. Due to the shaping work of selective forces in our evolutionary past, human beings have minds that easily and quite naturally entertain religious concepts. And for equally natural reasons, religious concepts can easily become personally compelling. The ordinary properties that structure representations of gods activate the brain's most powerful inference systems, while the extraordinary properties of god concepts make them seem highly relevant to human life. These mental responses are governed by cognitive processes that are automatic, nonconscious, and shared by people everywhere—a claim supported by the ubiquity and similarity of god concepts the world over.

Yet an explanation of the cognitive foundation of religious ideas cannot end here. Until now, we have been considering how god concepts can become both plausible and relevant to the human mind, but plausibility and relevance do not equal belief. Although almost everyone knows what gods are, not everyone believes that they actually exist. Public surveys regularly measure the religious beliefs of people and, depending on locale, the number of those who say that they hold them remains quite high. The United States, for example, is "a nation where nineteen in twenty people say they believe in God" (*Time*, June 21, 2004). The point, however, is that just because a concept is possible does not mean that it will be accepted as real. What really calls for an explanation is not that some people do not believe in gods but that other people *do*. Why, in the end, do so many people decide that invisible, unproven, and, at least on the surface, quite unbelievable supernatural beings in fact exist and choose to live their lives in accord with this commitment? Answering this difficult question requires that we move from the "naturalness of religious ideas" to the "naturalness of religious belief."

"The Heart Has Its Reasons of which Reason Knows Nothing"

Conventional descriptions of the Enlightenment in Europe bespeak a celebration of reason, a vanity fair fomented by the intellectual and scientific revolutions of the seventeenth century: Descartes' mind, Galileo's cosmos, and Newton's physics. Amid the sentiments spilling into the public square were an exuberant sense of adventure and a newfound faith in the grandeur and centrality of the human race. Microscopes and mathematics revealed the world to be rational, mechanistic, and just waiting to be harnessed in the service of society. Many of the demonstrable new facts about nature stirred the imagination because they eclipsed traditional religious claims. It seemed that the human mind could now be reckoned as discoverer and master of the universe, a belief culminating in the slow, somber procession of intelligentsia that A. N. Wilson calls "God's funeral" (1999).

But as Voltaire and the *philosophes* ushered in a new age, a number of equally gifted contemporaries looked upon the promises of autonomy with despair and the powers of reason with doubt. Most notable among these was Blaise Pascal, one of the greatest luminaries of France's *grand siècle*. A groundbreaking mathematician, physicist, and inventor, Pascal was also a profound religious thinker. His conversion experience, as striking and dramatic as any recorded in history, was preserved on a scrap of parchment found sewn into the lining of a discarded doublet by a servant after his death:

> From about half-past ten in the evening until about half-past twelve.
> FIRE.
> The God of Abraham, the God of Isaac, the God of Jacob.
> Not of the philosophers and intellectuals.
> Certitude, certitude, feeling, joy, peace.

While Pascal's "night of fire" on November 23, 1654, was a boon to the Catholic Jansenist movement, it also became a thorn in Voltaire's side. Running throughout Pascal's apology for Christian faith was a conviction of the folly of man and, more iconoclastic, of the inadequacy of human reason. Pascal certainly believed in the utility of reason—he was a scientific prodigy after all—but he condemned the Enlightenment's belief in the sufficiency of reason as both hubris and delusion. In Shakespearean fashion, Pascal maintained that there is more to heaven and earth than is discernable by rational reflection alone. In order to apprehend God as an object of belief and not merely as a proposition, reason must be joined with the "heart."

What redeems this otherwise prosaic argument is what Pascal meant by this term. In Pascal's vocabulary, heart is not a word for feelings or emotions but for a *mode of thinking* best understood as "intuition." Intuition for Pascal is a compelling and effective method of comprehending certain things without having to reason our way to them. In addition to being a mode of thinking distinct from reason, intuition also supplies the basic apprehensions that reason requires for its own operation. Of course, Pascal's desire was to distance these two modes of thinking rather than to highlight their confluence. His final defense of faith was that belief in a supernatural entity is supported by intuition rather than by logical reflection, hence the most famous of his *pensées*: "The heart has its reasons of which reason knows nothing."

Pascal's arguments are rather different from the claims of cognitive science, but his thinking with respect to what stands behind religious belief is more in line with its findings than one might suspect. At the very least, Pascal's juxtaposition of logic and intuition offers a valuable starting point for discussing the nature of belief in general and for understanding belief in gods in particular. Exploring this phenomenon requires first thinking about the nature of belief itself. What does it really mean to *believe* something? What are the requirements for belief? Are all forms of belief the same? And what might Pascal be on to with respect to each of these queries? For the moment, this means leaving aside gods and religion and talking about belief in general. The act of belief is related to the object of a belief in the same way that a mental representation is related to the cognitive processes that formed it. Religious belief is no more a special category of believing than religious thought is a special category of thinking. Once again, the underlying processes of mind are responsible for its products—in the religious domain as well as in the secular.

As the following discussion strives to make clear, belief in gods indeed is largely an activity of the heart, the cumulative effect of intuitions that renders gods not only plausible but believable too. Pascal knew well what he was saying in implicating intuition as the seat of religious belief, though there is no reason to view intuition as somehow less intelligent or rational than other, more explicit modes of thinking. Indeed, much of the "reasoning" we do, as well as many of the "reasonable" conclusions that we come to, owe their existence to the supporting work of the kinds of intuitive thinking processes discussed in this and previous chapters. With regard to belief in gods, few people ever truly "reason" their way to it. "I believe in order that I may understand," Anselm's summary of Augustine's famous position on the relationship between faith and reason, is more typical of religious commitment. But the same is true of many secular beliefs and opinions.

So, what does it mean to believe something? And is believing in a god or gods different from believing in, say, the Easter Bunny, hard work, or a heliocentric solar system? A thought-provoking story recounted by Boyer provides a nice entrée into the subject of belief, one that helps by blurring any lingering boundaries between a religious and a secular form of belief, and, equally, by calling into question the tactic of referring to religious belief as "faith" and secular belief as "knowledge":

> Many people in the world would find it strange if you told them that they "believe in" witches and ghosts or that they have "faith" in their ancestors. Indeed, it would be very difficult in most languages to translate these sentences. It takes us Westerners some effort to realize that this notion of "believing in something" is peculiar. Imagine

a Martian telling you how interesting it is that you "believe" in mountains and rivers and cars and telephones. You would think the alien has got it wrong. We don't "believe in" these things, we just notice and accept that they are around. Many people in the world would say the same about witches and ghosts. They are around like trees and animals—though they are far more difficult to understand and control—so it does not require a particular commitment or faith to notice their existence and act accordingly. In the course of my anthropological fieldwork in Africa, I lived and worked with Fang people, who say that nasty spirits roam the bush and the villages, attack people, make them fall ill and ruin their crops. My Fang acquaintances also knew that I was not too worried about this and that most Europeans were remarkably indifferent to the power of spirits and witches. This, for me, could be expressed as the difference between believing in spirits and not believing. But that was not the way people saw it over there. For them, the spirits were indeed around but white people were immune to their influence, perhaps because God cast them from a different mold or because Western people could avail themselves of efficient anti-witchcraft medicine. So what we often call faith others may well call knowledge. (2001: 9–10)

Of the several lessons taught by this example, one of the most important is that people largely hold their beliefs unselfconsciously. Personal beliefs and personal knowledge are part of the same system of reflection, and both are drawn on to perceive, interpret, and interact with the objects and events that make up daily life. Belief itself is not unnatural, even beliefs about unnatural things. In fact, judgments about beliefs are generally made from the outside, by people who do not share them, and most often it is only when someone else calls a particular belief into question that you step back to look at it with a critical eye. Nor is belief to be regarded as a diminutive or unsubstantiated form of knowledge. Every bit of information one holds, like every opinion one arrives at, needs to be recognized with the term "belief."

But this is frequently the bone of contention in discussions of faith and reason, belief and knowledge. Blaise Pascal's well-educated and imminently "reasonable" contemporaries pinned their hopes and lavished praise on reason precisely because they deemed it capable of cutting through unfounded beliefs and superstitious faith and arriving at true knowledge logically evaluated and clear-mindedly obtained. The problem, though, is that only someone wearing blinders can argue for this view of knowledge acquisition. While such careful, calculated thinking certainly takes place—scientists, for example, try very hard to emulate this process and hold their compatriots accountable to it—in everyday life the formation of the majority of our beliefs, even for the well educated and reasonable, follows a less rigorous course.

Discussing how people arrive at and use beliefs requires first considering what beliefs are. While most definitions of mental phenomena are unsatisfactory, beliefs can be roughly described as representational states that are observable through the behaviors they cause. This suggests that beliefs are somehow housed in the mind as propositions or dispositions where they maintain the potential to influence behavior and further thinking under the right circumstances. A common explanation for the way beliefs are retained is that our minds include a kind of mental storehouse, a "belief box," whose representational contents are accessed as needed.

While the idea of a belief box is attractive—having much in common with the way we think about memory—it does not fully account for the way beliefs are generated by the mind. First, it is simply impossible from the perspective of storage capacity that every bit of propositional knowledge could be retained by the mind in representational form. Fred Attneave has used the same argument to illustrate the feat of visual perception, pointing out that the volume of a brain needed to literally represent every image we can immediately recognize would be measured in light years (1954). Second, many of our beliefs are formed spontaneously, on the spot, and are not otherwise held in the mind. As an example, it's highly probable that you believe that this book cannot swim. It is equally probable that you did not have a representation of that belief until this very moment. We all have innumerable *unrepresented beliefs* of this sort. If this is the case, then the belief box approach explains lots of beliefs we maintain throughout life but not all, or even most, of them.

The ease with which an unrepresented belief becomes a represented belief suggests that a now-familiar cognitive process is at work as we form and express many of our beliefs. Just as various concepts are the products of mental inference devices that automatically and nonconsciously enrich conceptual structures with a host of intuitive expectations, so many beliefs are products of a process in which one belief is inferred from others. It remains possible, even highly probable, that we possess a belief box containing a set of basic beliefs from which additional beliefs are inferred, but one must also recognize a quick, nonconscious inference device as an integral part of the system.

Another issue to consider when discussing human belief is the fact that beliefs can originate in different ways. Clearly not all of our beliefs arrive by the same route or are held for the same reasons. Your previously unrepresented belief that this book cannot swim became represented instantaneously. Neither this nor any book can swim, and your assent to that fact required no encouragement or proof. In fact, if someone suggested that a book could swim, it would become quite clear just how strong your unrepresented belief had been. By contrast, a large percentage of our beliefs arise from precisely that source—communication. From the moment of birth we start to store up beliefs, which, through life, are variously solidified, transformed, or discarded. Many of our most cherished and important beliefs are acquired from others and continue to be held on the basis of authority.

The social scientist Dan Sperber has produced one of the most useful cognitive accounts of how people acquire, hold, and employ beliefs, one that takes seriously the multifaceted and dynamic nature of belief formation. According to Sperber, there are two fundamental kinds of beliefs represented in minds, and these two kinds of belief differ in their origins, application, and strength (1996, 1997). Sperber calls the first of these kinds of beliefs "intuitive beliefs" and the second kind "reflective beliefs."

Intuitive beliefs, the kind of basic beliefs that ought to be found in a belief box, are concrete, commonsense descriptions of the real world derived from perception and spontaneous, nonconscious inferences. Intuitive beliefs are intuitive both in the sense that they are products of innate cognitive mechanisms and in that you need not be aware of holding them, even less of the reasons why. Nonetheless, because intuitive beliefs arise from reliable perceptions and inferences, they are rigidly held. Examples of intuitive beliefs include the belief that when you are tired you should sleep, that you cannot walk through walls, and that books cannot swim. Notice that this is precisely the kind of knowledge equated in chapter 2 with intuitive biology, physics, and psychology. Intuitive beliefs are so obvious that they hardly seem like "beliefs" at all, yet they are. Countless such beliefs continually operate in the background of daily thought, supporting conscious reasoning and guiding behavior.

Reflective beliefs are what people normally understand by the word "belief." Instead of being derived automatically and nonconsciously, reflective beliefs come from conscious, deliberate reasoning or from external sources of authority like parents, teachers, and books. Reflective beliefs are usually explanatory and interpretative rather than descriptive. Reflective beliefs may or may not be fully understood or well grounded and, consequently, people's commitment to them vary widely, from loosely held notions to dogmatic convictions. The range of reflective beliefs includes everything from learned in-

TABLE 4.2 Differences between intuitive beliefs and reflective beliefs.

Intuitive Beliefs	Reflective Beliefs
1. Concrete, commonsense descriptions of the world	1. Explanations and interpretations of the world
2. Derived from perception and spontaneous inference	2. Derived from deliberate thought and sources of authority
3. Usually implicitly held	3. Usually explicitly held
4. Support conscious reasoning and guide behavior	4. Embedded in intuitive beliefs and other reflective beliefs
5. Universal, homogenous, and consistent	5. Local, heterogeneous, and variable

formation ($a^2 + b^2 = c^2$) to knowledge derived from experience (sisters don't like to be teased) to matters of opinion (drink red wine with beef).

A final difference between intuitive and reflective beliefs is that because intuitive beliefs are derived from cognitive processes that are innate and common to all human minds, they are not only homogenous in kind—comprising concrete descriptions of the world—but are also universally and consistently held, regardless of cultural context. Reflective beliefs, by contrast, may or may not be universal, are heterogeneous in kind, and, because they generally amount to flexible interpretations, display great variability based on local influences. Reflective beliefs, therefore, are the variety of beliefs that have frequently given rise to notions of cultural relativism.

The differences between intuitive and reflective beliefs tell us quite a bit about the knowledge content of our minds and how it comes to be. At the very least they make clear the fact that "belief" is a more complex, and in many ways a less introspective mental activity than general discussions of the subject would suggest. Indeed, while each of the differences between intuitive and reflective beliefs is significant, the most illuminating is that reflective beliefs often rest on intuitive beliefs. In Sperber's words, reflective beliefs are "interpretations of representations embedded in the validating context of an intuitive belief" (1996: 89). That is, reflective beliefs are shaped and supported by other, innately derived beliefs, though they might be embedded in other reflective beliefs as well.

Reflective beliefs are influenced by intuitive beliefs primarily because intuitive beliefs provide the default assumptions that underpin reflective beliefs. As an example, most of us believe that any two objects will fall to the ground at the same rate. This is a reflective belief concerning gravity that was taught to us and probably required a demonstration before it was accepted. What this reflective belief requires, though, is a previous understanding that objects in fact fall to the ground when released. This is an intuitive belief—derived from our intuitive physics—that all people share and that, interestingly, is neither itself in need of demonstration nor made an explicit part of the final reflective belief. Similarly, intuitive beliefs are routinely operating in the background of most of our reflective beliefs, supplying the host of default assumptions that make conscious reasoning possible but nevertheless go largely unnoticed.

Furthermore, reflective beliefs frequently derive their veracity from their connections with intuitive beliefs. As Sperber puts it, reflective beliefs are "believed in virtue of second-order beliefs about them" (1996: 98). The closer the fit and the wider the connections between a reflective belief and the intuitive beliefs that support it, the more plausible the reflective belief appears. Not all reflective beliefs are directly linked to intuitive beliefs. Some reflective beliefs, like $e = mc^2$, are (at least to most of us) just plain abstract propositions held for purely explicit reasons. But reflective beliefs that are grounded in intuitive beliefs are easily assimilated, less provisional, and more firmly held. What all this means is that many of our reflective beliefs, like all of our intuitive beliefs, ultimately owe their existence to the operation of the innate mental mechanisms our minds use to organize and interpret the world. The intuitive beliefs generated by these mental mechanisms serve as building blocks for reflective thought.

The question we are interested in here, of course, is which kind of belief is religious belief? Is belief in gods intuitive or reflective? And does it matter to the explanation of why so many people exercise belief in supernatural agents? The immediate answer is that belief in gods is surely a reflective belief. Despite the claims of apostles and theologians, humans do not simply infer the existence of divine beings from consideration of the natural world. God concepts are communicated, and they must be acquired before they can be believed. However, belief in gods is hardly assenting to an abstract proposition, the way that belief in $e = mc^2$ is. Belief in god, rather, is a textbook example of a reflective belief that arises from and is supported by intuitive beliefs.

Whenever people talk about gods, they are always exchanging reflective beliefs. Whether a god is trinitarian or singular in being, whether a god answers prayers, whether a god likes the smell of burnt offerings—all such theological pronouncements are examples of reflective beliefs. Nevertheless, all of these reflective beliefs also require the support of intuitive beliefs if they are to make any sense. The reflective belief that a god likes burnt offerings, for instance, rests on the intuitive belief that the god actually has desires. Yet no one, not even the theologian, stops to consider why *that* claim should be true. People do not need divine scriptures or special religious education to teach them basic facts about supernatural agents. The mental mechanisms we use to understand agents in general supply this information automatically.

Intuitive beliefs and the mental mechanisms that generate them play the same supporting role in the foundational reflective religious belief: that a god(s) actually exists. The first chapters of this book strove to isolate the mental mechanisms of the human mind that contribute to thinking about gods and that make them seem both plausible and relevant to our lives. In spite of some extraordinary, counterintuitive properties, god concepts fit nicely into the mind's natural ontological categories and therefore activate a rich array of inference systems. Mental modules like ADD and ToMM recognize these concepts as important and fill in extensive details about what supernatural agents should be like, drawing in particular from intuitive psychology. In addition, gods are represented in such a way that they engage the mind's powerful faculties of social intelligence, rendering them of immediate interest in the ordering and management of social interaction.

So god concepts activate a number of prominent mental mechanisms and, as a result, our thinking about gods is closely supported by a large number of intuitive beliefs. We can see, then, how the close fit between god concepts and the mind's ordinary cognitive processes not only contributes to the plausibility of god concepts but also strongly encourages people to believe in them. God concepts are not merely supported by intuitive beliefs, but *richly so*. Barrett argues for the general principle that "the more mental tools with which an idea fits, the more likely it is to become a reflective belief" (2004: 15). If this is indeed the case (a proposition backed by study of a wide range of beliefs), then god concepts ought to be profoundly compelling (a conclusion proven by the ubiquity of religious faith). Belief in gods is particularly common and particularly tenacious because gods fit with the principle particularly well. In fact, Barrett finds belief in gods to be so "natural" to the human mind that arguments are actually needed to explain why someone would *not* believe in gods: "Being an atheist is not easy. In many ways, it just goes against the grain. As odd as it sounds, it isn't natural to reject all supernatural agents" (2004: 108).

Boyer explains the phenomenon of religious belief in similar terms. For Boyer, the question of "belief" loses its edge amid the web of interconnected mental systems involved in the acquisition, representation, and transmission of religious concepts. The notion of religious belief is usually associated with a clear, direct, and conscious intellectual assent to propositional claims. It is thought that religious systems provide reasoned descriptions of supernatural agents and their moral demands, and that people are then convinced (or not) that these propositions are true and that their related moral behaviors are necessary. From Boyer's point of view the process is somewhat less clear, considered, or conscious. The phenomenon of religious belief is the result of *"aggregate relevance*—that is, of successful activation of a whole variety of mental systems" (2001: 298). People's general ontological and inferential systems render supernatural concepts intuitively plausible. Believable supernatural concepts are ones that also trigger important social effects and create strong emotional states.

Inevitably, this picture of religious belief raises questions concerning its "reasonableness" and "rationality," just as it did for Blaise Pascal's contemporaries. But as the preceding conversation suggests, beliefs—religious or otherwise—may only rarely meet the demands of thought that the intelligentsia deem reasonable and rational. Not many of our reflective beliefs are the result of a close, logical evaluation of empirical proofs or of a careful weighing of all the relevant evidence. Indeed, from the perspective of cognition the very notion of "rationality" is as misconstrued as the notion of "belief." Rational thought might better be defined not on the basis of syllogistic reasoning or some system of procedural rules but, rather, on the consistency of our cognitive processes and how well the mental representations produced by those processes correspond with our environment. In order words, do epistemological conclusions make good *biological* rather than philosophical sense? Are our mental inferences consistent with and warranted by perception and cognition?

This line of thinking relates directly to humankind's evolutionary journey.

The mental mechanisms we use to form beliefs were designed to contribute to survival in a hostile world and success in a competitive society. Displaying fear at a rustling bush may qualify as "irrational," but it is a perfectly sensible response for minds like ours. It might be "unreasonable" to assume without hard evidence that a friend has lied to you, but we arrive at such conclusions all the time. Our mental systems are not concerned with degrees of rationality or careful logic. They exist to produce rapid and reliable beliefs that aid survival. Nor are our mental systems interested in abstract questions of truth. Still, while minds are fallible and their perceptions sometimes wrong, intuitive beliefs turn out to correspond remarkably well with reality because they are the products of adapted, time-tested mental systems. On the other hand, discursive thought is certainly no guarantee of truth. Many reflective beliefs prove false because they are based on faulty reasoning, inadequate or inaccurate evidence, and matters of opinion.

From the standpoint of cognition, then, rationality is *cognitive consistency*. Intuitive beliefs owe their rationality to the innate perceptual and inferential mechanisms involved in organizing and interpreting the world. Reflective beliefs owe their rationality to compatibility with intuitive beliefs or with supportive reflective beliefs formed in the same way. Religious beliefs are rationally held, according to this account, because god concepts activate a number of prominent mental mechanisms and, as a result, reflective thinking about gods is consistently supported by a large number of intuitive beliefs. This process constitutes a rather powerful system of "reasoning"—the mind is hard at work constructing, understanding, and deciding—it just may not square with ideals held by purveyors of Reason.

When Pascal spoke of the "reasons of the heart" he may not have been envisioning intuitive knowledge processes in relation to literal mental systems in the mind, but he still managed to capture the fundamental nature of belief formation, including religious belief. Belief in gods is indeed based on reasons of which Reason knows nothing. Human thought and behavior is guided in large part by intuitions produced by cognitive processes that are innate, automatic, and nonconscious. In a religious context, these intuitions help to render gods not only plausible but believable too.

Pascal's critics insist that people have good reasons for their beliefs, yet that's not the way belief generally works. Many of the "reasons" that we put forth to explain particular reflective beliefs we hold are simply post hoc justifications that had little to do with the belief's actual formation. Furthermore, a good number of our reflective beliefs have *no* explicit reasons for support because none are called for. If intuitive beliefs get the job done, we don't stop to draw up more reflective arguments. Explicit reasoning or elaboration only comes later. The same is true of religious belief. Lots of people can give explicit reasons for their belief in gods, but few if any of these explicit reasons were actually part of the mental process that formed the original belief. Religious belief, rather, arises from that mode of thinking correctly identified by Pascal as intuition—the output of mental systems that find god concepts eminently workable. To minds like ours, gods are naturally conceived and naturally believed.

5

Gods and Religious Systems

What Does Religion Have to Do with Gods?

The lessons of the first part of this book are simply put. People have minds that easily and quite naturally entertain religious concepts. And for equally natural reasons, religious concepts can easily become personally compelling. Given evolutionary history and the human need to take seriously all sorts of agents, including those that are ethereal, it is not at all unreasonable—as many "straight-minded" atheists would have it—for well-educated individuals to confess belief in, and adjust their lives in response to, the kinds of non-natural agents that ground religion.

Yet religious ideas do not stay confined to individuals' heads. Ideas about non-natural agents, like many other kinds of ideas, make their way into the world. Gods of sundry names and natures are everywhere, for sale if you will, in the public marketplace. It is this public presence of religious ideas, also like many other kinds of ideas, that allow different people to browse among them, pick them up and look them over, perhaps take them home. Sometimes something even more extraordinary happens to religious ideas—and here quite *unlike* many other kinds of ideas—once they enter the public square. Around the supernatural agent concepts that people like best there begins to swirl systematized reflection (doctrines), prescribed behaviors (rituals), and social structure (community). It is this visible concatenation of human activities centered on supernatural agents that we call "religion."

Interestingly, neither this particular ordering of events nor this implicit definition of religion is widely accepted (Stark 2003). Strange as it may sound at first, religion scholars are wont to ask: "Is 'religion' really about gods at all?" The most influential figures have regarded the presence of gods in religious systems as, if not irrelevant, then at least of secondary significance. The three enduring explanations for religion appeal instead to human psychology, wonderment, and social longing. Psychological explanations for religion see it as a means for assuaging daily anxiety in a troubling world and for allaying more distant existential concerns like death. Intellectualist explanations regard religion as the way inquisitive humans fill gaps in knowledge, from small queries like the reason for thunder to big ones like the meaning of suffering and the origin of life. Social explanations for religion see it as a powerful tool for creating communal identity, cohesion, and order. According to each of these perspectives, the roles that gods play in religion are instrumental rather than foundational.

What "religion" is and how—even *if*—it relates to god concepts is a crucial question. And it is precisely this question that will be addressed from various angles throughout the last chapters of this book. Answering this question correctly requires first getting the definition of religion right. What one chooses to call "religion" determines both the method of study and its final outcome. For example, defining religion in terms of function—"religion is what it *does*"—means that religion can be interpreted, but never explained. Similarly, speaking of religion in purely symbolic terms—"religion *represents* this or that"—means that literally anything can be construed as "religious."

In stark contrast, most scholars approaching the phenomenon of religion from the perspective of cognition recognize that it displays at least one recurrent feature: attention to supernatural agents. While religion *does* function in ways that serve a range of human needs—psychological, intellectual, and social—and while religion *does* take on rich symbolic meanings, it is clear from libraries of anthropological work that supernatural agents are not merely ornaments in religious systems but are the objects around which religious belief, behavior, and community coalesce. As Pascal Boyer has come to see, the notion of superhuman entities and agency is the only substantive universal found in religious ideas (1994a: 9). If a ubiquity of gods is indeed the case, then it would seem that contrary to the dominant views of religion just mentioned, gods are in fact foundational and it is *religion* that is instrumental.

Illka Pyysiäinen recently used just this argument to take on some of the heavyweights of functionalist and symbolist thought—thinkers like anthropologist Clifford Geertz and sociologist Emile Durkheim. Among the many failings of Geertz's famous definition of religion as a "cultural system" are its refusal to root things "symbolic" in real cognitive mechanisms and its inability to delimit (from a profound vagueness) what is distinctive about religion. This, according to Pyysiäinen, takes reference to the appearance and use of counterintuitive agents: "Religion is a phenomenon based on the human ability to form counterintuitive ideas, metarepresent them, and treat them symbolically" (2001b: 53). As for Durkheim, who equates religion with the maintenance of society, Pyysiäinen shows that although religion has important social functions, these functions cannot be the *cause* of religion. Again, we must move to the level of psychological mechanisms to explain the arising of the very beliefs that are put to social use: "The social effects of religion would not be possible in the absence of a belief in agents that have counterintuitive capacities to bless, condemn, revenge, save, protect, etc." (2001b: 72).

These arguments illustrate that the strength of the cognitive approach to religion does not lie in empirical observation as such, but in empirical observation *from a particular vantage point*. Cognitivists look at the phenomenon of religion from below rather than from above—religion as the product of thought rather than as a *sui generis* entity—and the view from "down here" yields a telling description of its weave. This vantage point also directly challenges some of the most sacrosanct presumptions of contemporary social science, including the highly touted notion of "cultural relativism." If all human cultures are distinct and bounded, as many anthropologists believe, then on what basis can a study of one or more products between two or more cultures be thought to be meaningful? If cultural products are purely local, can there be such pan-cultural categories as "religion"? Finally, given the diversity of singular cultures, shouldn't we acknowledge that religious beliefs and practices are simply too broad ranging and too different to be enveloped into one explanatory model?

The unique vantage point of cognition turns the long-standing notions of cultural relativism upside-down. While not denying a considerable variation in knowledge from person to person, let alone from culture to culture, cognitivists studying the *noncultural* foundations of knowledge have found that human thought is neither as relative nor as diverse as culturalists assume. As Steven Pinker points out, "contrary to the widespread belief that cultures can vary arbitrarily and without limit, surveys of the ethnographic literature show that the people of the world share an astonishingly detailed universal psychology" (1997: 32). This shared psychology is the result of minds that operate according to biologically prescribed rules—rules that are not culture- but *species*-specific. This means that mental products are equally tractable between family members, neighbors, and cultures. In the final analysis, cultural variation has much more to do with the *use* to which ideas are put than to their genesis or content.

This is as true of religious ideas as it is of other kinds. "Religion" is a pan-cultural phenomenon precisely because all people everywhere are naturally predisposed to acquire it. Nor are warnings concerning diversity or difference more worrisome to students of religion. As the first part of this book demonstrates, when we cut beneath the variegation in religious representations found around the world, we find a basic set of cognitive building blocks that simultaneously constrains possible variation and betrays an underlying unity to the diversity that does exist. Contrary to the assumptions of cultural relativism, the menu of religious options is nowhere as diverse as it is taken to be. The types of ideas that lie at the core of religious systems are surprisingly limited. The use to which *these particular ideas* are put can and do vary greatly from time to time and place to place, but *these particular ideas* are selected from a short list of choices that proves to be universal and recurrent because it is supported by a psychology that is itself trans-historical and cross-cultural. It is attention to this shared psychology, and to the conceptual unity beneath cultural diversity, that revivifies the "comparative" study of religion, providing it, as Luther Martin notes, with "a non-ethnocentric framework for analogical religious constructs" (2000: 54).

The finer points of this discussion are academic, having to do with matters of theory and method, but they lead to the second major theme of this book. When it comes to talk of "religion," we cross a border from cognition to culture, from ideas as they are held in individuals' heads to their public use. Loosely speaking, religious ideas and religion are two different things. This is a problematic statement for a number of reasons. As this and the next chapter explain, cognition and culture are intimately connected, the later identifiable *only* with reference to the former. Yet it is also crucial to see that things happen to "private" ideas once they become "public." In the process of enculturation, mental concepts are expanded on, manipulated, and transformed. Some of these changes are beneficial, contributing to a concept's social success. Conceptual transformation is not boundless, however. There is a limit to the kinds of changes that can be imposed on religious representations. The same cognitive processes that constrain thinking about gods are also at work shaping the religious systems that form around them.

So the complete answer to the question of what religion has to do with gods lies in the relation of cognition and culture. The study of human thought does not stop at the skull but has important things to say about the public life of ideas. As we'll see next, cognition and culture stand in a hierarchical relationship. Rather than regarding culture as the principal composer of mental knowledge, as many social and behavioral scientists do, cognitivists emphasize how minds influence the content and organization of culture. The flaws of traditional explanations for religion result from considering culture (religion) before the psychology (religious ideas) that makes it possible.

Connecting Cognition and Culture

Of all the doctrines of modern anthropology, the most sacred is the belief that culture is a real, autonomous entity residing, somewhere, somehow, "out there." In recent times, many who work daily with culture have come to find this perspective, and even the term itself, to be troubling. Bruce Lincoln's ongoing quest to pin down the ambiguity of "culture" offers a fine illustration:

> Although the term "culture" is a seemingly indispensable part of my professional and everyday vocabulary, whenever I have tried to think through just what it means or how and why we all use it, the exercise has proved both bewildering and frustrating. As a result, I am always on the lookout for serviceable alternatives and my list now includes such items as discourse, practice, ethos, *habitus*, ideology, hegemony, master narrative, canon, tradition, knowledge/power system, pattern of consumption and distinction, society, community, ethnicity, nation and race, all of which manage to specify some part of what is encompassed within the broader, but infinitely fuzzier category of "culture." (2000: 409)

Staking out with precision one's subject matter is notoriously difficult in many disciplines. What is "art"? What is "politics"? What is "economics"? What is "society"? Some who study "religion" have serious reservations about using that term as well (McCutcheon 1997; Fitzgerald 2000). So the problem of defining culture is not necessarily all that grave. We all use fuzzy concepts like "culture" every day without fretting over their meanings or worrying that others have failed to understand our intent. What *is* grave about the modern anthropological handling of culture, however, is the ontological status that has been bestowed upon it. Culture—or more correctly *a* culture—is treated as a real, independent "thing"—or at least the totality of a gathering of discrete things—that exists just outside one's door, and anthropologists spend their time engaged in the representation and interpretation of this totality. Furthermore, culture is not only understood to be the repository of social knowledge but is also empowered as the primary molder and mediator of each individual's thought and behavior. In more common phrasing, this perspective constitutes the social science side of the nature-nurture debate, which sees the human mind as a *tabula rasa* that develops in ways commensurate with a given culture through experience, instruction, and socialization.

Both facets of this standard view of culture are problematic. As to what culture is, precisely, Tomoko Masuzawa notes that the "wholeness" of culture is "anything but immediately apprehendable or readily demonstrable" (1998: 78). Indeed, the best defense for culture as an object for study is to admit it as a *hermeneutical* reality. But holding up a culture, however constructed, as an independent, external entity that orchestrates the mental development of its members is much more problematic. Bradd Shore points out that this model of culture begs a number of questions, two of the most important being: *How is cultural knowledge organized in time and space?* and *How are public forms of knowledge transformed into personal forms of knowledge?* (1996: 11). For those who dismiss naturalistic models of human behavior, these questions are profoundly challenging. Just where is culture located? And just how can cultural input—or external input of any sort, for that matter—register with minds conceived of as blank slates? Today the nature-nurture debate has grown in sophistication as the gap between social and biological theories is closed, but on the whole cognitive models of culture are still met with suspicion.

The crux of the nature-nurture debate involves the kinds of knowledge and mental skills newborn infants are believed to possess. As chapter 2 strove to demonstrate, evolutionary and developmental psychology provides compelling evidence that human brains are genetically engineered to do all kinds of work from the moment of birth. From intuitive ontology to face recognition to language acquisition, human beings arrive hardwired with an array of mental tools—what David and Ann Premack call "original intelligence" (2002)—designed to make sense of an otherwise confusing world. What is more, these fundamental cognitive skills lead on, naturally and with breathtaking speed, to advanced levels of conceptual proficiency. Nowhere is it denied that cultural input plays a significant role in the accumulation and production of mental knowledge, but the essential point is that cultural input is meaningful only because people are already biologically equipped to receive, organize, and transmit it as such. Boldly put, culture is the manufacture of the noncultural machinery of minds.

One of the reasons for ascribing such weight to culture in the nature-nurture debate is the sheer volume of information that each person assimilates from the world around them. We are all born into a booming, cacophonous world of sensations, and from the very start that world seems to have designs for our lives—the clothes we wear, the rules we follow, the way we set table, the education we obtain. But consider for a moment whether all of this external stimuli is equal in kind or relevance. Certain external stimuli, let's call them "environmental cues" (sights, sounds, objects, other beings, and so on), directly engage the innate mechanisms of the brain and serve as the building blocks for higher prehensions. Continued interaction with environmental cues brings about the maturation of minds, including the progressive fruition of the mental competencies charted by developmental psychologists. There are also external stimuli that are properly "cultural" in nature (art, writing, customs, values, and so on), which, while taken to be terribly important by social scientists, are actually inconsequential from a biological standpoint. One can get along quite well without mastering the techniques of cubism, reading *Les Miserables*, participating in a Hopi rain dance, or affirming the benefits of democracy. Cognitivists also find it telling that the mind is predisposed to acquire some forms of knowledge with remarkable ease and speed, while other forms of knowledge require rigorous training to grasp. In very short order and with no formal education, all normal children achieve the astounding feat of speech; proficiency in molecular chemistry takes a bit more effort and instruction. But notice, language has noncultural foundations; molecular chemistry does not.

Reversing the standard line on culture by arguing that culture is not a real, autonomous entity but is instead the commodity of minds, and that cultural knowledge does not form otherwise empty brains but is itself rested on noncultural foundations of thought, requires a model of cognition and culture that successfully explains how "mental" ideas become "public," how they diversify, and how they are shared by others. The most fruitful "naturalistic" approach to culture is championed by Dan Sperber (1996). Sperber's originality lies in talking about culture in the same way that the medical community studies the transmission of infectious disease. In the science known as epidemiology, researchers strive to understand and track how contagion takes hold and spreads through a population. Periodically—consider today's worldwide AIDS/HIV epidemic or the localized SARS outbreak of 2003—illnesses of various sorts invade communities and propagate. Once active, such illnesses may remain permanent fixtures of the social landscape, pass as quickly as they arrived, assume a dormant state, or mutate into something new. Part of the job of epidemiologists is to determine which of the huge number of illness-causing organisms alive in the environment are presently or potentially infectious, to isolate the particular factors that make these organisms contagious in the first place, and to describe how they get passed from person to person.

Why is the epidemiology of disease a useful model for exploring culture? First, culture like contagion is something that is shared across a group of people. At the same time, epidemiologists don't imagine that disease—as many anthropologists imagine culture—exists somewhere "out there," on its own, infecting people who unwittingly come into contact with it; rather, infectious agents reside *in individuals*. People infect other people. Communication and contraction are biological events. Second, the fundamental units of culture and contagion, ideas and viruses, are also analogous. Just as an individual human body is inhabited by organisms that may be spread to another body, so an individual human brain is inhabited by ideas that may be spread to another brain. Third, epidemiological models in general recognize that macro-scale effects are the result of micro-scale causes. One infectious person begins an epidemic; one clever notion starts a fade.

By reorienting the work of anthropology as the study of the distribution of ideas, as an "epidemiology of representations," Sperber points us directly to what culture actually is and how it works. Each of us entertains a multitude of ideas. The life of these ideas can follow several trajectories. They may arise for only a moment, barely noticed, part of the "noise" of normal cognition. They may belong to a chain of ideas carrying thought on to new places. They may reside in long-term memory, as images of personal experiences or part of one's general encyclopedia of knowledge. At this level, ideas are both invisible and inaccessible to others. Sperber calls ideas that exist in individual minds, which are "internal to the information-processing device," *mental representations* (1996: 61). Beliefs, desires, recollections, likes and dislikes—all are examples of mental representations.

The vast majority of ideas people have stay in their heads. But because ideas also determine behavior, some ideas spur actions and creations that are observable by others. People move, send signals, speak; they sing songs, write books, paint pictures, design tools, build. Because actions and creations like these are either direct forms of communication or can be interpreted, they give rise to ideas in the minds of those who observe them. And, because all people think very much alike, sharing species-specific properties of mind, these new ideas will often closely resemble the originals. Sperber calls ideas that are located outside of the information-process device—in the form of speech, texts, pictures, artifacts, and so on—*public representations.*

This model of transmission, from mental representations as the "output" of one mind to the processing of public representations as "input" by another, accounts for how ideas spread from person to person:

> An idea, born in the brain of one individual, may have, in the brains of other individuals, descendents that resemble it. Ideas can be transmitted, and, by being transmitted from one person to another, they may even propagate. Some ideas—religious beliefs, cooking recipes, or scientific hypothesis, for instance—propagate so effectively that, in different versions, they may end up durably invading whole populations. (Sperber 1996: 1)

This model also offers a tighter, more tractable definition of "culture":

> Culture is made up, first and foremost, of such contagious ideas. It is made up also of all the productions (writings, artworks, tools, etc.) the presence of which in the shared environment of a human group permits the propagation of ideas. (1996: 1)

To speak of culture, then, is to speak about ideas that stick. More precisely, culture is composed of the ideas that are *shared in the minds* or *represented in products of the minds* of the people who comprise a social group. The basis for this shared knowledge is communication between what are, quite literally, *like-minded* people.

So *defining* culture within the framework of a naturalistic epidemiology of representations is a relatively simple affair. *Explaining* culture, however, requires a bit more work. Having a general description of the causal process that carries representations between people is a good start, but this general description raises some specific questions that need answering if the epidemiological approach is to be deemed of practical rather than merely analogical use. The first might be phrased something like this: It would seem that the number of mental representations is unlimited. One mind alone produces a staggering number of representations daily. If this is the wellspring of culture, then why does culture appear to have limited, organized patterns? Why isn't there simply a senseless jumble of ideas in the environment, a chaos of culture?

It is certainly true that at any given moment in any given mind there exists a great wealth of representations. But it is also true that the lion's share of these representations enjoy only private lives. As Sperber acknowledges, just as there are many more viruses and bacteria in a human population than those that end up causing widespread illness, so there are also many more mental representations than public ones (1996: 25). Of the millions of representations extant in the minds of individuals, only a few end up getting communicated. Of the few mental representations that are communicated as public representations, fewer still are communicated with enough regularity that they become mental representations in the minds of every member of a population. Culture displays limited, organized patterns in part because only some of the limitless range of mental representations becomes widespread and enduring.

But here, then, comes a second question: Why do only some ideas stick and not others? What factors make specific ideas "catching" such that they spread easily from mind to mind and ultimately wind up as the stable, durable features of culture we recognize across time and place? This is the crucial question, and it lies at the heart of any epidemiological model. In the study of contagion it is understood that not all pathogens are infectious. Of the many bugs that make individuals sick, only certain ones are readily communicable between individuals. An epidemiology of disease seeks to explain the reasons for this. An epidemiology of representations must do the same for ideas. "To explain culture," Sperber writes, "is to explain why and how some ideas happen to be contagious" (1996: 1).

The recognition that only some ideas thrive in the social environment while many others go unheard or soon wither away has led in recent years to Darwinian explanations of cultural transmission. On the surface, at least, there appears a provocative similarity in the way ideas and genes are selected for transmission within a population. Indeed, the work of population genetics is another application of epidemiology. The most compelling example of a Darwinian model of cultural transmission belongs to biologist Richard Dawkins. In his book The Selfish Gene (1976) Dawkins likens ideas and culture to genes and bodies, coining the term "meme" to refer to the fundamental units of culture—beliefs, values, habits, skills, songs, stories, and so on. Essentially, culture can be understood as a population of memes competing for mental space the way genes compete for physical space. Also like genes, memes influence people's behavior in ways that help facilitate their replication, though in the case of memes the process of replication takes place via communication and imitation.

Conceiving of ideas as self-replicating memes competing for survival in a cultural meme pool is engaging, and it certainly overturns the traditional social science model of the culture–mind relationship. The enduring popularity of memes since they were first introduced is itself a confirmation of the reproductive power of novel ideas. Yet there are two fundamental design flaws in what Susan Blackmore calls the "meme machine" (1999). The first flaw is that the analogy between genes and memes breaks down at its most crucial point. The defining characteristic of genes—and the reason that natural selection works—is that they are *replicators*. Replicators are things that make exact copies of themselves. Species retain a stable identity over time because their genes remain stable across many generations of copying. Periodically these replicators mess up and make random copying errors—mutations. Most often an inaccurate copy is detrimental to the replicator's survival and reproduction rate, and they quickly end up in the evolutionary trash heap. Occasionally, though, random copying errors enhance the survival and reproduction rate of the replicator and therefore continue to accumulate over generations. Still, *this* accumulation takes place precisely because the originally inaccurate copy continues its job of making accurate copies of its inaccurate self.

Ideas, however, are *not* replicators. They do not pass from person to person in the form of exact copies. In fact, when it comes to the reproduction of ideas, mutation is the rule rather than a mistaken exception. Brains are not copy machines that receive input from an external source and scan an identical version into memory. Brains are interpreting machines that put external input to use as new representations. As Sperber warns, "the most obvious lesson of recent cognitive work is that recall is not storage in reverse, and comprehension is not expression in reverse; memory and communication transform information" (1996: 31). Through the process of transmission from mental representations to public representations and back again, ideas undergo reconstruction, modification, and change. An obvious example of the speed and liberty with which ideas shift in the process of communication is the parlor game "Pass It On," in which one person speaks a thought into the ear of a second person, who in turn passes it along to a third, and so on down the line. With only a small number of individuals involved in the game, the resulting message is often a striking distortion of the original. Likewise, within a social group certain ideas may be generally stable *in kind*, yet they reside in the minds of individual members in a myriad of variant forms. Thinking of ideas—memes—as cultural genes overlooks the psychological processes they undergo as well as the range of conceptual variation that, if transferred to the biological domain, would quickly decimate a genome.

The second flaw of the meme model is that it still doesn't answer our primary question: Why are some ideas, or memes, better than others? Based on the recurrence of various ideas within and across people groups, it is clear that some representations—or variants of those representations—have a selective advantage, but what factors make these representations recurrent while others fail to catch on? Given that mental representations are not static but undergo transformation with every transmission, and given that every public representation stands in relation to countless mental variants, correctly answering this question requires that we approach the meme account of culture from the opposite angle. What makes a particular representation easy to catch—that is, to comprehend, remember, use, and communicate—is not intrinsic to the *representation* alone but to the representation-processing *device*. The selection of ideas takes place *in the minds* of individuals. So explaining the cultural success of ideas requires consideration of the types of brains that employ them.

A loose analogy provides a fresh starting point: With the advent of direct data exchange between computers—a marvelous idea that has changed all our lives—engineers solved the problem of communication by designing modems that allow one computer to receive information sent by another. At this basic level of transmission, the content of the information is irrelevant; what is important is the matching functionality of the information-processing devices. No matter the quantity or quality of the data, unless two modems are in synch, no inter-computer communication will take place. Nature has solved the same problem in the same way. People are able to send information back and forth, firstly, because their communications equipment is functionally equivalent. As the discussion of the early part of this book endeavored to show, human brains share species-specific design and wiring, including those systems involved in information exchange. Akin to a single line of computer models, all modern human brains can be called MHB 1000s. Furthermore, computers are able to send, receive, and execute common information not only because their hardware is functionally equivalent but also because they process data in the same way. The operating system of my office computer matches the one used by my PC at home, allowing for the easy transfer of digital representations between them. The opening chapters of this book also explored the suite of processing systems that are common to all normal human brains. Akin to computer models whose operating systems are the same right out of the box, all MHB 1000s run on MHB 1.0.

This analogy is germane to the current discussion because it highlights the fundamental relationship between representations and the devices that form and transform them, as well as between the devices that exchange representations. The form and meaning of representations are results of the minds that produced them, and representations can be successfully communicated because other minds recognize this form and meaning. Notice, this statement does not imply that the acquisition and transmission of representations are based solely on a similarity of attributed meaning—communication is not merely the result of a shared language or a correspondence in semantic knowledge—but that the acquisition and transmission of representations have a functional basis; receiving minds *reconstruct* a representation using the same mental processes used to *construct* it.

If this is true, then attention to the cognitive mechanisms underlying acquisition and transmission throws new light on everything from the psychological processes involved in the comprehension and communication of representations, to the types of representations produced by minds, to the properties that give certain representations a selective advantage over others. Consider the following ideas:

1. *Rock* is hard, immobile, and inanimate.
2. *Tigers* think, breathe air, and eat.
3. *Mickey Mouse* is an oversized, talking rodent.
4. *Ghosts* are reanimated deceased people.
5. *Memes* are cultural genes competing for mental space.
6. The first *Taylor polynomial* of $f(x) = e^x$ at $x = 0$ is $P_1(x) = 1 + 1/1 \cdot x = 1 + x$.

A moment's reflection reveals a couple of significant differences between these ideas. The first involves familiarity. It is safe to say that most people the world over would have little trouble recognizing ideas 1 through 4. Indeed, a very large number of people the world over already possess ideas 1 through 4 among their repertoire of mental representations. Many less people would recognize ideas 5 and 6. With regard to distribution, then, ideas 1 through 4 are more widespread than ideas 5 and 6. It is tempting to attribute familiarity solely to formal learning; ideas 5 and 6 demand particular avenues of communication (such as schools and books) that many people simply haven't accessed. While there is certainly truth to the statement that learning *is* the acquisition of ideas, it should also be pointed out that there are lots of "academic" ideas that are widely distributed among the educated and uneducated alike, such as the notions of a heliocentric solar system, evolution, and atoms. Interesting ideas have ways of spreading beyond their points of origin, so other factors must be involved than just formal instruction. Additionally, there *are* ideas—such as ideas 1 and 2—that are found in all normal minds *irrespective* of direct instruction. The innate processing systems of the brain construct a large body of knowledge, or learn, quite on their own.

Here's a second difference between these ideas: Even if all people were exposed to all of these ideas, such that they were all equally *recognized*, not all the ideas would be equally *understood*. It is a safe bet, for example, that most people the world over implicitly understand idea 1 while many fewer people grasp the calculus within idea 6. The "meme," too, is a marvelous idea in itself, but consider the background it takes before it fully makes sense. So another obvious lesson is that successful transmission requires comprehension—at both ends of the process. You cannot discuss polynomials with a friend if they are beyond either of you. Note well, though—novelty and comprehension don't necessarily go together. The notion of a "talking rodent," which is as synthetic an idea as a "cultural gene," is assimilated by everyone with very little set up.

Cognitivists are fascinated by these kinds of addenda, and their study has uncovered features of thought that are much less obvious yet also of much greater consequence to the acquisition-transmission process, and hence to the contents of culture. An important example is the recognition that minds are naturally *predisposed* to some kinds of ideas and not to others. As the first part of this book demonstrated, modern human brains interpret and organize the world using tacit inferential procedures grounded in intuitive ontology. One effect of MHB 1.0 is a bias for concepts with matching properties. Concepts that conform to the mind's intuitive ontology, and thus provide for rich inference connections, are easily comprehended and communicated. Natural kinds, animate/inanimate, color, and so on—such information is precisely what the brain was design to recognize as relevant and to process with alacrity. Ideas about "rocks" and "tigers" require little explanation because the mind itself makes the requisite connections. Sperber calls ideas like 1 and 2 "basic concepts" because, as the natural products of innate cognitive schemas, they are developed by people everywhere with minimal prompting (1996: 69). Predictably, basic concepts comprise the largest portion of shared public knowledge.

Recognizing the conceptual predispositions of minds not only explains the ubiquity of basic concepts but also helps to elucidate the presence of a more interesting set of representations. It turns out that being *predisposed* to specific kinds of concepts has a highly consequential side effect: it makes one *susceptible* to more general versions of those concepts, including versions featuring novel alternations. Ideas 3 and 4 above are examples of conceptual susceptibility. These kinds of ideas co-opt the mind's innate inference systems by innovating otherwise well-grounded basic concepts. The idea of Mickey Mouse works because, striking as a "talking rodent" might be, it is still seen by the mind to be an "animal," invoking all of the inferences that accompany that ontological category. By contrast, the idea of a "talking rodent" is much more readily assimilated than a "cultural gene" precisely because it retains a rich field of background inferences. Similarly, you already have all the tools you need to construct the concept "ghost" simply by accessing the mental blueprint for "person" and adding an evocative twist. Mickey Mouse and ghosts are examples of counterintuitive ideas; they run against tacit expectations of what is normal for the basic concept in some respect.

The "striking innovation" and "evocative twists" that conceptual susceptibility allows can take the formation of representations in seemingly limitless directions. Even small departures from common assumptions about physical, biological, or psychological phenomena can produce ideas that range from slight variations on basic concepts to the wildly fantastical. Yet there is a benefit to difference. When a given concept violates your expectation it also grabs your attention. Against the frenetic landscape of ideas, being attention grabbing is a selective advantage. These kinds of ideas are more likely to remain in memory and get communicated to others.

Experiments into the process of acquisition and transmission confirm a connection between a concept's form, recall, and transmission (for example, Barrett and Nyhof 2001; Boyer and Ramble 2001). A less obvious finding is that not all conceptual innovations are equally effective. It might seem that the more unusual a concept is the more memorable it would be. Yet recent tests demonstrate that this isn't true. Creativity is not a guarantee of communication. In fact, all else being equal, the most memorable concept is one that falls between the banal and the bizarre. In experiments pitting "mundane," "expectation-violating," and "bizarre" ideas against each other, Justin Barrett and Melanie Nyhof found that the concepts best suited for both recall and transmission are those that conform in most respects to the mind's intuitive ontology, making them recognizable, while at the same time possessing a single counterintuitive feature, making them provocative. As Barrett and Nyhof surmise, "this transmission advantage for counterintuitive concepts may explain, in part, why such concepts are so prevalent across cultures and so readily spread" (2001: 91).

A great many mental and public representations are the result of conceptual susceptibility. Mickey Mouse and ghosts fit nicely into this category of representations, and one is bombarded daily by a myriad others, as well as by ideas that are far more abstract. Clearly this phenomenon plays a major role in cultural diversity. In addition to their expansive repertoires of basic concepts, minds are also capable of remarkable feats of conceptual innovation, and people with differing backgrounds will inevitably ply their imaginations in differing ways. However, we cannot get lost amid cultural diversity the way many social scientists have. Pondering the expansive vista of human activity, it is easy to miss the fact not only that individual minds are responsible for the existence of what one chooses to call culture, but also that, from the standpoint of ideas, cultural diversity may not be as diverse as it seems.

An important lesson of recent studies of acquisition and transmission is that we often fail to see the *trees* for the *forest*. Not only is it the case that most mental representations fail to become public, but also within the dense woodland of human ideas many turn out to be of the same variety; beneath assorted variations lay common conceptual structures. This is a second consequential ramification of cognitive constraint: it narrows the range of concepts that are easy to spread. Cognitive constraint is the result of innate conceptual biases intent on interpreting and formulating information in prescribed ways. Cognitive constraint even has a hand in guiding personal judgments regarding the cogency and veracity of concepts. As Barrett and Nyhof further point out, "too many counterintuitive features undermine the structure of the concept" (2001:

93), resulting in a representation disconnected from its normal suite of expectations. Such concepts, while perhaps imaginative, are less likely to be kept as mental representations or get passed on to others.

Viewed against the backdrop of mental mechanisms like these, the world of ideas looks different than it once did. In 1959 Noam Chomsky brilliantly parried the behavioral psychology of B. F. Skinner, offering the cognitive revolution in riposte. Chomsky suggested that contrary to the then dominant views of language acquisition, verbal maturation is the result of a shared language faculty that reveals itself as a universal grammar underlying all particular grammars (1986). Cognitivists are now extending the rule-government nature of language to cultural knowledge in general, showing how obvious diversity in particular forms of knowledge nevertheless possesses underlying unity that is attributable to a consortium of mental faculties. Put another way, explaining the contents of culture requires the anthropological equivalent of reverse engineering. What proves most illuminating is moving from the study of diversity (the many) to unity (the few). A good bit of what gets transmitted in and across cultures—the *reason* this material gets transmitted—is built up from a relatively small set of conceptual structures employed by all people. In the final analysis, culture is the result of a natural selection, but one that takes place all the time in all minds.

Here are two rough and ready examples for skeptics. The first concerns the nature of "culture" itself; the second illustrates underlying unity amid diversity:

- "Shaker culture," like "Amish culture" or any other traditionally recognized bounded society, got its start at a particular time (the 18th century) in a particular place (England). Clearly, what was to become "Shaker culture" began with a set of ideas. These ideas passed between, and became shared in, the minds of a small group of people. These shared ideas produced specific kinds of behaviors (ecstatic trembling, celibacy, simplicity, pacifism, communalism, and so on) and specific kinds of artifacts (architecture, inventions, menus, clothing, and so forth)—the whole complex of which we naturally call "Shaker culture." Interestingly, cultures don't necessarily stay put because people don't. In 1774 Ann Lee led the first Shakers from Manchester, England, to a site near Albany, New York, and "Shaker culture" suddenly took up residence in New England. Yet culture moves not only because people move but also because they talk. The early Shakers traveled throughout New England communicating their ideas. At times this attracted converts, other individuals who were impressed by Shaker ideas and decided to share them. Each time this happened "Shaker culture" expanded. It finally reached its high point in the mid-1800s with an estimated 5000 members ranging from the East Coast to the Midwest.

Of course, Shaker culture only spread so far. Why? Many more people found Shaker ideas less then compelling and decided not to share them. In fact, many people shared instead the idea of persecution. Obviously, such people cannot be counted as members of "Shaker culture." Furthermore, Shakerism itself soon began a decline. With the advent of American industrialization and westward settlement, the "Shaker culture" began to shrink. Why? Fewer people *continued* to find Shaker ideas appealing. Each time this happened, "Shaker culture" diminished. Today there is but a single active Shaker community left at Sabbathday Lake, Maine. And, of course, the remaining members of this group could all change their minds too.

- For students of religion, there could hardly be a more diverse concept than "supernatural being." Whether or not one believes that religion is really about such entities, the fact remains that all religious systems have them, and these supernatural beings play a significant role in religious thought and practice. The point is that supernatural beings come in all shapes and sizes. Even the briefest of surveys reveals an astounding diversity found around the world. There are the all-powerful, singular "gods" that define the monotheistic faiths as well as the more specialized, multitudinous gods of Hindu, Roman, and African religion. There are less powerful but still notable "spirits" like those that populate Japan and animate Native American religion. There are also demons, and ghosts, and angels, and ghouls, and jinn, and so on and so forth. The nature of supernatural beings is as varied as their form. They can be good, evil, or indifferent. They may be embodied or amorphous, gendered or androgynous. They may be all-knowing, indifferent, or downright dumb. They may be self-sufficient or require care. The breadth of creativity brought to representations of supernatural beings is not only a classic example of cultural diversity but also one of the major arguments against the possibility of a "comparative" approach to the study of religion. As the argument goes, comparison among religious ideas is not possible because of the considerable variation that becomes obvious the moment we pay attention to actual religions in actual cultural situations. But hold on. Is there really nothing in common here? Is there really no unity to be found beneath the diversity? Undoubtedly the religions of the world present a remarkable variety of supernatural being concepts, but all of them are at bottom just *variations on a theme.* There are many kinds of beings, but all are beings just the same, and for the category-structured processing system of the human mind, "beings" are very specific things. To build a "god" a mind must first build a "person." And every mind does that in the same way.

So there is indeed a connection between cognition and culture and it is discernable in the relationship between the form, acquisition, and transmission of representations. A crucial factor determining the portability and durability of a given representation is how well it can be implemented on the mental processing system. When the structure and function of human brains are considered, it makes sense that certain kinds of representations turn out to be more easily acquired and transmitted than others, and therefore that culture is this way rather than that. Natural selection designed minds that produce and interpret representations in particular ways, and by doing so it simultaneously designed minds with particular conceptual predispositions. The result is that not all concepts are acquired with the same facility, and therefore not all concepts are equally conspicuous. Psychology has the dual effect of constraining both the form and distribution of ideas. In the end, Steven Pinker underscores the proper perspective:

> The geneticist Theodosius Dobzhansky famously wrote that nothing in biology makes sense except in the light of evolution. We can add that nothing in culture makes sense except in the light of psychology. Evolution created psychology, and that is how it explains culture. (1997: 210)

Connecting Gods and Culture

What does a discussion of culture have to do with religion? Religion is cultural. You learn it from others—parents, acquaintances, public displays. Like native customs, social manners, food choices, attire, and vocations, religion is related to local environments, and the religion one usually acquires (secularism, atheism, and conversions notwithstanding) is inherited. It is no mere coincidence that many Chinese adopt Confucian ideals, or that few Americans read the Adi Granth, or that toxcatl, the monthly human sacrifice in honor of Tezcatlipoca, is no longer in vogue.

As with Shakerism, religion of any stripe spreads through communication and imitation. It starts with exposure to a set of ideas and behaviors. These ideas and behaviors are then acquired and mimicked. As long as individuals continue to find this set of ideas and behaviors compelling, the religion will endure. Some forms of religion are short lived; others have staying power. A handful of religions have been part of the human experience for millennia. Of course, it was just argued that this process describes any aspect of culture, but that's just the point. There is no need for a special description for religion or to treat it as a unique or mysterious phenomenon that lies beyond the bounds of scientific explanation. While one could name name's—*which* religions have been short lived, *which* survived longer, *which* are counted among the "world religions"—it is the ubiquity of religious thought itself that is of interest and thus the forum in which that kind of thought takes place: the ordinary human brain.

What is especially fascinating about religion, however, is not that it is possible, but that everyone seems to have it. And here "everyone" is meant in the largest sense. As far as we know, no people group on this planet has been without some set of religious ideas and practices, and it appears, as the first chapter noted, that echoes of modern-day religious behaviors are detectable tens of thousands of years ago. It is perspective like this that often leads people to directly associate religion and society, naively assuming that religion arises naturally when people get together or that religion was invented to hold society together. While the first assumption is partly right, the latter is mostly wrong. Few societies are the harmonious wholes that sociologists like Durkheim imagine, and the presence of religion frequently offers counter-social beliefs, communalism, and violence. Religion does provide social cohesion at particular levels and influences the way people get on, but so do other factors beyond religion, such as law codes, ethnicity, and personal morality.

What's partly right about the first assumption, of course, is obvious: religion does appear when people get together. By now, though, it should be clear that the reason has nothing to do with some magical quality of society or with the devious machinations of political leaders; rather, religion begins as ideas in individuals' heads, and when individuals get together, these religious ideas, like lots of other kinds of ideas, spread from one head to another. So a proper explanation of public religious systems begins with the religious ideas privately held in people's minds. And what Sperber's epidemiological model highlights is the amazing success of religious ideas—they are easily acquired no matter what the cultural context.

Boyer finds this fact so curious that he has spent a large part of his career pursuing it. If one adopts a purely culturalist perspective, then religious thought ought to be a domain where, in Boyer's words, "flexibility should be maximal" (2000b: 93). If the claims of cultural relativism hold, then cultures, vis-à-vis religion, would likely have developed a range of responses. It is reasonable to assume, for example, that some cultures would find religious ideas like gods compelling and useful and come to organize personal and social life around them, while others would consider religious ideas ridiculous and reject them as meaningful for personal or social life. Likewise, one should expect that the autonomy of the world's many cultures would result in an amazing variety of god concepts, some as unlike as others are similar.

Life on the ground, however, matches theory but rarely, and in the present case not at all. Religion is not just concomitant with human social development, accepted and applied the world over, but it also everywhere consists of the same basic set of ideas—dressed to local tastes, of course, but structurally identical. Because this catalog of religious ideas is tightly constrained, similarity in religious behaviors and organizational arrangements follows suit. Boyer's work simultaneously illuminates a crucial feature of all religious ideas and demonstrates the central place of cognitive constraint in explanations of cultural evolution.

Religious ideas are everywhere it turns out, because the class of concepts they encompass are near-perfect examples of culturally successful representations. The gods, devils, ancestors, and angels that anchor religious systems display all the qualities of concepts that are attention grabbing, memorable, and highly portable. At the same time, these concepts are not simply striking; just as important to the durability of such ideas is the fact that they align with regular features of cognitive organization; that is, they come "naturally" to minds like ours. In focusing on universal cognitive structures, Boyer has demonstrated that religious ideas are not anomalies amid the more "believable" concepts people entertain but are in fact a *natural* product of the types of brains all normal humans possess. The sense in which Boyer uses the term "natural" refers to the fact that religious concepts arise from the same cognitive processes—intuitive ontology, inference systems, and so on—that generate all other kinds of representations. "Natural," then, are "those aspects of religious ideas which depend on noncultural constraints" (1994a: 3). Religious concepts make use of the banal but indispensable systems of cognition. They could not be acquired, represented, and transmitted if they were not anchored in these systems. Boyer is not suggesting that religious ideas are innate but that humans possess the types of minds that easily and naturally "catch" religious notions: "Having a normal brain does not imply that you have religion, all it implies is that you can acquire it, which is very different" (2001: 4).

It is important to note, though, that because religious concepts are parasitic on ordinary cognitive capacities, not all possible religious concepts are equally viable. People can learn a wide range of religious notions if exposed to them, but the specialized predispositions of brains mean that only specific kinds of religious concepts can be generated, acquired, stored, and passed on with ease. Innate principles of cognitive processing constrain how religious concepts are represented, thereby limiting the conceptual options to a surprisingly short list of possibilities. Only those religious concepts that retain a natural connection with intuitive knowledge promote salience and recurrence. Concepts that are abstract or obtuse are rare in real-world religion, and where they do exist, they are very often ignored as irrelevant.

This take on religious conceptualization not only shows the cognitive foundations of religious ideas and why religious representations share recurrent features, but it also helps explain the social transference of religious ideas over place and time. Because transmission is a process of translation and not simply of replication, concepts will be successfully passed from one person to another only if they align in significant ways with shared intuitive structures. The set of religious representations that are most ubiquitous the world over displays the qualities of "cognitively optimum" concepts described in chapter 4: they (1) remain within the acceptable limits of cognitive constraint and (2) are novel enough to capture the imagination. Such concepts hold a formidable selective advantage in the marketplace of ideas; they populate the public sphere as successful by-products of minds naturally tuned to cognitively optimal ideas.

What is more, religious ideas are not simply interesting and memorable—a great many ideas fit that bill. Nor are supernatural concepts like gods merely fanciful notions that people just happen to like to talk about. Cognitively optimal concepts are a dime a dozen, populating everything from children's stories to state holidays to local folklore. *Religious* ideas, however, engender mental ascent and stir serious emotional responses. God concepts are for many people eminently believable and worthy of considerable commitment. So there is a point at which the conversation regarding infectious ideas shifts from quantitative measurements of cognitively optimal characteristics to the psychological links between ideas and things like motivation and behavior. Few other outcomes of thought are as capable of garnering such dedication and devotion, of prompting such prepossession and passion. Few other outcomes of thought manage to gather into themselves the full range of human experiences, or of generating new ones.

Ultimately it is this *gestalt* of religious thought that gives it such staying power. At the personal level, commitment to religious ideas serves to structure not just a worldview but also *a way of life*. Religious ideas aren't simply contemplative propositions: they beget intellectual, behavioral, moral, and social responses. Religious ideas can easily become the basis of one's identity, the blueprint of one's epistemology, the catalyst of one's behavior, the wellspring of one's politics, the boundary of one's community. As a result, religious ideas are highly visible at the cultural level. We are all born into a world replete with religion. One constantly hears about it from others, encounters it through information, news, and entertainment forums, and sees its public products in the form of signs, symbols, buildings, and books. Factors of exposure, repetition, and emphasis in turn play an important role in the stability and longevity of religion. They boost the transmission potential of religious ideas by conscripting even those who find it unsatisfying. One does not need to be in a religious context to hear and talk about religion. Likewise, one does not need to *be* religious to participate in its communication. Harsh words for religion are as effective a carrier of religious ideas as evangelism. It is a testimony to the potency of religious ideas that, as Tom Lawson writes, "religious systems seem capable of consistently providing the conditions for their own transmission" (2000: 82).

So the statement that "religion is cultural" has a second, equally important dimension in addition to the process of acquisition just described. Religion is also cultural in the sense that it is a public production and not merely a set of private ideas. As Harvey Whitehouse puts it, religion is a distributed phenomenon: it "inheres not merely in the thoughts and feelings of an individual devotee but also in the recognizably similar or complementary thoughts and feelings of a population of religious adherents" (2004: 16). And here the presumption that "religion" and "society" seem to readily fit together finally does have validity. Religious concepts are compelling enough that public life as well as private life gets organized around them. Some religious individuals might worship their deities alone, but more often the activities of worship are undertaken with other people. Some religious individuals might have rituals that they conduct in private, but the really important rituals require religious gatherings and officiates. Some religious individuals might feel capable of developing their own theological, ethical, and political views, but most people defer to the intellectual work of educated elite. Some religious individuals might feel that they don't fit into a particular religious institution, but religion usually provides a well-organized, hierarchically arranged community that structures both religious life and its relation to the secular world.

It is in this sense, then, that "religious ideas" and "religion" are not the same thing. Anyone can entertain religious ideas as mental representations, but religion results from public representations and their artifacts. Whereas gods are ideas in the minds of individuals, religion is the culture of religious belief. Religious thought centers on intuitively generated supernatural agent concepts; religion is comprised of the systematized reflection (doctrines), prescribed behaviors (rituals), and social structure (community) that develop around them. However "religion" is depicted, two main lessons emerge from distinguishing between cognition and culture, between private religious representations and public religious systems. The first, as the following chapter attempts to show, is that differences between private religious ideas and public religion are differences of consequence. This does not just mean that cognition and culture are phenomena operating at different levels, or that culture comprises a social consortium in which a given individual may or may not play a part. What it means is that at the level of cognition, mental representations and public representations are often not a perfect match. Things happen to ideas once they migrate to the public sphere. Theological notions of gods (culture) are not equivalent to the god concepts that ordinary people use in everyday thought (cognition). In this as in so many other cases, basic concepts are acquired and processed with ease while lots of cultural knowledge can be assimilated only through rigorous training. Barrett's insight that "when it come to gods not just anything goes" will be used throughout the remaining pages of this book as a key for unlocking puzzling aspects of religious behavior as well as explaining some equally confusing changes that religious systems commonly undergo.

The second lesson—to return to this chapter's opening query—is that *religion has everything to do with gods.* Here, too, more is meant than merely an answer to long-standing academic debates over definition. While the history of religious studies is marked by an inability to yield a working definition of "religion"—to say nothing of universal agreement that gods are even a necessary component of such a definition (Idinopulas and Wilson 1998)—focus on human cognition makes the troublesome task of defining religion easier by showing, in an empirically testable fashion, that the common variable in discussions of religion at any level—from its slate of beliefs to its system of rituals to its organizational principles—is indeed commitment to superhuman agents. Regardless of *how* religion comes to take its particular forms, it nevertheless remains true that what *does* become "religion" still ultimately revolves around god concepts.

The full case for gods as the defining feature of religion, then, lies in the nature of the relationship of cognition and culture described above. Ideas about counterintuitive agents begin quite naturally in people's heads, and from there they spread to the public domain. A handful of these provocative public ideas are given such credence that they generate expansive reflection, peculiar behaviors, and distinctive social arrangements. Insisting on a definition of religion linked to the presumption of supernatural agents is neither ideologically derived nor value driven, but instead arises out of its own subject matter.

Connecting Gods and Religion

Pausing to further defend the claim that gods are integral to religious thought and behavior has polemical as well as pedagogical value. In the business-as-usual tradition of religious studies, this claim is illustrative of the methodological malaise the discipline has long experienced. Does religion include gods? Maybe. But, maybe not. The approach typically taken in comparative religion is to test such hypotheses against case studies of "religion" in different settings. Tautologies notwithstanding, the evidence has never been thought conclusive. Do Buddhist's worship gods or don't they? Has Confucius taken on divine status or not? The result of many years of grappling with such questions is what religious studies scholars call "family resemblance." What a "game" is to Wittgenstein, so "religion" is to students of religion. If enough of a set of agreed upon characteristics is present in a particular cultural phenomenon, then it can legitimately be deemed "religion." This is clearly a subjective call, but more importantly, a lack of gods in a given system can be trumped by a quorum of other "religious" characteristics.

The cognitive science of religion offers a more powerful method of evaluating religious phenomena than this I-know-it-when-I-see-it approach. True it strives to minimize subjectivity, as all science strives, but it also looks below the surface characteristics of religion to the psychological processes that animate them. Fully demonstrating the role of gods in religion requires more than surveying diverse religious systems; it requires explaining them. And doing that requires rummaging in the basement of these already well-developed edifices, examining the mental machinery that powers the cultural contraption. Doing so reveals that religious doctrines aren't happenstance, that religious rituals aren't accidents, and that religious social structures aren't optional. Religion has the set of "characteristics" that it has because these characteristics are the outgrowth of minds committed to supernatural agents. Without them, not only would there *not* be a family resemblance between religions but there would not be *religion*.

This chapter closes with a powerful example of the cognitive approach to religion. Any facet of human thought or behavior that we call "religious" could be dissected in this manner, revealing some significant connection with representations of and commitment to supernatural agents of one sort or another. It is fairly clear, for example, that religious doctrine, though appearing in various levels of sophistication, nevertheless intends to explicate the meaning, nature, history, activities, desires, and implications of specific supernatural agents. Even when theological discussion extends to such topics as ethics, politics, and the like, such reflection remains rooted in—indeed, takes the form it does precisely because of—a specific understanding of divinely inspired admonitions and sanctions. Likewise, the several yet similar sociopolitical arrangements assumed by religious communities are the result of top-down hierarchical relationships that begin with a recognition of the headship of supernatural beings. Shamans and popes may be looked to for worldly, temporal leadership, but they hold their positions because they are understood to be the representatives or conduits of higher powers.

A particular interest of religion scholars and anthropologists alike is the use and meaning of religious rituals. Many such individuals have found it difficult to determine common connections between ritual activities, let alone to presume that it all has to do with human traffic with supernatural beings. It is interesting, then, that some of the work that broke ground on the new cognitive science of religion comes specifically from the study of religious rituals. In their seminal book *Rethinking Religion* (1990), in their most recent collaboration, *Bringing Ritual to Mind* (2002), and in numerous articles that spin off these important volumes, Bob McCauley and Tom Lawson have advanced a rigorous and apparently bullet-proof description of religious rituals that clearly denotes the central role of supernatural agents in religious actions.

Drawing on recent research in cognitive science, particularly work in generative linguistics, McCauley and Lawson have constructed a "theory of religious ritual competence" showing that people are capable of making intuitive judgments about the proper forms, relationships, and efficacy of religious rituals. This seemingly striking capacity, which is now being confirmed by early experiments (Barrett and Lawson 2001), is not striking at all when it is pointed out, as Lawson and McCauley do, that religious rituals, while perhaps understood to be "special" kinds of actions, are nevertheless still actions. Because humans possess cognitive equipment for assessing "everyday" actions, they quite naturally extend that skill to "religious" actions as well.

The basis of this skill, according to McCauley and Lawson, is the presence of a mental "action representation system." People intuitively understand that all actions include three connected elements: an *agent acting* upon a *patient*, usually by means of some instrument (see Figure 5.1). It's important to note the role of agency here, since the identification of action *as action* is concomitant with the identification of agents. An event such as *man washes baby* with water matches the structural description of actions. Any number of substitutes can be made within any of the three structural "slots"—*cat eats mouse*, say— but the particular grammar of what comprises an action remains unchanged. In a direct echo of Chomsky's work with language, McCauley and Lawson's formal theory of ritual competence is built on this structural description of action, together with a set of generative rules that stems from it.

How are religious rituals different from mundane actions? They differ in but one crucial respect: religious rituals presume that *supernatural* agents are involved in some way, thereby lending the whole activity a special quality. As an action, a priest baptizing an infant is structurally different from a man washing a baby only in that a deity is thought to play a role in it. A careful look at *any* religious rite will reveal a special connection between gods and either the agent, the patient, or the instrument involved.

Extrapolation from this basic theoretical framework has yielded a compelling set of "universal principles of religious ritual" (Lawson and McCauley 1990: 6). The most basic is that religious rituals divide into two types or "forms," based on where gods connect with the action structure. Rituals in which gods are implicated in the agent slot are called "special agent rituals." Rituals in which gods are connected with either of the other two slots are called "special patient/instrument rituals." The role gods play in a given ritual may be immediate or indirect, in which case the present ritual is legitimated by any number of prior "enabling rituals." In the case of baptism, for example, the priest (agent) has received his special status through a chain of prior ordinations that lead ultimately to Jesus' christening of the apostle Peter.

In addition to delineating a typology of religious rituals, McCauley and

FIGURE 5.1. McCauley and Lawson's "action representation system."

Lawson's work shows that, even with rituals, form relates to function. *Bringing Ritual to Mind*, for example, is dedicated to unpacking some practical implications of the authors' early abstract model, including explanations for why some religious rituals are rarely performed, sonorous, highly emotional experiences while others are commonplace, mechanical, and dull; why some religious rituals can be undone while the effects of others are thought to be permanent; and how the balance of ritual arrangements impacts the overall stability of a religious system.

McCauley and Lawson's contribution to the study of religious rituals is much more complex than this brief summary suggests. What is important about it for the present context, however, is that it offers a concrete demonstration that what makes actions "religious" rather than ordinary is their explicit connection to supernatural agents. All human behaviors that are religious in nature are the result of supposed engagement with gods, just as all religious doctrines talk about gods, and all religious communities exist for them. Structurally speaking, communism is different from Soka Gakkai in that there is no supernatural agency underwriting its ideas. Likewise, the ritual pomp and circumstance of college graduations differ from bar mitzvahs in that a god is not thought to be involved. Religious thought centers on supernatural agents, and it is the visible concatenation of public beliefs (doctrines), behaviors (rituals), and social structure (community) that we call "religion." The window that provides us with these very valuable, very fruitful insights is—once again—the study of the human mind itself.

6

Cognition and Religious Systems

What Do Gods Have to Do with Religion?

Gods, religion, and culture belong together because gods, religion, and culture are products of cognition. The great achievement of cognitive science is the bridge it has built between the worlds we think and the worlds we make. Both of these forms of construction rely on complex mental mechanisms whose origins lay in human evolutionary history. A full-orbed understanding of who we are, why we are as we are, and why we do the things we do pivots on the adapted mind. As Jerome Barkow, Leda Cosmides, and John Tooby have so successfully demonstrated, "focusing on the evolved information-processing mechanisms that comprise the human mind supplies the necessary connection between evolutionary biology and the complex, irreducible social and cultural phenomena studied by anthropologists, sociologists, economists, and historians" (1992: 4).

In connecting the world of cognition with the world of culture, the last chapter showed that the power of religion as a social reality is due to its comprehensive nature. Religion is not merely a set of isolated propositions; rather, it is an integrated system of beliefs and behaviors with both personal and public dimensions. What is essential to see, though, is that at the center of the doctrinal-ritual-communal systems we call religion stand god concepts, or, more roundly, psychological commitments to supernatural beings. It is the supposed existence of supernatural beings that anchors religious teachings. It is the power of supernatural beings that provide ritual acts with their purpose and power. It is perceived involvement with supernatural beings that creates religious experiences and fosters emotional responses. It is the juridical attributes of supernatural beings that give moral injunctions their teeth. It is the presence of supernatural beings that ground institutional hierarchies. People allow religion to structure their lives because they believe in and are motivated by the gods at the heart of their religious systems, not because they especially enjoy communion wafers or bloodletting. A public display of the Ten Commandments becomes a political hot potato because members of a particular religious community view them as divine mandates, not because the negative social implications of acts like murder and adultery are particularly controversial.

So exploring the dynamics of religion from its central feature makes good sense. But it also turns out that concentrating on god concepts and the cognitive processes that form them throws fresh light on the behavior of religious people and the development of their religious systems. Take, for example, some standard anthropological fare. It has long been noted that *religious people* and their *religions* are not always harmonized. Reformed Christianity teaches that people's destinies are predetermined by divine decree and that humankind, by virtue of an inherited state of depravity, lacks free will. Believers within this religious tradition, however, not only report intellectual problems with these church views but also clearly conduct their day-to-day lives as if their attitudes and behaviors are the result of personal choice. Theravada Buddhism teaches that the worship of gods is a waste of precious time since they are powerless to alter the nature of existence and, theologically speaking, are actually in a worse position to achieve the goal of Buddhist practice than humans. Yet even in the strictest of Theravadan lands Buddhists regularly appeal to gods and supernatural beings and maintain a rich array of syncretistic practices that have little in common with the "Doctrine of the Elders." The Islamic faith counts idolatry as the worst of human sins, yet the veneration of saints is one of the most visible, and for many Muslims one of the most moving, components of religious observance.

The disparity between formal religious ideas and practices and the way that ordinary folks think and behave—what might be called "divergent religion"—has been described as two different faces of religious practice, one corresponding to an "official" set of beliefs and actions prescribed in texts, maintained by institutions, and communicated by specialists, the other a "popular" form of religion pursued by regular people in everyday life. Less well documented are satisfactory explanations for divergent religion. To the wonder of many, religious individuals appear to simply fail to correctly mirror their own tradition's orthodoxy.

Pascal Boyer has also noted the discrepancy between "official" and "popular" religion and given the phenomenon an interesting slant. The problem of divergent religion is really one-sided. Part of the business of religious leaders and literati is instilling in laypeople the meaning and relevance of their theological concepts. Yet this task is never fully successfully achieved. The "tragedy of the theologian," as Boyer nicely puts it, is that in spite of efforts by religious specialists to define what is theologically correct for their people, "there *always* seem to be some nonstandard beliefs and practices left sticking out." And though theologians attempt to get people to *think* according to official concepts, "people always add to or distort the doctrine" (2001: 281).

But why? This question is as fascinating as it is confounding. If the knowledge that informs religious thought is wholly cultural, then the beliefs and behaviors of adherents should line up quite closely with what is taught by their traditions. Furthermore, any divergence from traditional teachings and practices could be construed as a conscious act of dissent since each believer should know better. Even more compelling, religious people seem to have the *potential* to think and act correctly (they usually have at least a basic grasp of their faith's teachings) but they do so only under specific conditions. In other words, religious people commonly display duplicity of thought. Sometimes they use the religious knowledge their tradition has provided, and sometimes they employ a less formal—and what will shortly prove to be a more *intuitive*—brand of thinking.

Traditional theories and methods of religious studies can provide no meaningful explanation for divergent religion. While they are good at describing episodes of religious dissent or change, particularly those with sociological causes, they have little to say about the possible role psychological factors play in divergent thought and action. Lee Cronk warns staunch culturalists that when beliefs and attitudes that people profess at the cultural level do not line up with daily behavior, it's likely that the behavior has a biological foundation (1999). This book has highlighted the vital links between biology and culture and tried to demonstrate that the operation of the mind is far from incidental to explanations for religious phenomena. Here again attention to the noncultural foundations of human thought is instructive. Exploring the nature of *religious ideas* reveals quite a bit about *religion*.

The untold story behind divergent religion is that incorrect thinking and unorthodox behaviors are often both unintended and unnoticed. They are unintended and unnoticed because they are encouraged by private cognitive processes over which public teachers and teachings have no control. A cognitive explanation for divergent religion begins with the individual mind, the source of cultural products, and it goes on to suggest a more satisfying explanation for what are, at least to religious leaders, the foibles and follies of ordinary believers.

This final chapter introduces a dual-process model of cognition to the study of religion, suggesting that a crucial influence on how religious people think and act is the way the human brain handles religious concepts. Evidence drawn from cognitive psychology, social psychology, neuroscience, and comparative religion suggests that religious concepts—as well as other kinds of concepts—

can proceed along two contrasting mental pathways to differing effect. If correct, this account of cognitive processing provides a new way of understanding duplicitous forms of religious thought, of explaining common episodes of religious change (for example, doctrinal and ritual innovation, syncretism, conversion, and the formation of new religions), and of mapping an important set of selective forces at work on the shape and stability of religious systems.

A Dual-Process Model of Religious Thought

The most telling piece of psychological evidence bearing on the puzzle of divergent religion is Justin Barrett's identification of "theological correctness." In clever experiments with subjects from diverse cultures and religions, Barrett cut beneath the public appearance of religious knowledge to how such knowledge is privately represented and employed (1998, 1999; Barrett and Keil 1996, Barrett and VanOrman 1996). These experiments were introduced in chapter 3 to support the claim that people represent gods and humans with the same cognitive resources. But this research also demonstrates that people actually hold *more than one* representation of gods in their minds and that built-in cognitive biases make some god concepts easier and more natural to use than others.

Expanding on research into what scientists call "causal cognition" (Sperber, et al. 1995), Barrett's experiments are underwritten by the finding that concepts often reside in people's minds on "multiple levels of representation" (1999: 325). Intriguingly, these parallel versions of concepts may even be contradictory. Almost everyone knows, for example, that the earth revolves around the sun. When observing the sun in normal daily situations, however, such as watching a sunset, almost everyone, including scientists, ascribes the movement to the sun itself. Parallel representations of the same concept can range from the complex and abstract to the simple and concrete. Barrett calls these parallel understandings of single concepts "the theoretical level and the basic level; the level used in formal discourse and careful reflection, and the level used on-the-fly to solve problems quickly" (1999: 326). The discovery that minds actually work this way was the result of studying differences between reflective thought and real-time problem solving, what Barrett calls, respectively, "off-line" and "on-line" reasoning.

Barrett hypothesized that if religious knowledge is like nonreligious knowledge—that is, if the same cognitive biases that operate on nonreligious concepts also operate on religious ones—then parallel representations should also be found in religious thought. Barrett chose to call the coexistence of multiple representations of religious concepts "theological correctness" because the theoretical-level representations found in religious thought mirror the dominant theological dogma of the systems in which they arise (1999: 326). He also proposed thinking of religious representation in terms of a continuum. A tradition's orthodox theological dogma anchors the conceptually abstract end of this continuum, while native intuitive knowledge informs the simple, concrete concepts found at the other.

Strong evidence for theological correctness can be found in anecdotal form, as when Christian doctrine speaks of Jesus as being at once fully human and fully divine, yet Barrett wished to capture theological correctness at work in real minds in real time. His experiments with adult participants from faith traditions in both the United States and India successfully demonstrated that religious concepts, like nonreligious ones, *are* subject to cognitive biases consistent with intuitive knowledge. Using narrative recollection experiments to get at representations of the divine, Barrett was able to move beyond people's professed theological knowledge to the nature of god concepts they use in daily life. In keeping with predictions, Barrett found that people have at least two parallel, even contradictory god concepts and that the one based on intuitive rather than theological knowledge is functionally more meaningful. Specifically, "in contexts that demand using a god concept for rapid generation of inferences or predictions, the abstract, theological properties of gods that characterize reflective discourse disappear" (1998: 328).

According to Barrett, the inconsistency between off-line and on-line representation is most simply explained by cognitive constraint, "usually in the form of processing limitations" (1999: 325). Which concept will be selected in a given context—the basic, intuitive one or the more complex, theologically correct one—is largely the result of processing limitations. In on-line thinking tasks requiring quick, efficient solutions to an immediate problem, the basic concept rooted in intuitive knowledge is employed. In less demanding situations, where slower, more careful reflection is possible, complex theologically correct concepts are used. The cognitive demands of a given situation determine where along the continuum of theological correctness a concept will be found.

Such experiments reveal a distinct gap between theological and intuitive representations of supernatural beings. While members of religious communities are quite capable of working with the abstract theological concepts of their traditions, in on-line reasoning they nevertheless employ a concept of god with "few abstract, 'god-like' properties" (Barrett 1999: 329). Because representations of superhuman agents are constrained by the default assumptions covering all intentional agents, god concepts are represented and utilized on the basis of intuitive knowledge, despite professed theological beliefs. Theological concepts are simply received and stored as propositions. As such, they make no significant inference connections and therefore are not used in spontaneous tasks. In experiments with Christian subjects, for example, such theologically correct yet cognitively cumbersome conceptions of god as omniscient, omnipotent, and omnipresent are replaced with more anthropomorphic representations in which god is limited according to the expectations of folk psychology, biology, and physics. It is this intuitive concept of god that people use, largely without being aware of it, to make judgments in real time:

> The "theological God" is radically different from the "intuitive God" normally described in everyday discourse. Even individuals who explicitly endorse the theological version of God might nonetheless implicitly embrace a very different version in most of their daily thoughts. (Barrett and Keil 1996: 223)

Barrett's work shows that people simultaneously hold in their minds two parallel, often incompatible representations of gods, one an explicit, "theological-level" representation learned through instruction, and the other an implicit, "basic-level" representation rooted in intuitive expectations about intentional agents. This exciting finding, which has already informed a number of important discussions of religion, makes a valuable contribution to our present search for an explanation for divergent religion—and on several fronts. First, it highlights an important feature of cognition: in some domains at least, brains employ parallel conceptual/computational strategies. Second, it confirms the claim that built-in cognitive biases operate on religious and nonreligious concepts alike, and that these biases render some religious concepts easier to use than others. Third, it distinguishes between people's professed religious knowledge and the form of religious knowledge they utilize in everyday thought. Together these insights cast new light on one cause of divergent religion.

To see how, it is helpful to first take a closer look at the contrasting characteristics of the two types of representations Barrett's experiments identify (see Table 6.1). Several terms have been used to capture the differences between the two types of representations that people hold as well as the two modes of processing that each type requires. Theological representations are *explicit, analytical,* and *abstract* while basic representations are *implicit, intuitive,* and *inferentially rich.* In terms of the computational process each type of represen-

TABLE 6.1 Barrett's parallel conceptual/computational strategies.

	Theological Level	Basic Level
Representation	1. Explicit 2. Analytical 3. Abstract	1. Implicit 2. Intuitive 3. Inferentially rich
Computation	4. Slow 5. Reflective 6. Conscious	4. Fast 5. Reflexive 6. Unconscious/automatic

tation engages, theological representations employ *slow, reflective* thinking while basic representations provide for *fast, reflexive* thought. This is because theological representations require *conscious* activation while basic ones are *unconscious* and *automatic*.

The coexistence of two fundamentally different conceptual/computational strategies leads one to wonder how both reside in the mind at once. A fruitful approach to this problem is thinking about the brain using the dual-process models of information processing discussed in social psychology. Since the 1950s social psychologists have been interested in identifying the mental mechanics of human social life, from the basic building blocks of social intelligence—person perception, attribution theory, memory, decision making, attitude formation, and so on—to the kinds of dispositions and behaviors that arouse political concerns, such as stereotyping and prejudice. It has become obvious to many researchers that even these unattractive attitudes have biological foundations that defy environmental influence.

Recently some social and cognitive psychologists have attempted to account for various psychosocial phenomena using dual-process models of information processing. This approach, which, given its breadth, might best be viewed as a "family" of psychological theorizing, proposes that social attitudes and behaviors can be constructed in more than one way. While current dual-process models and theories have a broad range of interests and goals, most connect the presence of two alternative processing modes (with discrete problem domains, rules of operation, brain systems, and affective links) to the way people think about and respond to information—often with great inconsistency. If social psychologists are indeed on to something here, then this take on the mind has implications for the study of human thought and behavior more generally, including religious thought and behavior. Connecting dual *representation* with dual *processing* can elucidate Barrett's discovery of theological correctness and perhaps instances of duplicitous thought in nonreligious domains as well, such as differences between "folk" explanations for natural events and scientific ones (McCauley 2000; Keil 2003).

Interestingly, dual-process theorists use precisely the kinds of terms listed in Table 6.1 when speaking of two qualitatively different modes of information processing: "In essence, the common distinction in dual-process models is between a fast, associative information-processing mode based on low-effort heuristics, and a slow, rule-based information-processing mode based on high-effort systematic reasoning" (Chaiken and Trope 1999: ix). An intriguing example of dual-process model-building is the "Cognitive Experiential Self-Theory" (CEST) offered by Seymour Epstein and Rosemary Pacini (see Table 6.2). According to these researchers, the theological-level processing mode, which they would call the "rational system," is a "deliberative, analytical system that operates primarily in a medium of language and is relatively affect-free." It is "capable of high levels of abstraction" but is "inefficient for reacting to everyday events." It also has a "relatively brief evolutionary history." In contrast, the basic-level processing mode, what they would call the "experiential system," is a "relatively crude, albeit efficient, system for automatically, rapidly, and effortless processing information." It "encodes information in a concrete, holistic, primarily nonverbal form; is intimately linked with affect; and is inherently highly compelling." This system has a "very long evolutionary history and is the same system through which nonhuman, higher-order animals adapt to their environments" (Chaiken and Trope 1999: 463).

Parsing mental activity in terms of parallel or concurrent processes is neither new nor confined to social psychology. As reported in earlier chapters, the human brain is now commonly understood to be a complex of specialized processing systems evolved to solve specific computational problems. Research in cognitive psychology, neuroscience, and other related fields has ingeniously teased many of these systems apart, demonstrating some phenomena of mentation, such as vision, to involve analytic, concurrent processing (Van Essen and DeYoe 1995); others, such as memory, to involve independent, parallel systems (Tulving and Schacter 1990). Crucial cognitive faculties such as attention and language also fit into dual-process frameworks. Indeed, a more gestalt perspective on the brain suggests distinctions between cognitive processes that are cortical and subcortical in nature, as well as between processes related to hemispheric specialization.

Of particular importance here is the brain's use of dual pathways for information processing. Extensive investigation of the nature of cognition suggests that information proceeds along two discrete routes, one involving conscious reasoning and decision making, the other involving automatic, unconscious responses (Sternberg 1999). It is also becoming clear that conscious reasoning is itself built on tacit inferences and internal calculations beyond phenomenal awareness and voluntary control: "The vast majority of mental processes that control and contribute to our conscious experience happen outside our conscious awareness; we are conscious only of the content of our mental life, not what generates the content" (Gazzaniga et al. 1998: 532).

The evolutionary development of a brain organized to process knowledge

TABLE 6.2 Features of the CEST dual-processing model.

Rational System	Experiential System
1. Deliberative, analytical	1. Automatic, rapid, effortless
2. Medium of language	2. Holistic, nonverbal form
3. Relatively affect-free	3. Intimate affects, highly compelling
4. High-level abstractions	4. Crude, concrete conceptions
5. Brief evolutionary history	5. Long evolutionary history

along conscious and unconscious pathways is explained in part by Steven Pinker's cost/benefit analysis of information processing. In designing brains best fitted to the "cognitive niche," natural selection had to take into account the cost of space, the cost of time, and the cost of resources—costs that necessarily limit access-consciousness. As a result, brains are comprised of specialized processors that achieve computations in the quickest, most efficient way possible. Time consuming, cognitively expensive reflection is one available option, but real-time thought proceeds with access restrictions: "Only information *relevant* to the problem at hand" is allowed, or "routed" in (Pinker 1997: 138). Leading neuroscientists agree with Pinker's evolutionary scenario, pointing out the tremendous savings in brain volume facilitated by independent processing systems. Such a division of labor should also naturally result in different processing strategies: "Independent processing systems would be more likely to evolve non-identical computational capacities" (Gazzaniga et al. 1998: 341).

The language used to describe conscious versus unconscious processing varies in the literature. Rigorous models have distinguished between "automatic" and "controlled" processing (Schneider and Shiffrin 1977; Shiffrin and Schneider 1977), between "implicit" and "explicit" thought (Holyoak and Spellman 1993), between "reflexive" and "reflective" mental systems (Lieberman, et al. 2002), between "experimental" and "rational" cognition (Epstein 1994), and between "associative" and "rule-based" reasoning (Sloman 1996). One can also refer to the *contents* of these processing paths, as when distinctions are made between "declarative" and "procedural" knowledge, "implicit" and "explicit" memory, and "intuitive" and "reflective" beliefs. Illka Pyysiäinen has collated the many terms used to describe dual processing along with their affiliated functions, brain structures, computational characteristics, and psychological effects (2003, 2004b).

As summarized in Table 6.3, "explicit processing" (to settle on one of the available terms) is both accessible to and requires conscious control, is performed serially, and is slow in execution. The representations this processing system yields are explicit, analytical, abstract, and affect-free. In contrast, "implicit processing" (to pick a contrasting term) takes place automatically and reflexively, demands no effort or attention, and performs fast, parallel operations. The products of this processing system are implicit, intuitive, inferentially rich, and highly affective. Three additional though less technical terms have been added here to further highlight the qualitative differences between these representations—differences that bear directly on links between cognition and culture. Explicit representations are "learned," their full content acquired through instruction, while implicit representations are "tacit," acquired through innate inference-based construction. Explicit representations are also "malleable," readily open to manipulation or revision, while implicit representations are "rigid," the result of incorrigible default assumptions. Lastly, explicit

TABLE 6.3 Summary of dual processing/representational modes.

	Explicit processing	Implicit processing
Computation	1. Slow	1. Fast
	2. Serial	2. Parallel
	3. Reflective	3. Reflexive
	4. Conscious	4. Unconscious
	5. Controlled	5. Automatic
Representation	1. Explicit	1. Implicit
	2. Analytical	2. Intuitive
	3. Abstract	3. Inferentially rich
	4. Affect-free	4. Highly affective
	5. Learned	5. Tacit
	6. Malleable	6. Rigid
	7. Propositional	7. Experiential

representations are stored as "propositional" data, while implicit representations are stored as personal, "experiential" data.

At a minimum, dual-process models can help make sense of duplicitous thought, including the kind of religious duplicity identified by Barrett. The fact that brains employ parallel conceptual/computational strategies contributes to answers for long-standing questions in religious studies, such as why people simultaneously hold multiple, incongruent religious representations and how abstract theological reflection exists side by side with intuitive forms of religion. Theological-level representations and basic-level representations are the products of different processing systems, and are therefore naturally co-extant in the same mind.

But possessing the *capacity* to simultaneous entertain multiple representations does not in itself explain the *occurrence* of divergent religious thought and behavior. From a purely mechanical standpoint, recognizing that minds handle information in two contrasting ways is not yet to explain why one processing path is chosen over the other (though Barrett's emphasis on "processing limitations" is generally considered to be a sufficient cause). With respect to religious thought, the question might be put this way: Why is it that even individuals who understand theological concepts do not employ them in everyday thought and may even adjust them in undesirable ways? This question is particularly acute since one might easily assume that a concept like "god" is a perfect example of a theological-level representation that requires coherent and constant instruction to stabilize and therefore necessarily engages the explicit processing mode.

Though logical, this assumption is flawed. While it is true that some knowledge of what a particular god is like (purpose, powers, principalities, and so on) is the result of deliberate, conscious reflection, it is *not* the case that explicit processing is the most natural mental pathway for thinking about gods in general. Foundational to any discussion of religious representations is the insight that gods are, first and foremost, *intentional agents*. For this reason many cognitivists studying religion have focused their efforts on the role of agency in religious thought, whether explicating the naturalness and ubiquity of god concepts (Boyer 1994a, 2001), charting their place in the structure of religious rituals (Lawson and McCauley 1990; McCauley and Lawson 2002), or defining their "counterintuitive" features (Pyysiäinen 2001b; Barrett 2004). Much of the headway made in the new cognitive science of religion is the result of demystifying its subject matter. That gods are intentional agents means that they should be treated not merely as imaginative fictions for hermeneutics but as computational facts of social cognition.

Herein lays the real value of looking to cognitive models from social psychology. While social psychologists lack agreement on the actual mechanics of dual processing, they largely agree that humans employ unconscious, spontaneous inferences and associative categories to help them construct and negotiate the social world (Moskowitz 2005). God concepts also belong to the social world. So in studying the human perception of and response to agents—whether concrete and familiar or ethereal and counterintuitive—students of social psychology and students of religion are working with the same mental apparatus.

As indicated in earlier chapters, thinking about god concepts automatically activates key features of the social mind. In keeping with tacit assumptions about agents in general, god concepts are naturally represented as beings that are subjective, personal, interactive, and consequential. What is crucial here, however, is seeing that the contract for this mental work is held by the implicit processing system. Mentally building a "god" requires first building a "thinking agent"—a task that all minds carry out with alacrity. Regardless of the theological attributes applied to god concepts, they are continually underwritten by the default inferences that make agency detection and theory of mind the powerful adaptations that they are (Guthrie 1993; Barrett 2000).

The default operation of much of our mental activity suggests that, in addition to the qualitative differences between theological and basic representations already mentioned, there is also priority within the alternative processing modes. Not only are theological representations structurally parasitic on basic representations but, given this consolidative relationship, the implicit processing system remains the default mode in on-line thought. Explicit processing, as a discrete system whose inputs are symbols, language, and logic, is not engaged without conscious effort. Both of these relationships—consolidation in content and priority in processing—are clearly exposed by Barrett's experiments, where cumbersome abstract concepts are shown to rest on first-level, first-use ontology. So this model suggests a second explanation for theological correctness in addition to processing limitations. The argument that on-line, implicit processing saves time and effort is certainly correct, but where the representation of intentional agents is involved, people default to basic concepts because, more fundamentally, the implicit processing system is the *controlling* system. As manifested in phenomena ranging from taxonomic classification to stereotyping to theological correctness, basic representations govern social thought unless care is taken to override them.

> People use intuitive expectations about how a mind works, which are available automatically since they are constantly activated to make sense of people's behavior at all times. When the task allows for conscious monitoring, we get the theological version; when the task requires fast access, we get the anthropomorphic version. This not only shows that the theological concept has not displaced the spontaneous one but also that it is not stored in the same way. Very likely the theological concept is stored in the form of explicit, sentence-like propositions. In contrast, the spontaneous concept is stored in the format of direct instructions to intuitive psychology, which would explain why it is accessed much faster. (Boyer 2001: 89)

But there is more to this story. Though the representation of intentional agents—including *supernatural* intentional agents—falls primarily to the implicit processing system, people can and do think about gods using explicit reasoning. Indeed, this processing shift is responsible for the construction of complex theological representations; it is the *modus operandi* of "official" religion. Nevertheless, such "cross-system" concepts exist in cognitive tension. The fact that theological representations are easily inserted into our mental repertoires does not mean that they are equally useful to the thinking mind. While the differences between theological and basic representations are manifold, two examples—referred to here as "computational utility" and "psychological relevance"—will suffice to illustrate the cognitive tension inherent to religious thought:

- *Computational utility:* One of the distinctions between the two types of representations is that the theological are *abstract* while the basic are *inferentially rich* (see Table 6.3). In light of the procedural requirements of information processing, this is a distinction of consequence. Because they connect directly with the natural ontological categories and intuitive knowledge bases underpinning implicit processing, basic representations are computationally robust. By contrast, abstract theological representations are not only slow and effortful, grounded as they are in explicit processing, but also offer less inference potential. Theological gods are learned propositions with little functional utility; they do not lead to further inferences. In Sperber's words, "the cognitive usefulness of religious and other mysterious beliefs may be limited"

(1996: 90). Abstraction decouples the many inference connections that make agent concepts useful in the first place. From a processing standpoint, abstract agents make poor computational tools. Barrett seems to be saying much the same thing when he observes that a theological concept might not be "a full-blown concept" that can naturally generate predictions, explanations, and inferences (1998: 616). Rather, theological representations are stored simply as "a list of rehearsed, nonintegrated attributes, and have no causal efficacy" (1998: 612).

- *Psychological relevance*: We should expect, then, that the utility of basic representations—what Dan Sperber and Deirdre Wilson describe as the relationship between inference potential and computational effort (1986)—would lend them greater relevance in the marketplace of ideas. Evidence presented in the last chapter showed this claim to be true. But equally significant to the "relevance" of god concepts are the noted contrasts between theological representations as *propositional* and *affect-free* and basic representations as *experiential* and *highly affective* (see Table 6.3). In addition to utilizing the natural ontological categories and intuitive expectations that are needed to represent agents as such, the implicit processing system also assigns intentional agents social meaning and personal relevance by connecting theory of mind with theory of self. Furthermore, implicit processing does not operate in an affect-free way but is tied in directly to the brain's emotion systems. As Smith and DeCoster report, the implicit processing mode "generates what are experienced as affective responses to objects and events" (1999: 328). Representations produced via this processing system come complete with emotional coloring that makes them more evocative and, as a result, psychologically relevant. It is this experiential characteristic of basic representations that lead researchers to attribute the mediation of motivation to the implicit processing system; many agree, for example, that in the realm of social cognition, "experiencing is believing." All of this is unlike the affect-free propositions of theological reasoning, whose abstract qualities both minimize their computational utility and reduce their psychological relevance. Abstractions not only make poor computational tools, but they also make poor agents. Again, Boyer seems to be saying the same thing when he writes that the distortion of standard representations is inevitable since "they must produce inferences to make them coherent or relevant" (2001: 283); or Whitehouse, when he maintains that "a complex body of doctrine cannot 'live' in people's minds" (2000: 152).

Initially, then, computational utility and psychological relevance have to do with cognitive function—specifically, the fit between particular ideas and human social and emotional intelligence—but ultimately they elucidate such cru-

TABLE 6.4 Important contrasts between representational modes.

	Theological representations	Basic representations
Processing	Explicit (optional)	Implicit (default)
Computational utility	Low	High
Psychological relevance	Low	High

cial issues as belief and motivation. The processing disconnects just described not only make theological concepts less useful and salient but also less believable. As discussed in chapter 4, "belief" is in part the result of what Boyer calls "aggregate relevance." The combined activation of the mind's inference systems that makes the representation of religious agents *possible* also makes them *plausible*. But this phenomenon is dependent on implicit processing, which maximizes the suite of nonconscious mental tools used to produce quick, concrete inferences. Explicit processing decouples these same tacit connections, undermining aggregate relevance. In short, there is a direct correlation between the way the brain forms representations and the beliefs that we hold—a correlation highlighted in chapter 4 as the causal relationship between "intuitive" and "reflective" beliefs.

So "theological *incorrectness*," as Jason Slone dubs it (2004), is inevitable in part because in each person there are both "explicit" and "implicit" concepts that they can use, but more completely because explicit, theological-level concepts—while mentally manageable and publicly managed—are in fact conceptual overlays on tacit knowledge people bring to functional, coherent, and meaningful thought about intentional agents, real or imagined. Even amid theological trappings and well-rehearsed dogma, intuitive understandings of supernatural agents continually undermine abstract presentations of such beings. The real "tragedy of the theologian" is that he or she is shopping second-rate wares. Given the dynamics of dual processing and social cognition, basic representations provide robust computational utility and psychological relevance. Abstract, theological representations can be dispensed with, and often are. None of this, of course, requires conscious intent: "Empirical evidence of preconscious and subconscious precepts, memories, and thoughts reminds us that we are not always aware of why we do what we do" (Kihlstrom 1999: 198).

Cognition and Religious Change

Nonconscious mental processes are the scientist's stock in trade. As commented on here by John Kihlstrom and earlier by Michael Gazzaniga, people's minds often resemble an airplane flying on autopilot. Some incredibly sophisticated operations are at work keeping the craft aloft and sailing smoothly along, but the complex computations and mechanical procedures constantly being executed take place on their own, out of view. The autopilot won't suddenly decide to bank the plane hard to right and execute a roll—that sort of behavior requires some conscious commands from the pilot—but much of the flight is successfully carried off by unseen equipment that evaluates input conditions and responds in preprogrammed ways.

The idea of an autopilot unsettles lots of people who have a fear of flying. They would prefer that a well-trained, well-aware human being take hold of the controls and keep them. So imagine such people's reactions to the suggestion that on their flight today some hard banks and rolls might suddenly occur after all, and for no apparent reason. The cognitive scientist knows that, like many of our thoughts, many of our behaviors—even consciously undertaken behaviors—are also guided by nonconscious mental processes. All of us frequently do things without having firm conscious reasons for doing them. How we respond to the information and activity around us is informed by unseen, preprogrammed equipment.

This is true of religious behavior as well. Religion may seem like a domain of life over which we have complete control. After all, religious knowledge is not part of intuitive knowledge and therefore is only used when we choose to use it. Religious actions, though similar to secular actions in many ways, are only done when and where we decide to do them. Nevertheless, if, as Barrett as shown, religious thought like secular thought is influenced by cognitive biases, then religious behaviors like secular behaviors ought to be influenced in part by them also. A second benefit of a dual-process model of religious thought, then, is that it reveals some unseen causes of divergent religious behaviors. Divergent religion not only includes thinking that fails to mirror theological ideas but also the behavioral outcomes of such thinking.

There are, of course, various possible responses to the cognitive tension created by theological representations. It may, for instance, simply go unnoticed. Few religious people are theologians, and few theologians, like scientists off the job, are always theological. Indeed, an appreciable number of religious adherents display little understanding of their tradition's formal conceptual schemes and operate, for all intents and purposes, beneath them. Even those who do possess abstract theological representations naturally default to basic ones during on-line thought. But cognitive tension may manifest itself more visibly, as Boyer points out, in people's willingness to add to, distort, or modify their religion. So there is reason to suspect that some common episodes of religious change occur in response to overly abstract or psychologically irrelevant religious ideas and practices. Pyysiäinen, for example, suggests a direct relationship between psychological and social factors in some cases of religious conversion (2004a, 2005). Similarly, attention to cognition might well cast new light on a wider range of religious change, from historic shifts in mainstream traditions, to the arising of revival movements, to the acceptance of syncretistic teachings and practices, to the genesis of entirely new religions. One working hypothesis that arises from a dual-process model of religious thought is that when public religious systems perpetuate ideas distanced from the cognitive constraints imposed by implicit processing, divergent religious behaviors will likely result (Tremlin 2002, 2005).

Admittedly, this is a hard prediction to validate. One of the obstacles of religious studies throughout the years has been the sheer diversity of religion around the world. Confining one's gaze just to a handful of religions reveals multiple ways of doing religion. The Zen monk strikes an inexorable, pre-reflective pose, the meditative practice of *zazen*, as a means of displaying his Buddha-nature. The Catholic finds solace in a set of well-orchestrated, authoritative rituals that keeps her acceptable in the eyes of God. The Sunni Muslim diligently pursues regular prayer and a divinely prescribed lifestyle as outward expressions of his pious submission to Allah. The practicing Jew identifies most closely with the study of ancient texts and adherence to traditional customs, signs of the suzerain covenant struck between Yahweh and his people. The Hindu fosters positive karma and inner spirituality through a cornucopia of sacred rites and practices. And the variety of religious expression only expands as we consider the discrete traditions that have developed within each of these religions.

In addition to differences in content, religions also display differences in method and organization. Some faiths feature strong leadership and are acted out within highly structured institutions; others find the aid of leaders and teachers optional and solitude preferable. Some religions communicate their beliefs through standardized, repetitive doctrines and practices; others place a premium on personal experiences and stimulating services. Some religions open themselves to everyone and instigate staunch missionary efforts; others define themselves according to limited boundaries based on ethnicity or locale. These are just some of the ways religious traditions can be weighed against each other and such contrasting styles of religion can just as easily be found *within* traditions, as small coteries of people or even large sects choose alternative forms of religious expression that contrast noticeably with the mainstream.

An interesting set of questions revolves around just what drives divergent religion at both the personal and group level. Why would an individual switch their faith commitments or embrace alternative religious practices? Why do religious traditions frequently split into different branches? What leads to revival movements and to the formation of new sects? Is there something inherently unstable about mainstream religion that leaves it vulnerable to divergent practices? Conversely, is there something special about history's enduring religious traditions that provides for their relative stability and longevity? Finally, what if anything does the whole subject of private cognition have to do with the shape and development of public religion?

The specific cause of religious change proposed here touches on each of these questions. To restate this cause in direct terms, people use their religion to serve practical rather than intellectual purposes and expect their gods to behave like people—that is, as meaningful social agents. Religion that achieves and maintains these qualities—qualities that fit with natural cognitive biases—remains relevant to adherents and succeeds as a stable cultural system. Religion that becomes detached from daily life or promotes abstract theological concepts and practices will become irrelevant to adherents and undergo either revision or decline. Certainly adherents within such traditions can be expected to visibly display theologically incorrect thought and behavior.

Is there evidence for such bold claims? We don't have to look far to find hints that a constraint-based explanation for religious change captures at least some of the influences behind divergent religion, whether it takes place on the private or public level. First, consider some hard evidence for the presence of divergent religious thought in even a well-honed, timeworn religious system like Christianity. A decade ago a team of fifteen scholars headed by sociologist Robert Wuthnow conducted the first in-depth study of the extent, functioning, strength, and implications of "small groups," a religious phenomenon that has exploded on the American church scene during the last twenty years (1994a, 1994b). By definition, a "small group" is a small-scale gathering of individuals coming together in informal arrangements outside of institutional church structures for religious purposes: Bible study, prayer, fellowship, mutual support, and other "spiritual" concerns.

While the informational range of Wuthnow's study is of tremendous significance for understanding religion in America today—it reports data from different denominational settings around the country—the study also inadvertently reveals the influence of cognitive biases on religious thought. As Wuthnow documents, small groups promote an environment in which everyday concerns are pursued through everyday means. On the one hand, this is a boon to religious life, or so instigators of small-group gatherings believe. Small groups inherently foster religious identity, group solidarity, emotional attachment, and personal commitment. Yet creating a context in which intuitive forms of thinking dominant has some unexpected side effects:

> It [the small-group dynamic] rejects the received wisdom embodied in formal creeds, doctrines, and ideologies, often diminishing the importance of denominational distinctions, theological tradition, or the special authority of the clergy. Instead, it offers a pragmatic approach to solving one's problems by suggesting that the best proof of God's existence is whether one has received an answer to some

personal problem or by asserting that the Bible is true because it works in everyday life. These groups apply spiritual technology to the life of the soul, implying that the sacred can be realized by following simple guidebooks or formulas, and they often substitute powerful unstated norms of behavior, focusing especially on the value of being a group member and on achieving happiness as part of one's spirituality, for the formalized creeds and theological ideals of the past. The group is often able to define what is right or wrong, encouraging members to pay attention to their feelings, but also evoking these feelings and helping members to interpret them in certain ways. Thus, the movement makes faith more relevant but also risks turning belief into something that people can manipulate for their own selfish purposes. (Wuthnow 1994b: 5)

More telling still, the study also reveals that small groups create a context in which explicit representations of gods are rapidly replaced by implicit concepts. Intriguingly, people even frequently vocalize their personal struggles with thinking about and relating to "God" according to the official concepts used by their churches. Wuthnow's study thus further supports both Barrett's experiments with theological correctness and the proposal made here that theological concepts are not only expendable but also rife with cognitive tension. As Wuthnow's work describes, the god concepts used in small groups are eminently practical and eminently personal:

For the God who is experienced in small groups to be real, it is not enough to have rational arguments about the nature of the universe. Such arguments seem hopelessly arcane to most members of small groups. Reality is now tantamount to being concerned with "real-life issues," especially the ones individuals experience in their everyday lives. God has to be a deity who cares about one's moods, finances, worries, and relationships. If spirituality makes some practical difference to these issues, then God exists. If God is simply a theological teaching, then it makes little difference whether the sacred exists or not. The advantage of this conception of God, as most group leaders we talked to see it, is that God becomes more relevant in individuals' daily lives. The disadvantages are less apparent, but are nevertheless worth considering. One is that God ceases to be a supreme being who is in all respects superior to humans. Rather than being the inscrutable deity of the Reformation, for example, God is now a buddy. God no longer represents such awe-inspiring qualities as being infinite, all-powerful, all-knowing, and perfectly righteous. God is now on the same level as yourself, except perhaps a little warmer and friendlier. (1994b: 238–239)

The practice of small groups, which at the time of Wuthnow's study garnered the participation of more than 75 million people in the United States, is altering the character of American Christianity. Church leaders and small-group advocates themselves proclaim the practice to be the best means available for "revitalizing American religion" (Wuthnow 1994a: ix). But it is worth asking what, precisely, is being "revitalized" and why religious people find small groups to be so much more engaging than traditional church life. If our understanding of the history and operation of human cognition is correct, and if religion is parasitic on garden-variety mental processes, then the style of religion promoted in small groups aligns quite closely with how people naturally think and behave. We should not be surprised that people are finding small-group religion attractive.

The emergence of small groups is an example of religious change that displays the influence of cognitive biases. Divergent religion can be even more consequential, however. Those who participate in small groups may be seeking a more relevant form of religion, yet they are not consciously distancing themselves from mainline religion. Small groups are understood to be accents on more traditional religious practices. But consider some instances of divergent religion that *have* led to permanent changes within Christianity. Often efforts to revive or revise what Bob McCauley and Tom Lawson call theologically "deflated" religious systems (2002) result in the development of breakaway groups and new sects.

Pentecostalism, which arose at the turn of the twentieth century, is an evangelical movement that has its roots in the practices of Catholic and Anglican mystics. Identified as a "second blessing" movement alongside such parallel developments as John Wesley's "holiness" teachings, Pentecostalism has today emerged as a distinct Christian tradition second in size only to Catholicism (Synan 1997). Among the emphases of Pentecostalism is a belief in "baptism in the Holy Spirit," the courting of spiritual gifts such as healing, prophecy, and speaking in "tongues," and the use of ecstatic worship practices. While some of these emphases are highly theological in their own ways, they nevertheless evidence a move away from deflated doctrines and rituals and toward a more personal and practical use of religion and a more intuitive and psychologically relevant conception of god. Pentecostalism's early success as a revival movement resulted in the formation of an autonomous church that remains the fastest growing branch of Christianity and continues to spin off new "waves" of revival, the most recent identified as the "Toronto Blessing."

The more relevant expression of religion offered by Pentecostalism also precipitated the "charismatic movement," another distinctive expression of the Christian faith begun in the 1950s. While owing its roots to Pentecostal influences, the charismatic movement exists almost completely outside of official Pentecostal denominations (Fahlbusch et al. 1991). Indeed, it is because charismatic Christianity has arisen in and remains across the full range of historic churches that it is referred to as a "movement" rather than as a separate faith tradition. This makes charismatic Christianity an example of divergent religion residing within a mainstream framework. Sharing most of the emphases cultivated by Pentecostalism, charismatic Christianity has also evolved as an effort to revive the deflated theological systems in which charismatic Christians find themselves. It is interesting to note that the start of the charismatic movement coincides with efforts within mainline Protestantism to make Christian faith more theologically savvy and politically minded. In the mid-twentieth century, mainline churches enjoyed growing prestige in the media and within intellectual circles by touted liberal social agendas and embracing philosophically oriented theologians like Paul Tillich. But the price of *bon ton* has been heavy. Today these same denominations are still reeling from a backlash of irrelevance. Sociologists and church leaders alike report the sharp declines in membership and financial support experienced by mainline churches over the past half century (Vallet and Zech 1995).

Another—and perhaps the most visible—form of divergent religion that betrays the influence of cognitive biases is syncretism. In the context of religion, syncretism involves the mixing of two or more normally distinct faith traditions. Religious syncretism is actually rather common. As Charles Stewart and Rosalind Shaw argue, "all religions have composite origins and are continually reconstructed through ongoing processes of synthesis and erasure" (1994: 7). It is also true that the many sociopolitical facts surrounding episodes of religious syncretism cannot be readily reduced to the psychological. Nevertheless, attending to the nature of cognition can illumine some instances of people blending their religious views and practices. Consider this time a less parochial and more colorful religious tradition—Sri Lankan Buddhism.

The nation of Sri Lanka provides a laboratory setting for studying a wide range of phenomena, from the unique development of island society to the impact of colonialism on indigenous culture. With respect to religion, Sri Lanka provides a textbook example of syncretism in action, in this case between Theravada Buddhism, local spirit religion, and sundry Hindu practices. Yet religious life in contemporary Sri Lanka is, to say the least, highly controvertible. Today political ideologies, a struggle for social identity, and decades of civil war are inextricably intertwined with religious thought and practice (Tambiah 1992). Any attempt to unravel the factors of religious mixing on the island is fraught with danger. Yet in spite of the many sociopolitical forces that have contributed to change in Sri Lankan religion during the past two centuries, it is also evident that cognitive influences are at work shaping the form of Sinhalese religiosity (Tremlin 2000). In fact, it's hard to imagine a more powerful explanation for the existence of a remarkable range of religious practices antithetical to the "Doctrine of the Elders"—a religious moniker that, nevertheless, is being fought for, quite literally, with bombs and guns.

The most thorough work to date on the development of Sri Lankan Buddhism is that of Indologist Richard Gombrich and anthropologist Gananath Obeyesekere (1988). Concomitant with shifts in the social, political, and organizational aspects of Sri Lankan Buddhism due to historical, ideological, and economic factors are a wide range of religious innovations, some rooted in indigenous practices and others completely new. This transformation of Sinhalese religion, which Gombrich and Obeyesekere call "post-Protestant Buddhism" (1988: 9), can be characterized as a synthesis of traditional Therevadan ideals and spirit religion. Buddhism in Sri Lanka has long existed alongside spirit religions of Hindu origin. Today, however, these two religious expressions are well along in a process of syncretism.

The distinctive differences between these two forms of religion are what are of interest here. Theravada Buddhism is characterized by mental and emotional detachment. Spirit religion, on the other hand, is anything but. Part of what has changed in Sinhalese religiosity, according to Gombrich and Obeyesekere, is a heightened emotionalism. In contrast to the "quiet" and "equanimity" fostered by Buddhist devotional exercises, the spirit religions evoke ecstatic responses. The emphasis on possession, trance, *bhakti*-style worship, and emotionally loud cult practices stand in stark contrast to the austerity of Theravada Buddhism. The religious center of Kataragama, which was taken over from Hindu Tamils and "Buddhicized," has become the locus of religious innovation. It is here that Obeyesekere first noted the appearance of ecstatic priests and priestesses who constitute an entirely new religious class—the "Hindu-Buddhist religious devotees" (Obeyesekere 1981: 3). Yet such developments are by no means confined to Kataragama or Sri Lanka's rural environs. The island's cities and suburbs have also become wellsprings of spirit religion. Shrines abound, alone and in tandem with Buddhist temples, and freelance priests and priestesses host a steady stream of clients from across the social spectrum seeking oracles, exorcisms, astrological readings, and divine assistance for living.

For Gombrich and Obeyesekere, the contemporary dominance of spirit religion signals a sea change in Sri Lankan Buddhism. When considering the nature of Sinhalese religiosity today, with its concern for worldly advantage, its devotion to Sinhalicized gods, its unbounded emotionalism, and, in the case of kavada dancing, its flirtation with the sexually illicit, it must be acknowledged that "nothing could be further from the ethos of Buddhism" (1988: 195). Nor is spirit religion merely being grafted onto Buddhist practice; rather, Buddhism itself is being transformed. As Gombrich and Obeyesekere argue, many of the religious changes now unfolding in Sri Lanka are not only new historically but also either violate or reverse basic postulates of traditional Buddhism. Specific examples include the social movements known as Sarvodaya, the revival of nun orders, the implementation of Buddhist marriage, a deepened role for astrology, dramatic claims of Buddhahood by ordinary men, and the self-ordination of Uttama Sadhu, who, in addition to leading his own breakaway *sangha*, has also rewritten the original Buddhist texts in accordance with spirit-revealed revelations from his nuns. Each of these examples stands in stark contrast to traditional Theravadan beliefs and practices. Certainly they challenge the Three Jewels traditionally used to identify a person *as being* Buddhist. Two further recent innovations illustrative of the synthesis between Buddhism and Hindu religious practices are the *Bodhi puja* ceremony and the Buddhist appropriation of fire walking.

Does attention to the nature of cognition help make sense of contemporary Sinhalese religiosity? As stated earlier, while the causes of syncretism may be multifaceted, cognitive biases at least influence the direction that religious innovations like those in Sri Lanka take. Gombrich and Obeyesekere feel, for example, that the impetus behind religious change in Sri Lanka is rooted in shifting socioeconomic conditions of island life. Confronted with rapid population growing, the emergence of a bourgeois and urban proletariat, the disintegration of traditional village and kin groups, the encroachment of foreign interests, and elevated economic ambitions, the Sinhalese have turned in new ways to gods for help in coping with—and hopefully overcoming—the exigencies of the daily round. Yet this is precisely how we should expect religion to function and religious people to behave. Moreover, we should actually predict divergent religion within a highly abstract religious system like Theravada Buddhism. For religion to be deemed relevant it must have practical application not merely philosophical appeal, and its supernatural agents must align with the assumptions of social intelligence. In Sri Lanka being a Buddhist is essential to Sinhalese identity, but Buddhist beliefs and practices offer few answers for what matters most to people. Local spirit religions and Hindu-inspired rituals fit that bill much better. As a result, Sinhalese people still take final refuge in a theologically absent Buddha, but they turn to *real* gods when facing the frustrations and misfortunes of life.

Examples like these suggest that mental predispositions do indeed influence religious behavior, sometimes in dramatic ways. They may even lead to changes in established religious systems that are attributed to other causes or simply left unexplained. At the very least, focusing on the functioning of human cognition reveals that religious change itself is not arbitrary or boundless. People's cognitive biases shape the direction of religious change because a religion's fit with these biases determines what works and what is irrelevant. With gods *and* religion, not just anything goes. People are guided by practical concerns, and they strive to reconcile them using everyday understandings of agency and social exchange. If religion is to remain meaningful to ordinary people, then it must conform to these constraints. This is by no means to claim that all events of conversion, revival, religious innovation and the like are brought about by purely cognitive factors. There are a host of ecological reasons for religious change. But many of the short and long-term shifts in religious behavior that commonly occur within and across religious systems can be better understood in light of cognitive and psychological biases.

Cognitive Constraint on Religious Systems

The phenomenon of divergent religion is not ascribed to the behavior of religious individuals alone. In fact it has most often been recognized, and with equal wonderment, as a characteristic of religion at the group level. Anthropological studies going well back in time—like the several case studies just discussed—note how entire religions bifurcate along "formal" and "folk" lines, or between "Great" and "Little" traditions. In many faiths there can be found two contrasting styles of religion, one corresponding to orthodoxy as defined by its religious elite, the other a popular form of religious expression.

The usual explanations for this development are sociopolitical in nature. Max Weber distinguishes between routinized and charismatic religious forms (1930, 1947). Ernest Gellner differentiates urban and rural religion (1969). Jack Goody contrasts literate and non-literate religion (1968, 1986). Richard Werbner notes distinctions between regional cults and local cults (1977). Stephen Sharot outlines disparities between a religion of the elites and of the masses (2001). Other descriptive terms from the past century could easily be added to this list. However, while each of these scholars appears to be capturing very real—and, likely, the very same—dichotomies of religious expression, none of them manage to construct a complete or satisfying explanation of their causes and interactions. The reason for this is that each approach lacks the most crucial piece of the puzzle: the way religion is handled cognitively. One notable exception is the recent work of Harvey Whitehouse, who proposes that religious systems are structured in accord with two modalities—a "doctrinal" mode and an "imagistic" mode—with differing styles of codification, transmission, political organization, *and* cognitive processing (1995, 2000, 2004).

While the previous chapter attempted to show that god concepts have everything to do with religion, this one is arguing that the way in which people naturally think about gods and use religion influences their thought and behavior vis-à-vis their established faith traditions. Divergent religion is influenced by cognitive constraints that lead people to favor basic, intuitively generated notions of gods in the service of practical concerns and at the expense of more abstract, theological ones. But there may well be a third, broader application of this principle. If, as Boyer points out, one of the implications of cognitive constraint "is that cultural transmission is an inherently *selective* process" (1994b: 392), then the shape and stability of public religious systems themselves ought to be linked to the same cognitive constraints that govern private religious thought.

This contention, like the entire argument presented here, begs an important question—one that can be posed in different ways. Why, if intuitive ideas about gods are most relevant, do more theologically correct representations exist at all? Why do more abstract and less relevant "official" religious systems continue if folk religion is what people prefer? Why do many public religions drift away from what are more natural forms of religious thought and behavior? These concerns query the history of religion itself. They require speculating on the genesis of human culture, which is always a dubious undertaking. Few cultural behaviors are preserved as archaeological artifacts, and records of "origins" never are. Furthermore, if religious ideas are based on natural processes of cognition that operate even in the absence of formal cultural systems, then the start of "religion," as it has been defined in this book, was surely preceded by less organized and less doctrinal forms of religious thinking and behavior.

For this reason it is probable that the phenomenon of human religion did not (and does not) take on its common institutional/doctrinal character until the advent of specific historical conditions. Scholars who pursue cultural evolution think it likely that the earliest expressions of religion beginning with the Upper Paleolithic hunter-gatherers only take on a more doctrinal tenor when and where new conditions for social organization and cultural transmission take hold, including the development of political associations and literacy (Diamond 1998; Donald 1991). Under these conditions religion becomes institutionalized, administered by religious specialists, and communicated in standardized texts and teachings. We've seen the same process at work countless times in our own age, as colonialism and missionary efforts inevitably restructure indigenous societies and religions.

Of course, religion doesn't *need* to become institutionalized and codified in the way that is so common today. Elaborately developed religious systems like Buddhism, Judaism, Hinduism, Islam, and Christianity may dominate, but there are still a number of localized, loosely organized, and minimally doctrinal forms of religion around. More importantly, religious people don't really need institutions and specialists to understand how religion works. Because religious thought and action are based on tacit knowledge shared by all, individuals are quite capable of handling religious concepts on their own. This is particularly true with respect to gods. Religious specialists contribute nothing essential to people's representations of supernatural agents. Earlier we saw that elaborate doctrine is a conceptual overlay on more natural ways of thinking. Now we see that theology is also the product of specific external forces.

True to intuition, then, less theologically developed forms of religion ought to be more successful, all things being equal. The psychological evidence marshaled in this book highlights the utility of tacit forms of thought over abstract reasoning in the domain of religion. Evidence from comparative religion confirms this finding at the public level. More often than not, the "official" religion is an illusion. This reality is inevitable because people do not naturally represent their supernatural concepts in accord with formal conceptual schemes.

Gods are represented as counterintuitive entities that engage a host of strategic capacities. By contrast, theological concepts rarely produce the inferences that make them both coherent and relevant. As a result, "people are never quite as 'theologically correct' as the guild would like them to be" (Boyer 2001: 283). Because people's thinking is guided by cognitive constraints rather than by literal memory, they will always be theologically incorrect.

In spite of these findings, doctrinal religion has clearly monopolized the marketplace. In terms of cultural success, the winning religions today are in fact those that have become the most institutionally and doctrinally developed. This is because all things are *not* equal. Once the requisite social conditions are in place it becomes rather difficult to escape them. Political institutions and standardized modes of communication overshadow—in many cases simply overwhelm—loosely developed, poorly codified systems. As Whitehouse has shown, religions with centralized authority, well-defined organizational structure, routinized practices, and standardized teachings are highly portable and rapidly spread (2002). In addition, institutions and doctrine take advantage of other powerful psychological forces. Institutions not only dictate and control social relationships and correct forms of practice but also foster group identity and draw coalitional boundaries that become costly to cross. Likewise, developed doctrine not only adjusts and solidifies beliefs but also establishes what counts as heresy. People have time and again rejected standing coalitions and teachings and broken away from mainstream religious systems, but they inevitably develop new coalitions and teachings that in turn function in the same way.

It must also be mentioned here—for an erroneous impression has perhaps been made—that doctrinal religion is not necessarily inchoate, cold, or irrelevant. If it were it simply wouldn't exist. Doctrinal traditions like the current world religions provide a wide variety of practices that give intuitive processing free reign in personal religious expression. Prayer, meditation, chant, confession, offerings, worship, and a lot of profoundly experiential rituals help to keep doctrinal religion relevant to those who practice it. Scholars such as Pyysiäinen have for some time been arguing for increased attention to the role of "experience" in explanations of religion (2001a, 2001b), and any aspect of religious life that strengthens or weakens intuitive modes of thought is pertinent to the success and stability of a religious system. This observation is not merely an aside. Because cultural products are the result of selective processes operative at the level of individual minds, the cognitive constraints that shape religious thought at the private level must also be reflected at the public level. As Robert Hinde points out, "it is with the everyday believer that we must be concerned if we are to understand the persistence of religious systems" (1999: 36).

This warning returns us to the original point that though religious thought remains parasitic on ordinary cognitive processes, things happen to mental representations once they enter the public domain, particularly in social conditions like ours. Public representations are frequently manipulated, expanded on, and transformed, all in ways that are characteristic of theological reflection and which can distance them from their moorings in intuitive processing. But because of this effect, conceptual transformation is not boundless. There are limits to the kinds of changes that can be imposed on religious representations. For religious systems to remain as stable cultural fixtures that are successfully transmitted to others, they must be driven by cognitive relevance rather than by theological profundity.

Both Boyer and Sperber recognize that cultural transmission is a "relevance-driven" process (Boyer 2000b; Sperber 1996). Just as information that fits well with intuitive expectations is easily understood and used, so too is it easily acquired, stored, and passed along to others. As Sperber and Wilson have convincingly shown, people attend most to information that richly engages the various inference systems of the mind (1986). This in turn plays out in the distribution of information. So we can describe relevance as an active force shaping cultural acquisition. More relevant information has a *natural* advantage over less relevant information. This applies to "religious" information as well. People build supernatural concepts in ways that maximizes inference potential using minimal processing effort. These same kinds of concepts are therefore advantaged over those that are abstract, impractical, and cognitively cumbersome.

What has all this to do with the stability and development of actual religious systems over time? The same cognitive processes that constrain thinking about gods are also at work shaping the religions that form around them. The various theoretical threads woven throughout this chapter, in fact, suggest two general rules of cultural selection in the domain of religion. First, the shifting dynamics that so often take place within religious systems are due to conflicting ecological and psychological pressures. Given the twin demands of public transmission and private cognition, most religious systems will display features of "official" and "popular" religiosity. On the one hand, organizing, communicating, and overseeing religion necessitates institutionalized techniques for transmitting pre-packaged ideology that takes theological forms requiring literal memory and explicit processing. On the other hand, religious acquisition and representation is largely an intuitive exercise that engages the implicit processing system of cognition. If religions are to remain relevant to participants, then they must find ways to satisfy both of these demands. Pyysiäinen, who also emphasizes that theological traditions are an epiphenomenal overlay on natural religiosity, adequately summarizes my position when he writes that the more intuitive forms of religion "provide individual motivation" while doctrinal features "offer systems-level tools for the preservation of stable traditions" (2005: 160).

This suggests, second, that the most stable and durable religions are those that gravitate toward a balance of explicit and implicit forms of religiosity. What we see, then, is a kind of "cognitive optimum" equation operative at the level of cultural systems. Private religious belief and practice are motivated and sustained by relevance. If public religion is to continue to be acquired and transmitted, it must conform to and foster this same functional requirement. Religious systems that fail to maintain this balance are likely to be revised or abandoned. Again, Pyysiäinen concurs that highly doctrinal religion is "constantly threatened by the fact that its concepts seem irrelevant and are difficult to use in everyday reasoning;" and yet, "only doctrinal religions have the potential to spread beyond the boundaries of the local community and unite large masses of people" (2005: 160). This perspective is also nicely compatible with Sperber's notion of "cultural attraction," which emphasizes how the content of cultural productions is readily influenced by both psychological and ecological factors (1996). The type of brains we have—even the specific mental modules of which they are comprised—must be seen as crucial causal factors in the development of cultural phenomena: "They tend to fix a lot of cultural content in and around the cognitive domain the processing of which they specialize in" (1996: 113).

The religion that we find in the world is directly related to the way that people think, whether that is immediately obvious or not. This should be expected if all things public are also the products of private minds. A book like this one exists both because it began as an idea in one person's private mental life and because of the public knowledge that book-making requires. In the same way, catchy songs spread because they resonate similarly from one mind to the next, and their existence, too, is due to a physical format—live instruments and voices, broadcasts, laser discs, and so forth. As a cultural phenomenon, though, religion is more like a catchy song than a printed book. While books may or may not be of interest, catchy songs somehow remain irritatingly catchy. Also one is usually capable of expressing one's response to a book while catchy songs evoke at another, less analytical level.

The more fundamental difference between a book and a catchy song—and what makes this comparison illustrative of religion—regards what, precisely, makes the song "catchy." The content of books can vary greatly, and to little formal effect. A book is a book and readers are drawn or not drawn to it for explicit reasons. Not all songs are catchy, however, and moreover, what makes a song catchy has everything to do with the interaction between particular sounds and the mental faculties of listeners. This takes us back again to the noncultural foundations of thought. The techniques of musical composition might not be innate to human minds, but the cognitive machinery that recognizes and responds to music assuredly is a part of our hardwired equipment—yet another mental module described by David and Ann Premack (2002). What makes music *music* rather than just noise—what music in essence is—is its qualities of tone, rhythm, and syncopation that our minds find harmonic rather than cacophonous. Furthermore, we naturally find many rhythmic and harmonic sounds pleasant, and this response too offers a fascinating study in evolutionary developments that are shared by animal species for which sound is integral to communication. "Catchy" songs, though, strike chords (figuratively speaking) that prosaic songs don't. Minds clearly have musical preferences that catchy songs, however accidentally, manage to match. This suggests that within the vast range of musical possibilities there are cognitive constraints on the forms of music that will become widely popular. One can picture this preferred structure of harmony and beat as a kind of melodious watercourse flowing through the middle of an expansive musical valley.

Religion is similarly constrained by innate cognitive biases. In the mental valley that harbors religious ideas rather than musical ones, some forms of religion are more relevant—another way of saying pleasing?—than others. Just as the range of musical possibilities is great, so also can religion be conceptualized and practiced in diverse ways. Yet catchy religions, like catchy songs, are found within a narrower basin of forms constrained by the operation of mental equipment with which nature has endowed us. Taking account of the way individual minds function ultimately explains the durability and development of religion itself.

Conclusion

The scientific study of religion is a relatively recent affair. For hundreds of years in the Western world, religion—or more correctly, Christian theology—was regarded as the "queen of the sciences," offering the framework in which all other knowledge was to be explained. Religion itself required no explanation. Divine revelation was accepted both as a sufficient condition for truth and as self-authenticating. Religion provided thought with its interpretive lens; few imagined that thought needed to explicate religion.

Today investigations of cognition are not only revealing the processes of the human mind but also explaining many of its products, including religion. From a cognitive standpoint, religion is neither revelatory nor enigmatic nor inextricable. Religion is simply one outcome of faculties of thought common to all normal brains. Explaining religion, however, is not to *explain it away*—a fear of those who eschew the naturalistic enterprise. Religion remains extremely noteworthy, and precisely for the reasons that it is so often newsworthy. Regardless of causal backgrounds, religious ideas are potent enough that multitudes of people take them with great seriousness and organize their entire lives around the practices of a chosen faith tradition. Because successful mental representations become public, religious ideas are equally influential in the social sphere, to the point of playing consequential roles in human history. Religion has supported institutions and empires, shaped ethnic narratives and national identities. Religion has inspired the sublime and instigated the gruesome, prompted acts of beneficence and launched wars.

Certainly it is difficult to call religion ordinary when it appears in so many ways to be quite extraordinary.

The introduction to this book began by highlighting the extent to which the cognitive approach to religion has advanced the discipline at the theoretical level. Cognitivists are today offering valuable insights into such engaging issues as the arising and persistence of religious thought, the place of religious ideas in the larger repertoire of mental representations, the ubiquity and similarity of religion across cultures, and the shape and development of religious systems. In each of these areas the focus of attention has been on the cognitive foundations of god concepts—the way human minds create and use them, and the way religious behaviors and communities take shape around them.

For students of religion, this approach is likely both new and, perhaps, a little disconcerting. The cognitive science of religion challenges long-held assumptions about the origins and nature of religious thought and religious systems. It also challenges long-used theories and methods in the study of religion. Traditionally there have been two ways to conceive and study religion as a natural human phenomenon. One way is to treat religion as a *sui generis* reality only amenable to interpretations of various sorts. Here one finds stories about the "sacred" versus the "profane" facets of life as well as numerous opinions about the inherent longings of *Homo religiosis*. The second way is to envision religion as an invention, which, like other human tools, can be explained in terms of utility, usually with reference to intellectual, emotional, or social needs. As it should by now be clear, this book tacks along a third course, one that sees religion as a cultural by-product of biologically based psychological commitments to god concepts, and that explains the various aspects of religion in relation to these foundational psychological commitments.

This "new" science of religion is new enough, however, to still be framing in its theoretical superstructure. Important empirical work and hard experimentation has certainly begun, but some of the approach's major claims and predictions remain only partially substantiated. At the same time, many additional lines of investigation continue to be drawn in rapid fashion. The constraint-based argument for religious change sketched out in chapter 6 is a perfect example of a research program in search of proofs. In keeping with its scientific ties, any predictions that come from the cognitive approach to religion need to look good on the ground and not merely on the blackboard. What is exciting about this developing enterprise, though, is its truly interdisciplinary profile. Interest in uncovering the cognitive origins and foundations of religion is bringing together researchers from diverse fields, linking what have historically been some deep gulfs separating the human, social, and natural sciences. Religious studies, previously among the most ghettoized of academic departments, is now making a significant contribution to human understanding.

The cognitive perspective on religion offered here might be especially disconcerting to people who are not engaged in the academic study of religion but who count religious faith and practice as important features of their personal lives. For such people the idea that gods are ideas and that religion, like every other human activity, is underwritten by hidden mental processes will be understandably unwelcome. Religious beliefs are among our most cherished and sacrosanct, and naturalistic explanations appear to diminish their significance and challenge our commitments.

Richard Dawkins has written about how, upon the publication of his first book, he began to receive letters and communications from people commenting on what they took to be the bleak, pessimistic message behind his portrayal of genetic programs and cosmic origins. One tearful woman whom he mentions in particular had been persuaded "that life was empty and purposeless" (1998: ix). Science is often accused of stripping away mystery and marvel and replacing them with barren facts and figures. In the process, science's cold calculations remove the joys and hopes that make life worth living.

But such intentions are quite beyond the endeavors of science and one can just as easily marvel at the human capacities displayed in the very act of science. What is more, let me suggest that rather than threatening or reducing the beauty or integrity of life, the discoveries made through science in fact enhances them. Is it really true that charting the intricate workings of the human body diminishes the magnificence of its design or the wonder of being? Is it really true that measuring the dimensions of the universe limits its grandeur or the possibilities it presents? Does an understanding of the building blocks of life really bleed existence of its meaning and purpose? It would seem instead that nature is sufficiently amazing to stir our imaginations and emotions. It would seem instead that daily life and relationships offer us plenty to enjoy, hope for, and believe in.

In the same way the cognitive science of religion does not set out to challenge the veracity of religious thought and behavior but, rather, to better understand them. Religion is one way that humans naturally express themselves, so the study of how religion works is integral to our understanding of what it means to be human. Nor does the cognitive science of religion seek to overturn religion. Religious belief persists *because of* not *in spite of* the reasons described in this book. It might even be pointed out that little of what has been discussed here is fundamentally at odds with religious teachings, save perhaps to fundamentalists for whom the idea of an evolutionary model (in any form) is anathema. Many scientists studying the human brain, including those who come at it from an evolutionary perspective, are themselves religious, and some researchers working in the cognitive science of religion openly practice a religious faith.

In the end—and this is the winning point—whatever we think, whatever we talk about, and however we feel, it is all the work of our brains. These three-pound cogitating organs composed of 100 billion nerve cells make us what we are—as a species and as individuals. We use them to organize and interpret the world around us. We use them to settle on decisions and to orchestrate actions. We use them to emote and to dream, and to share our feelings and thoughts with others. We also use them to debate questions of ultimate truth, such as whether gods exist or not. In every domain of human life, the brain is the seat of knowledge, including the knowledge of god. We may not qualify as the kinds of beings that possess divine minds—though, interestingly, some religions would say that we do—but we do have minds that are naturally well tuned to think divine thoughts.

Bibliography

Aiello, L. and C. Dean (1990). *An Introduction to Human Evolutionary Anatomy*. London: Academic Press.

Allman, J. (1999). *Evolving Brains*. New York: Scientific American Library.

Andresen, J. (ed.) (2000). *Religion in Mind: Cognitive Perspectives on Religious Belief, Ritual, and Experience*. Cambridge: Cambridge University Press.

Astington, J., P. Harris, and D. R. Olson (eds.) (1988). *Developing Theories of Mind*. New York: Cambridge University Press.

Atran, S. (1990). *Cognitive Foundations of Natural History: Towards an Anthropology of Science*. Cambridge: Cambridge University Press.

———. (2002). *In Gods We Trust: The Evolutionary Landscape of Religion*. Oxford: Oxford University Press.

Attneave, F. (1954). "Informational Aspects of Visual Perception." *Psychological Reviews* 61, 183–193.

Axelrod, R. (1984). *The Evolution of Cooperation*. New York: Basic Books.

Baillargeon, R. (1995). "Physical Reasoning in Infancy." In M. S. Gazzaniga (ed.), *The Cognitive Neurosciences*. Cambridge, Mass.: MIT Press.

Barkow, J. H., L. Cosmides, and J. Tooby (eds.) (1992). *The Adapted Mind: Evolutionary Psychology and the Generation of Culture*. Oxford: Oxford University Press.

Baron-Cohen, S. (1990). "Autism: A Specific Cognitive Disorder of 'Mind-Blindness'." *International Review of Psychiatry* 2, 79–88.

———. (1995). *Mindblindness: An Essay on Autism and Theory of Mind*. Cambridge, Mass.: MIT Press.

Baron-Cohen, S., A. Leslie, and U. Frith (1985). "Does the Autistic Child Have a 'Theory of Mind'?" *Cognition* 21, 37–46.

Baron-Cohen, S., H. Ring, J. Moriarty, P. Shmitz, D. Costa, and P. Ell (1994). "Recognition of Mental State Terms: Clinical Findings in Children with Autism and a Functional Neuroimaging Study of Normal Adults. *British Journal of Psychiatry* 165, 640–649.

Baron-Cohen, S., H. Tager-Flusberg, and D. Cohen (eds.) (1993). *Understanding Other Minds: Perspectives from Autism.* Oxford: Oxford University Press.

Barrett, J. L. (1998). "Cognitive Constraints on Hindu Concepts of the Divine." *Journal for the Scientific Study of Religion* 37, 608–619.

———. (1999). "Theological Correctness: Cognitive Constraint and the Study of Religion." *Method and Theory in the Study of Religion* 11, 325–339.

———. (2000). "Exploring the Natural Foundations of Religion." *Trends in Cognitive Sciences* 4, 29–34.

———. (2001). "How Ordinary Cognition Informs Petitionary Prayer." *Journal of Cognition and Culture* 1, 259–269.

———. (2002). "Dumb Gods, Petitionary Prayer, and the Cognitive Science of Religion." In I. Pyysiäinen and V. Anttonen (eds.), *Current Approaches in the Cognitive Science of Religion.* London: Continuum.

———. (2004). *Why Would Anyone Believe in God?* Walnut Creek, Calif.: AltaMira.

Barrett, J. L. and A. H. Johnson (2003). "The Role of Control in Attributing Intentional Agency to Inanimate Objects." *Journal of Cognition and Culture* 3, 208–217.

Barrett, J. L. and B. VanOrman (1996). "The Effects of the Use of Images in Worship on God Concepts." *Journal of Psychology and Christianity* 15, 38–45.

Barrett, J. L. and E. T. Lawson (2001). "Ritual Intuitions: Cognitive Contributions to Judgments of Ritual Efficacy." *Journal of Cognition and Culture* 1, 183–201.

Barrett, J. L. and F. C. Keil (1996). "Conceptualizing a Non-Natural Entity: Anthropomorphism in God Concepts." *Cognitive Psychology* 31, 219–247.

Barrett, J. L. and M. A. Nyhof (2001). "Spreading Non-Natural Concepts: The Role of Intuitive Conceptual Structures in Memory and Transmission of Cultural Materials." *Journal of Cognition and Culture* 1, 69–100.

Barrett, J. L., R. Richert, and A. Driesenga (2001). "God's Beliefs versus Mother's: The Development of Nonhuman Agent Concepts." *Child Development* 72, 50–65.

Barsalou, L. W. (1992). *Cognitive Psychology: An Overview for Cognitive Scientists.* Hillsdale, N.J.: Lawrence Erlbaum.

Bechtel, W. and A. A. Abrahamsen (1991). *Connectionism and the Mind: An Introduction to Parallel Processing in Networks.* Oxford: Blackwell.

Bell, C. (1997). *Ritual: Perspectives and Dimensions.* Oxford: Oxford University Press.

Berger, L. R. (2000). *In the Footsteps of Eve: The Mystery of Human Origins.* Washington, D.C.: National Geographic Adventure Press.

Bering, J. (2001). "The Biological Bases for Afterlife Beliefs." Paper presented at the Annual Meeting of the Society for the Scientific Study of Religion, Columbus, Ohio.

———. (2002). "Intuitive Conceptions of Dead Agents' Minds: The Natural Foundations of Afterlife Beliefs as Phenomenological Boundary." *Journal of Cognition and Culture* 2, 263–308.

Blackmore, S. (1999). *The Meme Machine.* Oxford: Oxford University Press.

Bloom, P. (1998). "Theories of Artifact Categorization." *Cognition* 66, 87–93.

Boden, M. A. (1991). *The Creative Mind: Myths and Mechanisms.* New York: Basic Books.

Boyer, P. (1994a). *The Naturalness of Religious Ideas: A Cognitive Theory of Religion.* Berkeley: University of California Press.

———. (1994b). "Cognitive Constraints on Cultural Representations: Natural Ontologies and Religious Ideas." In L. A. Hirschfeld and S. A. Gelman (eds.), *Mapping the Mind: Domain Specificity in Cognition and Culture.* Cambridge: Cambridge University Press.

———. (1995). "Causal Understanding in Cultural Representations: Cognitive Constraints on Inferences from Cultural Input." In D. Sperber, D. Premack, and A. J. Premack (eds.), *Causal Cognition: A Multidisciplinary Debate.* New York: Oxford University Press.

———. (2000a). "Functional Origins of Religious Concepts: Ontological and Strategic Selection in Evolved Minds." *The Journal of the Royal Anthropological Institute* 6, 195–214.

———. (2000b). "Evolution of a Modern Mind and the Origins of Culture: Religious Concepts as a Limiting Case." In P. Carruthers and A. Chamberlain (eds.), *Evolution and the Human Mind: Modularity, Language, and Meta-cognition.* Cambridge: Cambridge University Press.

———. (2001). *Religion Explained: The Evolutionary Origins of Religious Thought.* New York: Basic Books.

———. (2002). "Why Do Gods and Spirits Matter at All?" In I. Pyysiäinen and V. Anttonen (eds.), *Current Approaches in the Cognitive Science of Religion.* London: Continuum.

———. (2003). "Religious Thought and Behaviour as By-Products of Brain Function." *Trends in Cognitive Sciences* 7, 119–124.

Boyer, P. and C. Ramble (2001). "Cognitive Templates for Religious Concepts: Cross-Cultural Evidence for Recall of Counter-Intuitive Representations." *Cognitive Science* 25, 535–564.

Brain, C. K. (1983). *The Hunters or the Hunted? An Introduction to Cave Taphonomy.* Chicago: University of Chicago Press.

Bransford, J. D. and N. S. McCarrell (1974). "A Sketch of a Cognitive Approach to Comprehension: Some Thoughts about Understanding What It Means to Comprehend." In W. B. Weimer and D. S. Palermo (eds.), *Cognition and the Symbolic Processes.* Hillsdale, N.J.: Lawrence Erlbaum.

Braun, W. and R. T. McCucheon (2000). *Guide to the Study of Religion.* London: Cassell.

Brothers, L. (1990). "The Social Brain: A Project for Integrating Primate Behavior and Neurophysiology in a New Domain." *Concepts in NeuroScience* 1, 27–51.

Burenhuldt, G. (ed.) (1993). *The First Humans: Human Origins and History to 10,000 B.C.* New York: HarperCollins.

Burkert, W. (1996). *Creation of the Sacred: Tracks of Biology in Early Religions.* Cambridge, Mass.: Harvard University Press.

Byrne, R. W. and A. Whiten (eds.) (1988). *Machiavellian Intelligence: Social Expertise and the Evolution of Intellect in Monkeys, Apes, and Humans.* Oxford: Oxford University Press.

Call, J. and M. Tomasello (1999). "A Nonverbal Theory of Mind Test: The Performance of Children and Apes." *Child Development* 70, 381–395.

Carey, S. (1985). *Conceptual Change in Childhood.* Cambridge, Mass.: MIT Press.

Carruthers, P. and A. Chamblerlain (eds.) (2000). *Evolution and the Human Mind: Modularity, Language, and Meta-Cognition.* Cambridge: Cambridge University Press.

Chaiken, S. and Y. Trope (eds.) (1999). *Dual-Process Theories in Social Psychology.* New York: Guilford Press.

Chomsky, N. (1959). "Review of *Verbal Behavior* by B. F. Skinner." *Language* 35, 26–58.

———. (1980). *Rules and Representations.* New York: Columbia University Press.

———. (1986). *Knowledge of Language: Its Nature, Origins, and Use.* New York: Praeger.

———. (1988). *Language and Problems of Knowledge.* Cambridge, Mass.: MIT Press.

Coles. R. (1996). *In God's House: Children's Drawings.* Grand Rapids, Mich.: Eerdmans.

Cosmides, L. (1989). "The Logic of Social Exchange: Has Natural Selection Shaped How Humans Reason? Studies with the Wason selection task." *Cognition* 31, 187–276.

Cosmides, L. and J. Tooby (1992). "Cognitive Adaptations for Social Exchange." In J. H. Barkow, L. Cosmides, and J. Tooby (eds.), *The Adapted Mind: Evolutionary Psychology and the Generation of Culture.* Oxford: Oxford University Press.

———. (1994). "Origins of Domain Specificity: The Evolution of Functional Organization." In L. A. Hirschfeld and S. A. Gelman (eds.), *Mapping the Mind: Domain Specificity in Cognition and Culture.* Cambridge: Cambridge University Press.

Cronk, L. (1999). *That Complex Whole: Culture and the Evolution of Human Behavior.* Boulder, Colo.: Westview.

Damasio, A. R. (1999). *The Feeling of What Happens: Body and Emotion in the Making of Consciousness.* New York: Harcourt Brace.

d'Aquili, E. G. and A. B. Newberg (1999). *The Mystical Mind: Probing the Biology of Religious Experience.* Minneapolis, Minn.: Fortress Press.

Darwin, C. (1859). *On the Origin of Species by Means of Natural Selection.* London: John Murray.

———. (1871). *The Descent of Man, and Selection in Relation to Sex.* London: John Murray.

Dawkins, R. (1976). *The Selfish Gene.* Oxford: Oxford University Press.

———. (1982). *The Extended Phenotype.* Oxford: Oxford University Press.

———. (1998). *Unweaving the Rainbow: Science, Delusion, and the Appetite for Wonder.* New York: Houghton Mifflin.

DeCasper, A. J. and W. P. Fifer (1980). "Of Human Bonding: Newborns Prefer Their Mothers' Voices." *Science* 208, 1174–1176.

Denes-Raj, V. and S. Epstein (1994). "Conflict between Intuitive and Rational Processing: When People Behave against Their Better Judgment." *Journal of Personality and Social Psychology* 66, 819–829.

Dennett, D. C. (1987). *The Intentional Stance.* Cambridge, Mass.: MIT Press.

———. (1991). *Consciousness Explained.* New York: Little, Brown, & Company.

———. (1995). *Darwin's Dangerous Idea: Evolution and the Meanings of Life.* New York: Simon & Schuster.

de Waal, F. (1982). *Chimpanzee Politics: Power and Sex among Apes.* Baltimore, Md.: Johns Hopkins University Press.

Diamond, J. (1998). *Guns, Germs, and Steel: The Fate of Human Societies.* New York: W. W. Norton.

Donald, M. (1991). *Origins of the Modern Mind: Three Stages in the Evolution of Culture and Cognition.* Cambridge, Mass.: Harvard University Press.

Dunbar, R. I. M. (1992). "Neocortex Size as a Constraint on Group Size in Primates." *Journal of Human Evolution* 20, 469–493.

———. (1993). "Co-Evolution of Neocortex Size, Group Size, and Language in Humans." *Behavioral and Brain Sciences* 16, 681–735.

———. (1997). *Grooming, Gossip, and the Evolution of Language.* Cambridge, Mass.: Harvard University Press.

———. (1998). "The Social-Brain Hypothesis." *Evolutionary Anthropology* 6, 178–190.

———. (2000). "On the Origin of the Human Mind." In P. Carruthers and A. Chamberlain (eds.), *Evolution and the Human Mind: Modularity, Language, and Meta-Cognition.* Cambridge: Cambridge University Press.

Durham, W. H. (1991). *Coevolution, Genes, Cultures, and Human Diversity.* Stanford, Calif.: Stanford University Press.

Durkheim, E. (1995) (1912). *The Elementary Forms of Religious Life.* New York: Free Press.

Eddy, T. J., G. G. Gallup, and D. J. Povinelli (1993). "Attribution of Cognitive States to Animals: Anthropomorphism in Comparative Perspective." *Journal of Social Issues* 49, 87–107.

Elman, J. L., E. A. Bates, M. H. Johnson, A. Karmiloff-Smith, D. Parisi, and K. Plunkett (1996). *Rethinking Innateness: A Connectionist Perspective on Development.* Cambridge, Mass.: MIT Press.

Epstein, S. (1994). "Integration of the Cognitive and the Psychodynamic Unconscious." *American Psychologist* 49, 709–724.

Epstein, S. and R. Pacini (1999). "Some Basic Issues regarding Dual-Process Theories from the Perspective of Cognitive-Experiential Self-Theory." In S. Chaiken and Y. Trope (eds.), *Dual-Process Theories in Social Psychology.* New York: Guilford Press.

Eslinger, P. and A. Damasio (1985). "Severe Disturbance of Higher Cognition after Bilateral Frontal Lobe Ablation: Patient EVR." *Neurology* 35, 1731–1741.

Fahlbusch, E., J. M. Lochman, J. Mbiti, J. Pelikan, and L. Vischer (eds.) (1991). *The Encyclopedia of Christianity,* Vol. 1. Grand Rapids, Mich.: Eerdmans.

Festinger, L. (1957). *A Theory of Cognitive Dissonance.* Stanford, Calif.: Stanford University Press.

Festinger, L., H. W. Riecken, and S. Schachter (1956). *When Prophecy Fails: A Social and Psychological Study.* Minneapolis, Minn.: University of Minnesota Press.

Feuerbach, L. (1957). *The Essence of Christianity.* New York: Harper & Row.

Fiske, A. P. (2000). "Complementarity Theory: Why Human Social Capacities Evolved to Require Cultural Complements." *Personality and Social Psychology Review* 4, 76–94.

Fiske, A. P. and N. Haslam (1997). "Is Obsessive-Compulsive Disorder a Pathology of the Human Disposition to Perform Socially Meaningful Rituals? Evidence of Similar Content." *Journal of Nervous and Mental Disease* 185, 211–222.

Fiske, S. T. and S. E. Taylor (1991). *Social Cognition.* New York: McGraw Hill.

Fitzgerald, T. (2000). *The Ideology of Religious Studies*. New York: Oxford University Press.

Fodor, J. A. (1983). *The Modularity of Mind: An Essay on Faculty Psychology*. Cambridge, Mass.: MIT Press.

———. (1985). "Précis of 'The Modularity of Mind.' " *The Behavioral and Brain Sciences* 8, 1–42.

Fraser, C. and G. Gaskell (eds.) (1990). *The Social Psychological Study of Widespread Beliefs*. Oxford: Clarendon Press.

Freud, S. (1955). *Totem and Taboo*. New York: Norton.

Friend, T. (2004). *Animal Talk: Breaking the Codes of Animal Language*. New York: Free Press.

Gardner, H. (1983). *Frames of Mind: The Theory of Multiple Intelligences*. New York: Basic Books.

———. (1993). *Multiple Intelligences: The Theory in Practice*. New York: Basic Books.

Gazzaniga, M. S., R. B. Ivry, and G. R. Mangun (1998). *Cognitive Neuroscience: The Biology of the Mind*. New York: W. W. Norton.

Gellner, E. (1969). "A Pendulum Swing Theory of Islam." In R. Robertson (ed.), *Sociology of Religion: Selected Readings*. Harmondsworth: Penguin Education.

Ginsburg, H. and S. Opper (1969). *Piaget's Theory of Intellectual Development: An Introduction*. Englewood Cliffs, N.J.: Prentice-Hall.

Goleman, D. (1995). *Emotional Intelligence*. New York: Bantam.

Golinkoff, R. M. and J. L. Kerr (1978). "Infants' Perception of Semantically Defined Action Role Changes in Filmed Events." *Merrill-Palmer Quarterly* 24, 53–62.

Gombrich, R. and G. Obeyesekere (1988). *Buddhism Transformed: Religious Change in Sri Lanka*. Princeton: Princeton University Press.

Goody, J. (1968). "Introduction." In J. Goody (ed.), *Literacy in Traditional Societies*. Cambridge: Cambridge University Press.

———. (1986). *The Logic of Writing and the Organization of Society*. Cambridge: Cambridge University Press.

Gopnik, A. M., A. N. Meltzoff, and P. K. Kuhl (2001). *The Scientist in the Crib: How Children Learn and What They Teach Us about the Mind*. New York: HarperCollins.

Gould, S. J. and R. C. Lewontin (1997). "The Spandrels of San Marco and the Panglossian Program: A Critique of the Adaptationist Programme." *Proceedings of the Royal Society of London* 205, 281–288.

Greenfield, P. M. (1991). "Language, Tools, and Brain: The Ontogeny and Phylogeny of Hierarchically Organized Sequential Behavior." *Behavioral and Brain Sciences* 14, 531–595.

Griggs, R. A. and J. R. Cox (1982). "The Elusive Thematic-Materials Effect in Wason's Selection Task." *British Journal of Psychology* 73, 407–420.

Groome, D. (1999). *An Introduction to Cognitive Psychology: Processes and Disorders*. London: Psychology Press.

Guthrie, S. E. (1980). "A Cognitive Theory of Religion." *Current Anthropology* 21, 181–203.

———. (1993). *Faces in the Clouds: A New Theory of Religion*. Oxford: Oxford University Press.

———. (2001). "Why Gods? A Cognitive Theory." In J. Andresen (ed.), *Religion in*

Mind: Cognitive Perspectives on Religious Belief, Ritual, and Experience. Cambridge: University of Cambridge Press.

Harris, P. L. (1994). "Thinking by Children and Scientists: False Analogies and Neglected Similarities." In L. A. Hirschfeld and S. A. Gelman (eds.), *Mapping the Mind: Domain Specificity in Cognition and Culture*. Cambridge: Cambridge University Press.

Heider, F. and M. Simmel (1944). "An Experimental Study of Apparent Behavior." *American Journal of Psychology* 57, 243–259.

Heller, D. (1986). *The Children's God*. Chicago: University of Chicago Press.

Hinde, R. A. (1999). *Why Gods Persist: A Scientific Approach to Religion*. London: Routledge.

Hirschfeld, L. A. (1996). *Race in the Making: Cognition, Culture, and the Child's Construction of Human Kinds*. Cambridge, Mass.: MIT Press.

Hirschfeld, L. A. and S. A. Gelman (eds.) (1994). *Mapping the Mind: Domain Specificity in Cognition and Culture*. Cambridge: Cambridge University Press.

Holyoak, K. J. and B. A. Spellman (1993). "Thinking." *Annual Review of Psychology* 44, 265–315.

Humphrey, N. (1984). *Consciousness Regained: Chapters in the Development of Mind*. Oxford: Oxford University Press.

———. (1986). *The Inner Eye: Social Intelligence in Evolution*. London: Faber and Faber.

———. (1992). *A History of the Mind: Evolution and the Birth of Consciousness*. New York: Simon & Schuster.

Idinopulos, T. A. and B. C. Wilson (eds.) (1998). *What Is Religion? Origins, Definitions, and Explanations*. Leiden: Brill.

Johanson, D. C. and B. Edgar (1996). *From Lucy to Language*. New York: Simon & Schuster.

Jones, S., R. Martin, and D. Pilbeam (1992). *The Cambridge Encyclopedia of Human Evolution*. Cambridge: Cambridge University Press.

Karmiloff-Smith, A. (1992). *Beyond Modularity: A Developmental Perspective on Cognitive Science*. Cambridge, Mass.: MIT Press.

Keil, F. C. (1989). *Concepts, Kinds, and Cognitive Development*. Cambridge, Mass.: MIT Press.

———. (1994). "The Birth and Nurturance of Concepts by Domains: The Origins of Concepts of Living Things." In L. A. Hirschfeld and S. A. Gelman (eds.), *Mapping the Mind: Domain Specificity in Cognition and Culture*. Cambridge: Cambridge University Press.

———. (2003). "Folkscience: Coarse Interpretations of a Complex Reality." *Trends in Cognitive Sciences* 7, 368–373.

Keil, F. C. and R. A. Wilson (eds.) (2000). *Explanation and Cognition*. Cambridge, Mass.: MIT Press.

Kelemen, D. (1999a). "Beliefs about Purpose: On the Origins of Teleological Thought." In M. Corballis and S. Lea (eds.), *The Descent of Mind: Psychological Perspectives on Hominid Evolution*. Oxford: Oxford University Press.

———. (1999b). "Functions, Goals, and Intentions: Children's Teleological Reasoning about Objects." *Trends in Cognitive Sciences* 12, 461–468.

———. (1999c). "The Scope of Teleological Thinking in Preschool Children." *Cognition* 70, 241–272.

———. (1999d). "Why Are Rocks Pointy? Children's Preference for Teleological Explanations of the Natural World." *Developmental Psychology* 35, 1440–1453.

———. (2004). "Are Children 'Intuitive Theists?' Reasoning about Purpose and Design in Nature." *Psychological Science* 15, 295–301.

Kihlstrom, J. F. (1999). "Conscious versus Unconscious Cognition." In R. J. Sternberg (ed.), *The Nature of Cognition*. Cambridge, Mass.: MIT Press.

Kirkpatrick, L. A. (2005). *Attachment, Evolution, and the Psychology of Religion*. New York: Guilford Press.

Knight, C. (1990). *Blood Relations: Menstruation and the Origins of Culture*. New Haven, Conn.: Yale University Press.

Kundera, M. (1990). *Immortality*. New York: Grove Weidenfeld.

Larsen, C. S., R. M. Matter, and D. L. Gebo (1991). *Human Origins: The Fossil Record*. Prospect Heights: Waveland Press.

Lawson, E. T. (2000). "Cognition." In W. Braun and R. T. McCutcheon (eds.), *Guide to the Study of Religion*. London: Cassell.

———. (2001). "Psychological Perspectives on Agency." In J. Andresen (ed.), *Religion in Minds: Cognitive Perspectives on Religious Belief, Ritual, and Experience*. Cambridge: Cambridge University Press.

Lawson, E. T. and R. N. McCauley (1990). *Rethinking Religion: Connecting Cognition and Culture*. Cambridge: Cambridge University Press.

———. (1993). "Crisis of Conscience, Riddle of Identity: Making Space for a Cognitive Approach to Religious Phenomena." *Journal of the American Academy of Religion* 61, 201–223.

Leakey, M. G., F. Spoor, F. H. Brown, P. N. Gathogo, C. Kiarie, L. N. Leakey, and I. McDougall (2001). "New Hominin Genus from Eastern Africa Shows Diverse Middle Pliocene Lineages." *Nature* 410, 433–440.

Leakey, R.E.F. (1992). *Origins Reconsidered: In Search of What Makes Us Human*. New York: Doubleday.

LeDoux, J. (1996). *The Emotional Brain: The Mysterious Underpinnings of Emotional Life*. New York: Simon & Schuster.

———. (2002). *Synoptic Self: How Our Brains become Who We Are*. New York: Viking Press.

Leslie, A. M. (1984). "Infant Perception of a Manual Pick-Up Event. *British Journal of Developmental Psychology* 2, 19–32.

———. (1987). "Pretence and Representation: The Origins of 'Theory of Mind.' " *Psychological Review* 94, 412–426.

———. (1994). "ToMM, ToBy, and Agency: Core Architecture and Domain Specificity." In L. A. Hirschfeld and S. A. Gelman (eds.), *Mapping the Mind: Domain Specificity in Cognition and Culture*. Cambridge: Cambridge University Press.

———. (1996). "A Theory of Agency." In D. Sperber, D. Premack, and A. J. Premack (eds.), *Causal Cognition: A Multidisciplinary Debate*. New York: Oxford University Press.

Liberman, A. and I. Mattingly (1989). "A Specialization for Speech Perception." *Science* 243, 489–494.

Lieberman, M. D., R. Graunt, D. T. Gilbert, and Y. Trope (2002). "Reflexion and Reflection: A Social Cognitive Neuroscience Approach to Attributional Inference." *Advances in Experimental Social Psychology* 34, 200–250.

Lincoln, B. (1989). *Discourse and the Construction of Society: Comparative Studies of Myth, Ritual, and Classification.* New York: Oxford University Press.

———. (2000). "Culture." In W. Braun and R. T. McCutcheon (eds.), *Guide to the Study of Religion.* London: Cassell.

Marr, D. (1982). *Vision.* New York: W. H. Freeman.

Martin, L. H. (2000). "Comparison." In W. Braun and R. T. McCutcheon (eds.), *Guide to the Study of Religion.* London: Cassell.

Masuzawa, T. (1998). "Culture." In M. C. Taylor (ed.), *Critical Terms for Religious Studies.* Chicago: University of Chicago Press.

McCauley, R. N. (2000). "The Naturalness of Religion and the Unnaturalness of Science." In F. C. Keil and R. A. Wilson (eds.), *Explanation and Cognition.* Cambridge, Mass.: MIT Press.

McCauley, R. N. and E. T. Lawson. (2002). *Bringing Ritual to Mind: Psychological Foundations of Cultural Forms.* Cambridge: Cambridge University Press.

McCutcheon, R. T. (1997). "A Critique of 'Religion' as a Cross-Cultural Category." *Method & Theory in the Study of Religion* 9, 91–110.

McNamara, P. (2001). "Religion and the Frontal Lobes." In J. Andresen (ed.), *Religion in Minds: Cognitive Perspectives on Religious Belief, Ritual, and Experience.* Cambridge: Cambridge University Press.

Medin, D. L., and S. Atran. (eds.) (1999). *Folkbiology.* Cambridge, Mass.: MIT Press.

Meltzoff, A. and A. Gopnik (1993). "The Role of Imitation in Understanding Persons and Developing a Theory of Mind." In S. Baron-Cohen, H. Tager-Flusberg, and D. Cohen (eds.), *Understanding Other Minds: Perspectives from Autism.* Oxford: Oxford University Press.

Michotte, A. (1963). *The Perception of Causality.* London: Methuen.

Mitchell, P. (1996). *Introduction to Theory of Mind: Children, Autism, and Apes.* Oxford: Oxford University Press.

Mithen, S. (1996). *The Prehistory of the Mind: The Cognitive Origins of Art, Religion, and Science.* New York: Thames & Hudson.

Moskowitz, G. B. (2005). *Social Cognition: Understanding Self and Others.* New York: Guilford Press.

Müller, F. M. (1872). *Lectures on the Science of Religion.* New York: Charles Scribner and Company.

Newberg, A. B. and E. G. d'Aquili (2001). *Why God Won't Go Away: Brain Science and the Biology of Belief.* New York: Ballantine.

Obeyesekere, G. (1981). *Medusa's Hair: An Essay on Personal Symbols and Religious Experience.* Chicago: University of Chicago Press.

Pals, D. L. (1996). *Seven Theories of Religion.* New York: Oxford University Press.

Pannenberg, W. (1990). *Systematic Theology: Volume 1.* Grand Rapids, Mich.: Eerdmans.

Parker, S. T. and M. L. McKinney (1999). *Origins of Intelligence: The Evolution of Cognitive Development in Monkeys, Apes, and Humans.* Baltimore: Johns Hopkins University Press.

Perner, J. (1991). *Understanding the Representational Mind.* Cambridge, Mass.: MIT Press.

Persinger, M. A. (1987). *Neuropsychological Bases of God Beliefs.* Westport, Conn.: Praeger.

Pinker, S. (1994). *The Language Instinct: How the Mind Creates Language.* New York: William Morrow.

———. (1997). *How the Mind Works.* New York: W. W. Norton.

———. (2002). *The Blank Slate: The Modern Denial of Human Nature.* New York: Viking Press.

Poulin-Dubois, D. and T. R. Shultz (1988). "The Development of the Understanding of Human Behavior: From Agency to Intentionality." In J. Astington, P. Harris, and D. Olson (eds.), *Developing Theories of Mind.* New York: Cambridge Unversity Press.

Povinelli, D. and K. Nelson (1990). "Inferences about Guessing and Knowing in Chimpanzees." *Journal of Comparative Psychology* 104, 203–210.

Premack, D. (1976). *Intelligence in Apes and Man.* Hillsdale, N.J.: Erlbaum.

Premack, D. and A. Premack (2002). *Original Intelligence: Unlocking the Mystery of Who We Are.* New York: McGraw Hill.

Premack, D. and G. Woodruff (1978). "Does the Chimpanzee Have a Theory of Mind?" *Behavioral and Brain Sciences* 4, 515–526.

Pyysiäinen, I. (2001a). "Cognition, Emotion, and Religious Experience." In J. Andresen (ed.), *Religion in Minds: Cognitive Perspectives on Religious Belief, Ritual, and Experience.* Cambridge: Cambridge University Press.

———. (2001b). *How Religion Works: Towards a New Cognitive Science of Religion.* Leiden: Brill.

———. (2002). "Religion and the Counter-Intuitive." In I. Pyysiäinen and V. Anttonen (eds.), *Current Approaches in the Cognitive Science of Religion.* London: Continuum.

———. (2003). "Dual-Process Theories and Hybrid Systems: A Commentary on Anderson and Lebiere." *Behavioral and Brain Sciences* 25, 617–618.

———. (2004a). "Corrupt Doctrine and Doctrinal Revival: On the Nature and Limits of the Modes Theory." In H. Whitehouse and L. H. Martin (eds.), *Theorizing Religions Past: Archaeology, History, and Cognition.* Walnut Creek, Calif.: AltaMira.

———. (2004b). "Intuitive and Explicit in Religious Thought." *Journal of Cognition and Culture* 4, 123–150.

———. (2005). "The Modes Theory Helps Explain Conversion Phenomena." In H. Whitehouse and R. N. McCauley (eds.), *Mind and Religion: Psychological and Cognitive Foundations of Religion.* Walnut Creek, Calif.: AltaMira Press.

Pyysiäinen, I. and V. Anttonen (eds.) (2002). *Current Approaches in the Cognitive Science of Religion.* London: Continuum.

Reisberg, D. (1997). *Cognition: Exploring the Science of the Mind.* New York: W. W. Norton.

Ridley, M. (1996). *The Origins of Virtue: Human Instincts and the Evolution of Cooperation.* New York: Penguin Books.

———. (2003). *Nature via Nurture: Genes, Experience, and What Makes Us Human.* New York: HarperCollins.

Rochat, P. (2001). *The Infant's World.* Cambridge, Mass.: Harvard University Press.

Rorty, A. O. (1980). "Introduction." In A. O. Rorty (ed.), *Explaining Emotions.* Berkeley, Calif.: University of California Press.

Sagan, C. (1980). *Cosmos.* New York: Random House.

Sawaguchi, T. and H. Kudo (1990). "Neocortical Development and Social Structure in Primates." *Primates* 31, 283–290.

Schneider, W. and R. M. Shiffrin (1977). "Controlled and Automatic Human Information Processing." *Psychological Review* 84, 1–66.

Sharot, S. (2001). *A Comparative Sociology of World Religions: Virtuosi, Priests, and Popular Religion.* New York: New York University Press.

Shiffrin, R. M. and W. Schneider (1977). "Controlled and Automatic Human Information Processing, II: Perceptual Learning, Automatic Attending, and a General Theory." *Psychological Review* 84, 127–190.

Shore, B. (1996). *Culture in Mind: Cognition, Culture, and the Problem of Meaning.* New York: Oxford University Press.

Sloman, S. A. (1996). "The Empirical Case for Two Systems of Reasoning." *Psychological Bulletin* 119, 3–22.

———. (1999). "Rational versus Arational Models of Thought." In R. J. Sternberg (ed.), *The Nature of Cognition.* Cambridge, Mass.: MIT Press.

Slone, D. J. (2004). *Theological Incorrectness: Why Religious People Believe What They Shouldn't.* Oxford: Oxford University Press.

Smith, E. R. and J. DeCoster (1999). "Associative and Rule-Based Processing: A Connectionist Interpretation of Dual-Process Models." In S. Chaiken and Y. Trope (eds.), *Dual-Process Theories in Social Psychology.* New York: Guilford Press.

Spelke, E. S. (1991). "Physical Knowledge in Infancy: Reflections on Paiget's Theory." In S. Carey and R. Gelmann (eds.), *Epigenesis of Mind: Studies in Biology and Culture.* Hillsdale, N.J.: Erlbaum.

Sperber, D. (1975). *Rethinking Symbolism.* Cambridge: Cambridge University Press.

———. (1985). *On Anthropological Knowledge.* Cambridge: Cambridge University Press.

———. (1994). "The Modularity of Thought and the Epidemiology of Representations." In L. A. Hirschfeld and S. A. Gelman (eds.), *Mapping the Mind: Domain Specificity in Cognition and Culture.* Cambridge: Cambridge University Press.

———. (1996). *Explaining Culture: A Naturalistic Approach.* Oxford: Blackwell.

———. (1997). "Intuitive and Reflective Beliefs." *Mind and Language* 12, 67–83.

Sperber, D., D. Premack, and A. J. Premack (eds.) (1995). *Causal Cognition: A Multidisciplinary Debate.* New York: Oxford University Press.

Sperber, D. and D. Wilson (1986). *Relevance: Communication and Cognition.* Cambridge, Mass.: Harvard University Press.

Spilka, B., R. W. Wood Jr., B. Hunsberger, and R. Gorsuch (2003). *The Psychology of Religion: An Empirical Approach,* 3rd ed. New York: Guilford Press.

Staal, F. (1979). "The Meaninglessness of Ritual." *Numen* 26, 2–22.

Stanford, C. (2001). *Significant Others: The Ape-Human Continuum and the Quest for Human Nature.* New York: Basic Books.

Stark, R. (2003). *For the Glory of God: How Monotheism Led to Reformations, Science, Witch-Hunts, and the End of Slavery.* Princeton, N.J.: Princeton University Press.

Stern, D. N. (1985). *The Interpersonal World of the Infant.* New York: Basic Books.

Sternberg, R. J. (ed.) (1999). *The Nature of Cognition.* Cambridge, Mass.: MIT Press.

Stewart, C. and R. Shaw (eds.) (1994). *Syncretism Anti-Syncretism: The Politics of Religious Synthesis.* London: Routledge.

Strauss, C. and N. Quinn (1997). *A Cognitive Theory of Cultural Meaning.* Cambridge: Cambridge University Press.

Stringer, C. B. and C. Gamble. (1993). *In Search of the Neanderthals: Solving the Puzzle of Human Origins*. New York: Thames & Hudson.

Synan, V. (1997). *The Holiness-Pentecostal Tradition: Charismatic Movements in the Twentieth Century*. Grand Rapids, Mich.: Eerdmans.

Tambiah, S. J. (1992). *Buddhism Betrayed? Religion, Politics, and Violence in Sri Lanka*. Chicago: University of Chicago Press.

Taylor, Mark C. (ed.) (1998). *Critical Terms for Religious Studies*. Chicago: University of Chicago Press.

Thagard, P. (1996). *Mind: Introduction to Cognitive Science*. Cambridge, Mass.: MIT Press.

———. (1998). *Mind Readings: Introductory Selections in Cognitive Science*. Cambridge, Mass.: MIT Press.

Tillich, P. (1973). *What Is Religion?* New York: Harper & Row.

Tomasello, M. (2000). *The Cultural Origins of Human Cognition*. Cambridge, Mass.: Harvard University Press.

Tomasello, M. and J. Call (1997). *Primate Cognition*. New York: Oxford University Press.

Tooby, J. and L. Cosmides (1990). "The Past Explains the Present: Emotional Adaptation and the Structure of Ancestral Environments." *Ethnology and Sociobiology* 11, 375–424.

———. (1992). "The Psychological Foundations of Culture." In J. H. Barkow, L. Cosmides, and J. Tooby (eds.), *The Adapted Mind: Evolutionary Psychology and the Generation of Culture*. Oxford: Oxford University Press.

Tooby, J. and I. DeVore (1987). "The Reconstruction of Hominid Evolution through Strategic Modeling." In W. G. Kinzey (ed.), *The Evolution of Human Behavior: Primate Models*. Albany, N.Y.: SUNY Press.

Tremlin, T. (2000). "Iconoclasm and Catharsis: Seeking a Middle Way for Religion Studies." *Journal of Comparative Religion* 1, 20–29.

———. (2002). "A Theory of Religious Modulation: Reconciling Religious Modes and Ritual Arrangements." *Journal of Cognition and Culture* 2, 309–348.

———. (2003). "Thought and Emotion in the Scientific Study of Religion: A Critical Review of Ilkka Pyysiäinen's *How Religion Works*." *Journal of Cognition and Culture* 3, 255–263.

———. (2005). "Divergent Religion: A Dual-Process Model of Religious Thought, Behavior, and Morphology." In H. Whitehouse and R. N. McCauley (eds.), *Mind and Religion: Psychological and Cognitive Foundations of Religion*. Walnut Creek, Calif.: AltaMira.

Trivers, R. (1985). *Social Evolution*. Menlo Park, Calif.: Benjamin Cummings.

Tulving, E. and D. L. Schacter (1990). "Priming and Human Memory Systems." *Science* 247, 301–306.

Turing, A. M. (1950). "Computing Machinery and Intelligence." *Mind* 59, 433–460.

Vallet, R. E. and C. E. Zech (1995). *The Mainline Church's Funding Crisis: Issues and Possibilities*. Grand Rapids, Mich.: Eerdmans.

Van Essen, D. C. and E. A. DeYoe (1995). "Concurrent Processing in the Primate Visual Cortex." In M. S. Gazzaniga (ed.), *The Cognitive Neurosciences*. Cambridge, Mass.: MIT Press.

Walter, A. and P. Shipman. (1996). *The Wisdom of the Bones: In Search of Human Origins*. New York: Knopf.

Ward, T. B. (1994). "Structured Imagination: The Role of Category Structure in Exemplar Generation." *Cognitive Psychology* 27, 1–40.

Warrington, E. and T. Shallice (1984). "Category Specific Semantic Impairments." *Brain* 107, 829–854.

———. (1995). "What's Old about New Ideas?" In S. M. Smith, T. B. Ward, and R. A. Finke (eds.), *The Creative Cognition Approach*. Cambridge, Mass.: MIT Press.

Weber, M. (1930). *The Protestant Ethic and the Spirit of Capitalism*. London: George Allen and Unwin.

———. (1947). *The Theory of Social and Economic Organization*. Oxford: Oxford University Press.

Wellman, H. M. (1990). *The Child's Theory of Mind*. Cambridge, Mass.: MIT Press.

Werbner, R. P. (1977). *Regional Cults*. London: Academic Press.

Whitehouse, H. (1995). *Inside the Cult: Religious Innovation and Transmission in Papua New Guinea*. Oxford: Clarendon Press.

———. (2000). *Arguments and Icons: Divergent Modes of Religiosity*. Oxford: Oxford University Press.

——— (ed.) (2001). *The Debated Mind: Evolutionary Psychology versus Ethnography*. Oxford: Berg.

———. (2002). "Modes of Religiosity: Towards a Cognitive Explanation of the Sociopolitical Dynamics of Religion." *Method & Theory in the Study of Religion* 14, 293–315.

———. (2004). *Modes of Religiosity: A Cognitive Theory of Religious Transmission*. Walnut Creek: Calif.: AltaMira.

Whitehouse, H. and J. Laidlaw (2004). *Ritual and Memory: Towards a Comparative Anthropology of Religion*. Walnut Creek, Calif.: AltaMira.

Whitehouse, H. and L. H. Martin (2004). *Theorizing Religions Past: Archaeology, History, and Cognition*. Walnut Creek, Calif.: AltaMira.

Whitehouse, H. and R. N. McCauley (2005). *Mind and Religion: Psychological and Cognitive Foundations of Religion*. Walnut Creek, Calif.: AltaMira.

Whiten, A. (ed.) (1991). *Natural Theories of Mind: Evolution, Development, and Simulation of Everyday Mindreading*. Oxford: Blackwell.

Whiten, A. and R. W. Byrne (1997). *Machiavellian Intelligence II: Extensions and Evaluations*. Cambridge: Cambridge University Press.

Wilson, A. N. (1999). *God's Funeral*. New York: Norton.

Wilson, E. O. (1998). *Consilience: The Unity of Knowledge*. New York: Vintage Books.

Wilson, R. A. and F. C. Keil (eds.) (1999). *The MIT Encyclopedia of the Cognitive Sciences*. Cambridge, Mass.: MIT Press.

Wright, R. (1994). *The Moral Animal: Evolutionary Psychology and Everyday Life*. New York: Pantheon.

Wuthnow, R. (ed.) (1994a). *"I Come Away Stronger": How Small Groups Are Shaping American Religion*. Grand Rapids, Mich.: Eerdmans.

———. (1994b). *Sharing the Journey: Support Groups and America's New Quest for Community*. New York: Free Press.

Index

CPSIA information can be obtained at www.ICGtesting.com
Printed in the USA
BVOW071746270213

314306BV00002B/4/P